SNAFU EDU

TEACHING, ENGAGING, AND THRIVING IN HIGHER ED

James M. Lang and Michelle D. Miller, SERIES EDITORS

SNAFU EDU

Teaching and Learning When Things Go Wrong in the College Classroom

JESSAMYN NEUHAUS

University of Oklahoma Press : Norman

Publication of this book is made possible in part through the generosity of Edith Kinney Gaylord.

Library of Congress Control Numbers:
2024059303 (hardcover)
2024059295 (paperback)

ISBN: 978-0-8061-9545-2 (hardcover)
ISBN: 978-8061-9546-9 (paperback)

Snafu Edu: Teaching and Learning When Things Go Wrong in the College Classroom is Volume 6 in the Teaching, Engaging, and Thriving in Higher Ed series.

The paper in this book meets the guidelines for permanence and durability of the Committee on Production Guidelines for Book Longevity of the Council on Library Resources, Inc. ∞

The manufacturer's authorized representative in the EU for product safety is Mare Nostrum Group B.V., Mauritskade 21D, 1091 GC Amsterdam, The Netherlands, email: gpsr@mare-nostrum.co.uk.

*Captain, good news! We know when
the next disturbance is going to hit.
Bad news: it's in two seconds.*

—Lieutenant Sylvia Tilly,
Star Trek: Discovery, "Anomaly"

CONTENTS

PART IV. FAILURE

PART V. FEAR

ACKNOWLEDGMENTS

When I began a new job in 2024, I had to pack up the contents of my office at the State University of New York at Plattsburgh, including a filing cabinet crammed with teaching materials from over two decades in the classroom. Sorting through syllabi, SET forms, and assignments, I drew three conclusions about my teaching career: (1) My students are diverse, interesting people who inspired me to reflect on and improve my teaching; (2) I worked hard to help students learn, and many things went well; and (3) I made many mistakes and sometimes students really messed up too. Hoo boy, did some things go wrong! My first acknowledgment is to all the students with whom I've learned, struggled, stumbled, and succeeded. Sorry about my snafus and thank you for sharing your ideas with me.

I also want to thank the faculty and staff at SUNY Plattsburgh whose insights into student experiences helped shape this book: Elizabeth Bernat, Michelle Bonati, Wanda Carroll, Jenn Curry, Cody Dulaney, Kolleen Duley, Bridget Haina, Allison Heard, Karin Killough, Chiranjivi Lamsal, Regan Levitte, Shatawndra Lister, John Locke, John McMahon, Michelle Ouellette, Connie Shemo, Priyanka Singh, Kelly Theisen, and Yong Yu. Thank you too to everyone who participated in a Center for Teaching Excellence program or consultation. Thank you for trusting me and brainstorming with me.

One of the most surprising things that happened when my career shifted from history professor to educational developer was how easy it was to "network" with my new colleagues. These conversations and connections have fueled my research and this book. I'm particularly grateful for friendship and collaborations with

Leslie Bayers, Niya Bond, Flower Darby, Cate Denial, Jen Garret-Ostermiller, Cyndi Kernahan, John Kane, Lindsay Masland, Victoria Mondelli, Rebecca Mushtare, Lillian Nave, Chris Price, Jeremy Schiender, Maggie Schmuhl, Travis Thurston, and Jessica Tinklenberg. I'm especially indebted to Chavella Pittman for her keen insights, sense of humor, and powerful words of encouragement.

There is another group of people without whom *Snafu Edu* would not exist: the creators and authors of the Teaching and Learning in Higher Education series at West Virginia University Press. Being a part of that series completely changed how I thought about my work. Big thanks to Susan D. Blum, Derek Bruff, Sara Rose Cavanagh, Jenae Cohn, Joshua Eyler, Kevin Gannon, Kelly Hogan, Susan Hrach, Cyndi Kernahan, Derek Krissoff, James M. Lang, Viji Sathy, and Thomas Tobin.

I learned so much about teaching and higher education while editing *Picture a Professor*, a project that gave me hope and energy during the pandemic years of loss and fear. Thank you to all the authors: Celeste Atkins, Breanna Boppre, Alison Cook-Sather, Melissa Eblen-Zayas, Jesica Siham Fernández, Ashley JoEtta, Fenn Kennedy, Sarah Mayes-Tang, Donna Mejia, Emily K. Michael, Mona Minkara, Chavella T. Pittman, Rebecca Scott, Erik Simmons, Kelly Theisen, M. Gabriella Torres, Sheri Wells-Jensen, Chanelle Wilson, and Jacinta Yanders.

I'm thrilled to be a part of the Teaching, Engaging, and Thriving in Higher Ed series. Thank you to Derek Krissoff, James Lang, and Michelle Miller. Additional thanks to David Chesanow for his careful copyediting. I also cannot thank enough Alison Cook-Sather and Liz Norell, the amazing scholars and awesome human beings who read my manuscript. Their thoughtful input, constructive critiques, and all-around brilliance made *Snafu Edu* immeasurably better. I am especially grateful for the insightful, frank, and funny margin notes that Liz gave me.

I want to thank my friends Trina Brown, Kelly Douglass, Holly McCullough, and Erika Poethig for their spot-on advice and steadfast support when, right in the middle of writing this book, I was making a ginormous decision about accepting a new job.

For their lifelong cheerleading, and for reading virtually every word I've ever written, all my thanks and love to John and Lori Neuhaus, and to Alison Neuhaus, my favorite introvert and empath in the world. Thank you to Solomon Neuhaus, for all the ways you've helped me see school—and the world—in a new light. My deepest gratitude is always to Douglas Butdorf, for being the partner that makes it all possible. Doug, marrying you was the best decision I'll ever make. No mistake.

Snafu Edu is dedicated to everyone who read and told me they enjoyed *Geeky Pedagogy*. Nothing has brought me as much unalloyed professional delight as hearing from college teachers who liked my book about teaching. Thank you, you big nerds.

INTRODUCTION

Brace for Impact

A well-executed emergency landing in bad terrain can be less hazardous than an uncontrolled landing on an established field.

—"How to Land a Plane,"
The Worst-Case Scenario Survival Handbook

In a cartoon titled "Instinct Is Weird" by author and naturalist Rosemary Mosco, a bird looks at its new nest, saying, "I made this for some reason." In the next panel, the mama bird admires her freshly laid eggs: "These are my smooth round children." When a baby bird pokes its squawking head out of an egg, she's shocked: "Oh no now it's loud." In the final panel, the nest is full of screeching baby birds and the stunned mother just says, "Help."[1]

As a college educator, I can relate, because every new semester begins with me laying my own clutch of "smooth round" children, i.e., creating a set of fresh, pristine syllabi. It is not strictly necessary to toil for weeks over every teensy-weensy detail in one's syllabus. One can overstuff one's syllabus with too much information and unnecessary verbiage. But every time I start to plan a class, I just can't stop myself from nitpickingly mapping out every moment of what I dreamily envision as fifteen solid weeks of engaging class activities, useful assignments, and inclusive, supportive structures that will ensure student learning and success. Impeccable, silent, and utterly inviolate, my perfect syllabi eggs repose in an immaculate pedagogical nest . . . right up until the moment that reality breaks through and the actual noisy, hungry, messy life of the class begins. Oh no, my smooth, silent children are loud and needy now. Help!

For me, class planning always seems to include some denial of a highly predictable future reality, pretending that everything is going to work out precisely as I expect. It's magical thinking whereby my perfectly organized syllabus will wield the power to exactly determine the future unfolding of events. Spoiler alert: it won't. Double spoiler alert: turns out the syllabus itself also has flaws. I'm an experienced college instructor, so I'm fully aware that no class goes exactly like you plan. Never, ever, ever. Like, ever. I also know that some factors completely outside my control are constantly at play. As *Radical Hope: A Teaching Manifesto* author Kevin Gannon notes, widespread systemic problems and issues in higher education ensure that sometimes we can't "pedagogy our way out" when things go wrong.[2] Yet there's still a part of me that believes that this time, with this syllabus, every single thing will go according to my beautiful plan. There's a part of me that's still regularly taken aback when something goes wrong in my meticulously planned class.

Something *will* inevitably go wrong. It could be as small as a glaring typo on our first slide or as huge as a global pandemic. It could be a minor hiccup in the schedule, one assignment that didn't seem to quite land, or one lecture that bored everyone into a stupor. Or it could be a big, damaging situation, such as a troubled student upsetting others in class or a major plagiarism problem or a heartbreaking family crisis—a student's or your own—derailing your plans and making it a million times harder to concentrate on teaching and learning. It could be an ongoing challenge, such as grappling with students' stereotypes about embodied identities and academic expertise or trying to counteract the seductive enthrallment of our phones and devices. It could be something that's completely outside our control, such as fixed seating in the classroom when we'd really prefer flexible seating arrangements.

No amount of brilliant planning and skillful teaching will change the fact that when human beings undertake any endeavor whatsoever, including teaching and learning, mistakes will be made and some things will go awry. Students will struggle and instructors will be frustrated. Students will be frustrated and instructors will struggle. Words will be blurted and then regretted. Stereotypes and biases will flare up. Emotions will erupt. Bad choices will be made. The scholarship of teaching and learning (SoTL) and published advice to college instructors frequently ignores or significantly understates this fundamental truth: teaching and learning is never and will never be a perfectible activity. It encompasses an almost unlimited number of situations with the potential to go haywire. It predictably, inexorably entails moments of missteps and mistakes.

There's an almost Pollyannaish undercurrent bordering on toxic positivity subtext in a lot of SoTL and college teaching advice.[3] Often I see a teaching expert appearing to make a tacit assumption that teaching and learning problems can be fixed unilaterally if you just have the right know-how and can-do attitude. As highly skilled learners with agile brains packed full of sophisticated knowledge and extensive content expertise, college instructors are particularly vulnerable to the seductive idea that really understanding how something works will naturally lead to success. Without stating it outright, too much college teaching advice implies that there is a direct and uncomplicated line between these things. Just use the right evidence-based teaching technique and *presto chango*: your students will learn and succeed. Even on the rare occasion when a scholar or commentator in our field discusses "teaching mistakes," it's usually framed as something that's pretty much totally fixable going forward.[4]

Additionally, sometimes in the discourse about teaching and learning, I see an almost fetishistic belief that by knowing and applying psychology and science we can swiftly and painlessly untangle all our knotty teaching and learning problems and avoid all future mistakes. Without explicitly making this claim, some advice seems to suggest that when we encounter teaching and learning problem X, the answer is simply fact Y, based on all the things we know about the physiological functioning of Homo sapiens brains and psyches. When you know and plan for this fact, it seems to imply, then you've solved the problem for good and for all, amen.

True story: minutes after I first typed the previous paragraph, a webinar advertisement popped up in my email in-box and the subject line read: "Solve Your Teaching Problems." Not "Learn How to Understand and Cope with Your Teaching Problems." Not "Contend with Ongoing Teaching Problems." Not "Join Forces with Students to Collectively Address Teaching and Learning Problems We All Struggle with at Times." No: they promise, in one seminar, to *solve* your teaching problems. I mean, sign me up! This is an overt example of a shortcoming I see in the advice doled out to college instructors who want to be effective teachers. Too often it seems to be discussing teaching problems as if there is a permanent solution that will work everywhere for everyone all the time.

When I was doing research for my 2019 book about college teaching, *Geeky Pedagogy: A Guide for Intellectuals, Introverts, and Nerds Who Want to Be Effective Teachers*, there was a pesky little voice in my head that kept saying, Okay, yes, sure, that pedagogical technique or teaching practice or important classroom innovation could help me teach effectively.[5] But it won't work every time, for every instructor, in every teaching context. Right? Right!? Of particular concern to me was the failure of so much otherwise outstanding published research and advice about college teaching to address what sociologist Roxanna Harlow terms "disparate teaching realities."[6] I would read an article about "best practices" or a book about what all "excellent college teachers" do, and there would be little or no mention of the way that social and embodied identities, employment status, student populations, and other specificities of our individual teaching contexts create inequitable teaching labor.

So I set about collecting and editing evidence-based insights and intersectional teaching strategies crafted by and for college instructors who actively sought to increase student learning while at the same time challenging stereotypes about what a professor "looks like." The result was *Picture a Professor: Interrupting Biases about Faculty and Increasing Student Learning*, published in 2022.[7] I was working on editing that manuscript in the spring of 2020 when the world fell apart. That is to say, the predictable work-ings of higher education came to a screeching halt when the COVID-19 pandemic broke out. Talk about upended plans. Talk about stuff going wrong! Talk about overwhelmed birds trying to take care of nests full of fragile fledglings! One thing that really struck me about educators' own individual responses at that time was a widespread desire to do right by students and continue to facilitate learning. I include myself in this group. I publicly advo-cated for maintaining an educator's growth mindset and worked intensively to "pivot" to emergency remote instruction, to teach effectively online for the first time, and to help other faculty do the same. We started expending vast amounts of energy and goodwill implementing new teaching techniques in a whole bunch of new and new-to-us modalities. But as the pandemic dragged on, even the most dedicated educators' batteries ran out of juice.[8]

In the context of economic precarity, social distancing, cogni-tive overload, "Zoom U," and trauma and traumatic stress—not to mention the political, economic, and cultural crises of our era—it became exponentially harder to learn.[9] It became exponentially harder to teach. Yet again and again I saw institutional leaders and educational developers like myself fail to fully acknowledge, let alone productively address, how enervating and unrewarding many aspects of teaching and learning were at that time. Here was the problem I'd already been having with so much advice about college teaching and SoTL, the thing that had been bugging me all along, resurfacing in a horrible new coronavirus-era iteration: discourse about education that included many unstated but nonetheless potent promises to "solve your teaching problems." Well before, all throughout, and long after the height of the COVID-19 lockdown, otherwise useful and insightful advice about college teaching rou-tinely implies that teaching is, primarily, an individual act consist-ing solely of potentially perfectible pedagogical skill. I'm calling BS.

Situation Normal, All Fouled Up

In *Snafu Edu*, I give a clear, loud voice to a reality too often brushed aside in teaching advice: sometimes things don't work out. Sometimes things go totally sideways. Teaching can be meaningful, personally rewarding work, and there is an abundance of research and scholarship about learning and teaching practices that can be implemented on an individual basis that often improves teaching and increases learning. But teaching can also be painfully frustrating and even fruitless, no matter how much SoTL you've read and utilized or how many webinars or workshops you've attended. Moreover, any one instructor's teaching efficacy can be significantly undermined by low wages, employment precarity, workplace dysfunction, illness, intersectional systemic discrimination, and other institutional factors outside our control. Crucially, sometimes *learning* is miserable work as well. It often entails struggle, sacrifice, dislocation, and, at the college level, an astronomically high financial toll. And, just like teaching, learning can be significantly undermined by personal circumstances and systemic and institutional factors outside students' control.

In short, sometimes things go wrong, both for instructors as well as for students. Contrary to its aim of increasing teaching skill and student learning, too much SoTL and other types of college teaching advice sets us up for failure by not adequately acknowledging this. It often does not pay enough attention to three irrefutable truths about humans and higher education.

Truth #1: People routinely make bad mistakes and badly mess things up in bad ways. Yet numerous systems and standard practices in higher education and academia leave little to no room for human error, messiness, and missteps. The fact that we, as teachers and learners, make mistakes is not a problem to be solved; it's just a reality of our existence on this earth. We ourselves, as teachers and learners, are not problems to be solved.[10]

Truth #2: Positionality—our intersectional embodied, economic, and social identities—influences how we interact with one another in educational settings. We cannot talk about effective teaching and learning without also talking about the role of racism, sexism, ableism, and other types of discrimination and stereotyping.

Truth #3: The Super Teacher myth damages teaching efficacy and self-efficacy. Prevalent in popular representations of and discourse about teaching, the Super Teacher is an extraordinarily gifted monologist and charismatic classroom performer who singlehandedly transforms the lives of his (it's usually "his") students and facilitates indelible learning experiences, all without ever having taken a teaching workshop or reading a book about teaching. He's just a "born teacher"! The Super Teacher myth undermines pedagogical self-efficacy and it creates stereotypes about what both effective teaching, as well as what professors themselves, "look like."

The Super Teacher myth is also one of the factors contributing to a lack of in-depth discussion and research about the reasons things go wrong in college teaching and learning. As the editors of a collection of personal essays about failure and teaching suggest, "Perhaps the push towards teaching stories that are always positive is influenced by the 'super teachers' immortalized in books and on film in our culture." That push toward the positive, they continue, does educators a disservice: "Very few stories of failure and discouragement appear in writing by teachers. These are stories that teachers need to tell—and hear, too. Teachers can find little in the literature that tells them what to do next when an activity stinks up the classroom or what can be learned as they mop up the pieces of a splattered innovation."[11]

Every college class in every modality, every college student at every type of institution, and every college instructor in every discipline will be influenced by these three higher education truths. These truths can, and do, sometimes "stink up the classroom" and "splatter innovation," not unexpectedly or occasionally but predictably and frequently. *Normally.* Recognizing, preparing for, and coping with these realities as they manifest in a variety of ways is the bedrock goal of this book. It's thoroughly threaded into what I identify in *Snafu Edu* as five major reasons things go wrong in the college classroom: inequity, disconnection, distrust, failure, and fear. These five things do not encompass or explain everything that may go wrong in the college classroom—which is, as I've previously mentioned, an infinity number of things. They do, however, form a large umbrella of overlapping and interconnected causes for why some things routinely go wrong in the college classroom.

I argue that while we can implement teaching strategies to recognize and reduce these five things at the root of so many teaching and learning mishaps and missteps, we must also deliberately and concertedly normalize things going wrong in the college classroom. There is no way for people to teach and to learn effectively without making some mistakes. If you're not making at least some mistakes, you're not learning, and that includes the ongoing learning that every educator who wants to be an effective teacher must do. We are constantly learning how to effectively facilitate student success because students constantly change, we constantly change, new knowledge about our content is always being generated, and the world itself constantly changes.

The word "snafu" is a noun, a verb, and an acronym, and in all senses it accurately describes this important aspect of teaching and learning: when we are working hard to learn how to do new things, and when we are working hard to teach effectively, we *will* make mistakes.[12] Because we are humans who mess things up sometimes, we will cause snafus. But that's normal. Let me repeat: snafus are normal. Can we, with effort and practice, recognize some of the causes of major snafus, and can we respond productively, mitigating the impact of those snafu-causing agents? Yes. A thousand times yes. But can we *eliminate* totally the causes of college classroom snafus? Can we work really hard and completely overcome inequity, disconnection, distrust, failure, and fear in higher education, and henceforth reign over classrooms of perfect peace, justice, and harmony where nobody struggles, and nobody screws up? Nope, not a chance.

"Snafu" has also acquired a slang definition as an acronym, commonly ascribed to military usage, suggesting that the normal and expected state of affairs will include major hassles and headaches. It stands for "situation normal all fouled [or the other f-word] up." In *Snafu Edu*, I show that feeling like things are "all fouled up" is not an unusual occurrence for educators; it's just another Tuesday. It's "situation normal." While careful preparation, pedagogical research, reflection, and ongoing revisions to teaching practices reduce the chances of things going irrevocably wrong in the college classroom, we can't ever eliminate mistakes, missteps, discord, and just plain trouble. The requirements of learning, the impact of entrenched institutional structures and systemic injustices, the complexities of human interactions, and the weight of individual and collective histories means that there will always be moments when things go wrong.

Snafu Edu begins by wholly recognizing the reality of things sometimes going poorly in our classroom, no matter how well prepared and engaged we are as learners or how skilled we are as instructors. But we can try to clearly perceive snafus when they happen and cultivate awareness of what strategies will help us navigate them. More than "classroom management" or "classroom conflict resolution," we need to more widely and deliberately recognize that in any teaching and learning situation, things will sometimes go wrong. Sometimes, carefully planned assignments and activities will fail to achieve our hoped-for outcomes. Sometimes people will be angry and upset. Teaching and learning are hard, and sometimes, no matter what we do, they generate tension, pain, and unrewarding struggle. We *will* encounter all the types of snafus that are frequently generated by the five causes I unpack in this book.

Effective educators cannot eliminate such snafus but we also do not throw up our hands and give up. As writing professor Glenda Bissex states: "The underside of teaching is not merely the things that go wrong but the way we view the things that go wrong."[13] "We" in this sense means higher education at large and also ourselves as individual educators. As individuals, we can work to get past the habit of lying awake at 2:00 a.m. asking ourselves what we did wrong to make this happen and if we're a bad teacher and maybe we're not smart/good/socially adept enough to be teaching. Perfectionism is its own special kind of sanctioned torment in academia, reinforcing the most restrictive and discriminatory kind of gatekeeping and posing a serious threat to individual instructor's self-efficacy.[14] Fighting perfectionism and assuming the normality of snafus, we can instead ask: *What can I do when this happens? How can I work together with students and with other educators to prevent or mitigate these problems and to respond productively when these things happen? Where can I go for help and support when things go wrong?* We figure out what mistakes and missteps we can work on correcting going forward while understanding that future mistakes and missteps await. We empower ourselves not by denying the normality of snafus in effective teaching and learning but rather by cultivating an in-depth understanding of the nuances of those snafus and figuring out ways we can chip away at diminishing their causes.

Snafu Edu explores in detail these five major and interconnected reasons for why things go wrong in our college classrooms. Each of the main sections focuses on one of the reasons—inequity, disconnection, distrust, failure, and fear—and explores why things go wrong from both the instructor's and the students' points of view, examining how each of these issues impact both learning as well as teaching. In my discussion of why things go wrong in the college classroom, I try to broaden the "us" (instructors) versus "them" (students) lens through which we so often view teaching and learning. Unlike most teaching advice books, including my own *Geeky Pedagogy*, that portray teaching mostly or solely through the lens of instructors' individual challenges and efforts to improve, *Snafu Edu* highlights the porousness of boundaries and intermingled activities of teaching and learning, emphasizing the important parallels between student and instructor experiences. I believe that consciously reducing the deeply entrenched, intellectual, emotional, and academic barricades between "us" and "them" in the college classroom is one of our most powerful tools for understanding and lessening the negative fallout from teaching and learning snafus.

Our snafus cannot be adequately understood, let alone productively moderated, unless we can see ourselves and our students as members together in the unique and finite (one semester, for example) community of a college class. We cannot view instructors and learners as entirely separate entities facing entirely separate problems if we want to recognize, prepare for, withstand, and recover from fouled-up situations that routinely occur while teaching and learning. Inequity, disconnection, distrust, failure, and fear do not affect learners and instructors in the same ways, and learners and instructors are varied and diverse, so these snafu-causing issues do not affect all learners the same way or instructors the same way. But, to a person, inequity, disconnection, distrust, failure, and fear in various guises affect all of us in higher education. By remembering that we as instructors must navigate those obstacles alongside our students, by recognizing the shared roots of our obstacles, we will be better able to find a way out when we're snarled up in a snafu.

To break from the clutches of our snafus, we must overcome the "closed-door" culture of college teaching by cultivating our personal pedagogical learning network and fighting the widespread isolation that so many instructors experience. Far too often, teaching college classes is viewed as a solitary undertaking. When we view our work teaching in the college classroom within a silo of our own intellect and abilities, when things go wrong—because things *will* go wrong—we're stuck there all alone in our silo, smothering under a pile of classroom conundrums and potential problems that just got dumped on us like a bumper crop of corn being stored for the winter.

I assert throughout this book that talking and learning from other educators who want to be effective teachers is a vital part of contending with teaching and learning snafus. We think, like that webinar title suggested, that something went wrong in class so therefore something must be wrong with what we're doing, and therefore we have a "teaching problem." Or, even worse, that we ourselves are the teaching problem and that there's something wrong with us. But consider how differently it would feel, when something goes wrong, to say to ourselves, *Something went wrong in class. Drat these pesky, reoccurring realities and humanity-based messes that everyone teaching and learning in higher education must navigate. What was that I read in* Snafu Edu *about disconnection? I'll pull that book out again and maybe I could also ask [Trusted Colleague/Wise Mentor/Supportive Pal on Social Media] what they did when this happened to them.*

I hope that anyone at any point in their teaching career will find *Snafu Edu* an energizing and thought-provoking read, but educators who've already logged some miles in the classroom and have subsequently accrued all-too-vivid memories of the times things went wrong will especially benefit from this in-depth examination of mistakes, muddles, and messes. Midway through our teaching career is prime time for restocking our teaching tool kit with strategies for reducing and mitigating snafus, building on the knowledge and experience we've gained thus far. I must note that "teaching career" applies to people in a range of professional roles. There is a sharp delineation and, usually, a hierarchy between "faculty" and "staff" in higher education, but numerous people in student support services, tutoring centers, and other campus offices frequently work in classroom settings and as teachers. Although I'm writing primarily with professors—including non-tenure-track faculty, instructors, and graduate-level teaching assistants—in mind, the snafus that I unpack in this book, and the strategies I suggest for reducing and mitigating them, are applicable in many college-setting teaching and learning configurations.

There is a subset of college educators who do not care—or have convinced themselves they don't care—about teaching effectively and/or who refuse to revise and improve their teaching practices no matter how much evidence accrues that their students are not learning and succeeding. In my experience, this is a statistically small percentage of people teaching college classes, yet they wield noteworthy power to negatively impact students' educational experiences.[15] This book isn't for them. Nor does it contain any blueprints for the revolutionary reform we'd need if we wanted to change all the systems and structures in higher education that allow demonstrably terrible teaching practices to continue unchecked.[16] But *Snafu Edu* does offer insights and actionable strategies for when things go wrong, written for people who willingly engage in ongoing pedagogical learning, reflection, and professional development because they want to be effective teachers and/or help other people be effective teachers.

Snafu Edu emphasizes that things routinely get fouled up when we're learning and teaching, and these things can frequently be traced back to inequity, disconnection, distrust, failure and fear. Understanding how these five things impact teaching and learning in overlapping ways can help us shift focus away from the negativity biases, individualized shame spirals, and, on the flip side, defensiveness and condemnation of students that engulf many college educators when things go wrong in the classroom. We can also proactively use specific course design principles and pedagogical practices to reduce big teaching and learning snafus by increasing equity, building connections, fostering trust, enabling success, and increasing agency.

In this book, I do not examine the most extreme example of something going wrong in the classroom: physical danger and life-threatening violence. The absolute worst worst-case scenario in any teaching and learning context is a mass shooting or any type of physical attack on instructors and/or students. Violence on college campuses, especially gun violence, sexual violence, and racially motivated violence, are not another part of the "situation normal all fouled up" day-to-day context for teaching and learning I'm addressing in this book. However, it's not so unimaginably rare that I can let the topic go unmentioned. I hate to have to say it but here goes: students and instructors should know security protocols and procedures on their campus, including active-shooter responses, and be aware of campus advocates and supports. This is true for everyone but especially for instructors from historically underrepresented groups, such as women faculty of color, who are more likely to experience threats of physical harm in their professorial roles. While I don't address acts of physical violence themselves in *Snafu Edu*, the trauma that occurs in the wake of such events contributes to how inequity, disconnection, distrust, failure, and fear manifest in the experiences of both students as well as instructors in higher education.[17]

Snafu Edu is also not a step-by-step to-do list that promises to magically disappear all the ordinary snafus we will encounter in teaching and learning. No guarantees here to "fix your teaching problems." Rather, it's a starting point for reflecting and strategizing during your ongoing pedagogical learning, when you're applying that big brain of yours to the next complicated teaching and learning dilemma you've just encountered and figuring out how to best address it in your specific and unique teaching context. *Snafu Edu* won't provide you with any simple solutions or easy-peasy-lemon-squeezy answers. But it can be a touch point for anyone trying to understand why things went wrong and give you some approaches to consider going forward while reminding you that we're not alone in facing these snafus.

Stop, Think, Identify, Repair

In *Snafu Edu,* I offer some specific repair strategies for productively recognizing and responding to these five overlapping categories of things that can go wrong for learners and for educators in the college classroom. I position these strategies as the last step in my variation of a common conflict resolution and classroom management technique known as SOAR (Stop, Observe, Assess, React).[18] My version draws on the scholarship of teaching and learning, published pedagogical advice, and my own years of experience of having oh-so-many things go oh-so-wrong in the college classroom. STIR stands for Stop, Think, Identify, and Repair, and it goes like this:

> **Stop:** Call a time-out, halt class business as usual, and pause. The pause can be a matter of minutes or it can be significantly longer—whatever time is needed to immediately interrupt reactive thoughts and silence all knee-jerk internal or external commentary.
>
> **Think:** Using that academically trained, highly skilled brain of yours, examine the situation, looking closely at exactly what the snafu is, considering what might be causing it, and reflecting on what you might need to do next. This could take place in the space of a minute or a few days or for weeks.
>
> **Identify:** Clearly speak to and inquire about what happened with open-minded curiosity, describing, defining, explaining, and asking questions as needed.
>
> **Repair:** In whatever way is within your power as an individual educator in your unique teaching context, apply the short-term patches or implement the long-term changes needed to mitigate and reduce the effects of the snafu and its potential for reoccurring in your classroom.

Some specific STIR strategies outlined in this book include things like apologizing when we've messed up; prepping for certain predictable interactions with scripted remarks; being able to revise course plans and class activities; and leaning into learning, i.e., embracing as much as possible the power of productive failure and the new knowledge it can generate.

I want to acknowledge that "STIR" is a somewhat hackneyed acronym, as in "stir yourself to action." Don't just sit there: get moving already! You can do it! Go, go, go! Ugh, so cheesy (although arguably not as cheesy as "soar"). Also, I'm aware that scholars of teaching and learning, myself included, have a weakness for jargony acronyms. But the unabashedly invigorating overtones of the word "stir" helps to counteract that overwhelming and disempowering feeling of futility that we educators might experience when we begin to truly grapple with exactly how reliably things can—and will—sometimes go wrong in the college classroom, for reasons both within and outside our individual control. Furthermore, when things go wrong in the college classroom, it's all too easy to give in to hasty reactions or flippant/passive-aggressive/immediately regrettable responses that further exacerbate the problem at hand. A highly memorable acronym like "STIR" can be a valuable tool for cutting through in-the-moment flare-ups of emotions and ego and enacting more productive and useful response strategies.

The "Stop" part of STIR will enable us to be more aware that when a snafu occurs, we can't just keep barreling onward, hoping it will sort itself out. When he was relatively new to college teaching, a friend of mine once had a student suddenly stand up in class, rush to the wastebasket, and throw up. "Oh, my gosh!" I said, when my friend described this incident to me. "What did you do?" "Oh, I just kept lecturing," he said. I didn't have the heart to tell him that not a single student in that class heard a single word he said after their classmate barfed right there in the room in front of everyone. Maybe even more problematically, when the professor ignored this unignorable commotion in class, his students couldn't help but wonder, What's the deal with this guy? Does he, like, not see us? Does he think we didn't notice what just happened? Student-upchucks-in-class is not a common teaching situation for professors, but students-and-instructors-get-trapped-in-a-snafu is an exceedingly common and damaging way things go wrong in the college classroom. And so too is the frequency with which professors try to ignore snafus, given how fraught such situations can be, how underprepared we may be for them, and what an emotional, cognitive, and psychological toll they can take on us.

Acronyms are our friends in times of stress and turmoil. The power of STIR for me as a teacher is the way it helps me to remember that things *will* sometimes go wrong and, when they do, to not freeze (which, as a wannabe Vulcan, is my natural response to heightened human emotions), fight (an unhelpful Klingon-like response in the college classroom setting), or flee (beam me up!). A handy mnemonic device can cut through the noise in our heads when our bodies and brains are under stress. STIR is easy to remember, even when you're facing something that's gone really, truly, awfully, terribly wrong, and every fiber of your being is in freeze, fight, or flight. I know, from years of experience falling flat on my teaching face and struggling to get back up, that

> When something goes wrong
> in the classroom or teaching,
> STIR can prevent me
> from totally freaking.

A Snafu Go-Bag

Snafu Edu is divided into five main parts focusing on one of the reasons why things go wrong in the college classroom.[19] Each of the main parts begins with a chapter briefly summarizing how that issue—inequity, disconnection, distrust, failure, or fear—fouls up learning and teaching. The next chapter in each main part outlines how to identify these types of snafus and building on the STIR formula, details some specific repair strategies for productively coping and responding when things go wrong. The final chapter in each part explores some of the evidence-based ways to proactively reduce and counteract the likelihood of this snafu with course design and ongoing pedagogical practices. In each chapter, samples of words we can use—in writing or spoken aloud—for responding to, mitigating, and reducing snafus are either italicized or italicized and further emphasized with an arrow bullet point. These "scripts" aren't meant to be memorized and recited verbatim but rather suggestions for helping you find and use the words that work for you and to have them ready before a snafu ensues. Scripts are an especially helpful tool for people like me who tend to either become suddenly speechless, begin babbling, or both during moments of stress.

Each chapter concludes with "Gear for Your Go-Bag"—a bullet point list of the chapter's central points, key takeaways, and suggested strategies to have at the ready, for quick consultation and implementation when things go wrong. Like a natural disaster preparedness kit in the basement or a zombie apocalypse bug-out bag hidden under our bed, our teaching and learning snafu go-bag is stocked with the items we need for survival and ideas we can use immediately when the sirens sound and we have to STIR and take action. Every educator has to pack their own go-bag, because every educator works in their own unique teaching context and must contend with unique snafus. But we can start building our go-bags with shared strategies proven in the research to be useful when inequity, disconnection, distrust, fear, and failure foul up teaching and learning.

Teaching, Learning, and Emergency Landings

While *Snafu Edu* frankly and realistically discusses reoccurring obstacles in teaching and learning, it is ultimately an optimistic book about the transformative power of education and communities of learners. It does not dwell unduly in the darkest, dreariest places of educational institutions and systems, nor does it call on readers to abandon all hope. In fact, more of this book describes things that we as individuals working in higher education can do to reduce the odds of things going wrong than it does describing the things that go wrong. But I do insist that we can never pretend that things won't go wrong, because they will. Teaching and learning are not perfectible activities, and they are never easy, but worthwhile, meaningful work rarely is. Hard things are hard, and authentic learning is a difficult and complex undertaking. Teaching effectively is a difficult and complex undertaking.

Without in any way suggesting that our individual pedagogical efforts alone can "fix" every higher-ed snafu, I do want to help readers better understand what is happening during some of the most unpleasant, difficult, and bewildering moments of college teaching and learning and help you build a go-bag of useful knowledge and actionable repair strategies for when something goes kerflooey in the classroom. I hope *Snafu Edu* can help us move a little more smoothly, as individuals and collectively, through all the muddles, miscommunications, mistakes, and outright fiascos, and to emerge knowing more about teaching and learning in our individual and unique teaching contexts. Snafus often have the potential to become vital moments of intellectual growth, helping us gain important new insights. Without sugarcoating the reality of how scary, maddening, or uncomfortable it is in the midst of a snafu, when we know that it's "situation normal," we may be able to allow mistakes and the problems to inform and increase our understanding and to help us build and practice new skills in the moment and going forward.

As the authors of *The Worst-Case Scenario Survival Handbook*[20] point out in their instructions for non-pilots who find themselves in a worst-case scenario that requires landing a plane, sometimes emergency landings actually work better than struggling to implement your original flight plan: "a well-executed emergency landing in bad terrain can be less hazardous than an uncontrolled landing on an established field." This book is all about the teaching and learning emergency landings we have to make in bad terrain. When we're piloting a class as instructors and learners, unexpected situations—obstacles, frustrations, mistakes, and errors—can also create opportunities for increasing our knowledge and abilities in real ways. We need to prepare for it, not panic when it happens or pretend it's not happening, and then we have to brace for the impact. When we prepare for an emergency landing, we are preparing not only for things going wrong but also for the real, meaningful, and sometimes life-changing impact that teaching and learning can have on students and instructors.

Fouled-up situations leading to effective learning and teaching in college classrooms? Yup, totally normal.

Gear for Your Go-Bag

- Teaching and learning are not perfectible undertakings because, as human beings, we will make mistakes and mess things up. Snafus are normal.
- Social and embodied identities are important factors in teaching and learning because they are important factors in how human beings interact with one another.
- The Super Teacher myth creates damaging stereotypes and expectations about what college teaching and learning—and college professors themselves—"look like."
- We can empower ourselves to effectively navigate snafus in the college classroom by using a STIR strategy when things go wrong: Stop, Think, Identify, and Repair.

PART I

INEQUITY

If the alligator gets you in its jaws, you must prevent it from shaking you or rolling over—these instinctual actions cause severe tissue damage.

—"How to Wrestle Free from an Alligator,"
The Worst-Case Scenario Survival Handbook

Chapter 1

INEQUITY FOULS UP
LEARNING AND TEACHING

Imagine higher education is a vast sea, teeming with knowledge and wisdom. On the far shore awaits a new life that's immeasurably improved by learning. All you have to do is get in and start swimming. Except: some people start out with expensive scuba gear and some people arrive with nothing. Some feel right at home in the water, so they jump in joyfully and immediately start splashing around, while, for others, merely wading in up to their ankles is a major endeavor. That guy over there has a yacht: he'll be in Advanced Degree Land in no time—but here's someone packed into a tiny rowboat trying to get their entire extended family across. Olympic-level swimmers jackknife in and zip through the waves like Aquaman, while beginners dog paddle in the shallows, working just to keep their heads above water. Alligators are everywhere, but they're hunting some swimmers and not others. A privileged few will make it through the whole ocean and never feel the alligators snapping at their heels, trying to drag them down. "Alligators?" they'll say. "What alligators? I didn't see any alligators."

We in higher education are awash in a bottomless ocean of inequity. We're soaking in it. Because higher education exists in the real world where human beings do human stuff, academia is wrought by the same historical systems of discrimination that crisscross our society. A plethora of entrenched intersectional biases and prejudices, such as racism, sexism, classism, ableism, and homophobia, negatively impact teaching and learning because these things negatively impact the world where we teach and learn. They don't miraculously disappear when we walk into a college classroom.

Yet often I read or hear advice about college learning and teaching that seems to presuppose a level or mostly level playing field for students and for instructors, as if there's an ocean of higher education knowledge that everyone enters wearing the exact same set of swim fins. Routinely, I see otherwise solid, evidence-based suggestions about effective teaching fail to even mention how an instructor's unique teaching context, including employment status and positionality, creates pedagogical challenges. I also regularly come across study guides for students that detail time management and academic skill building without paying adequate attention to how any single student's embodied and social identities, family background, age, disabilities, citizenship status, and economic resources will have a big impact on what they must do to complete their degree.

That said, research and published work about inclusive teaching practices is on the rise, although higher education researchers don't always agree on what exactly constitutes "inclusive teaching practices," and intersectionality remains an underexamined component of this work.[1] Even as it evolves and new debates emerge in the scholarship, and even as higher education faces virulent political and legislative attacks on DEI programming and curriculum, campuses and individual practitioners are increasingly aware of the need to utilize teaching practices that facilitate academic success for diverse learners with a wide variety of life experiences. The COVID-19 pandemic significantly increased many instructors' awareness of trauma-informed teaching practices and fueled widespread discussions about the ways in which a student's life circumstances can encumber or enhance their ability to learn and succeed in college.[2]

In my view, two things are largely missing in discussions about inclusive teaching. First, we need to pay a lot more attention to the fact that college instructors themselves are also swimming/barely staying afloat/drowning in the same ocean of inequity that students are traversing in higher education. Anyone engaged in academia and college teaching encounters numerous gendered, racialized, and other biases and expectations about scholarly expertise and pedagogical authority. Anyone who doesn't "look like" a professor[3] routinely and persistently encounters student resistance, incivility, and overt hostility that white able-bodied cisgendered men teaching college do not. Many of the newly emerging inclusive teaching "best practices" do not adequately account for how systemic discrimination shapes an instructor's ability to implement certain pedagogical strategies.[4] We can't talk about how inequity negatively impacts college learners without also talking about how inequity negatively impacts college teachers.

Second, as inclusive teaching practices become an accepted pedagogical imperative in higher education, it's vital that we more concertedly normalize making mistakes when we undertake the difficult task of reducing inequity in our classes. The work of making learning more equitable for every college student will include snafus. Tracie Marcella Addy and her coauthors of *What Inclusive Instructors Do* write that "being an inclusive instructor is an ongoing process that involves learning, mistakes, persistence, reflection, and willingness to adapt teaching practices to a diverse student population."[5] I would emphasize that being an inclusive instructor is an ongoing process that involves *repeatedly* making *a lot* of mistakes.

We can and must take steps as individual educators to recognize and respond to inequity. We can take steps to mitigate the negative impact of inequity when we encounter it. And we can implement strategies to build greater equity in the classroom, considering how systemic inequity constrains not only learners but also instructors and fully recognizing the reality that everyone will make some mistakes and things will go wrong when we are doing this work.

Inequity alligators are everywhere in higher education. The water is full of them. But we can't just bury ourselves in the sand and hide from these dangerous reptiles. We must wade into the water when we want to teach effectively. So, when an alligator of inequity, injustice, and discrimination grabs us or our students, we need to keep it from rolling over and dragging us down.

Inequity Fouls Up Learning

Every conscientious educator I know keeps an embarrassing mental list of "Things I Used to Do That Make Me Cringe Now." Near the top of my own list is this statement I used to put in my syllabus:

> I give every student in my classes an equal opportunity for success. Please do not ask me for any type of preferential treatment—especially deadline extensions or extra credit—that is not offered to all the other students! I understand that you juggle academic, family, athletic, personal, and employment responsibilities. I know that personal, health, or family problems may make completing the work for our class particularly challenging for a few of you. But for each student to have an equal opportunity to succeed in our class, the assignments, grading, and all deadlines in our syllabus apply to every student equally.

All my pedagogical intentions in crafting this syllabus statement—what I sometimes called my "Equal Opportunity Policy"—were good ones. I set out to convey that I wanted every student to succeed. I hoped to reassure students that I wouldn't play favorites. I thought that I was showing them that I understood the challenges and obstacles students faced. Last but not least, I was trying to make my own daily work life less stressful and proactively reduce negative interactions and conflicts with students that can regularly occur around missed deadlines and grades.

However, my good intentions to foster equality did not translate into an equity-minded teaching practice. My emphasis on treating everyone the same way, no matter what, did not account for the inequities some students have to navigate that other students do not. Isis Artze-Vega and coauthors write in *The Norton Guide to Equity-Minded Teaching* that "equity-minded educators work to ensure that every student has the opportunity to learn, succeed, and thrive. This work involves making adjustments to account for the imbalances in students' experiences and access to resources."[6] Unfortunately, the tone and content of my "Equal Opportunity Policy" not only failed to account for those imbalances but actually reinforced certain barriers. For one thing, the statement conveyed to students that if they found themselves falling behind or not able to complete work, they should not approach me for help. That's not what I was trying to say, but it's the message that I conveyed with this wording. By emphasizing what I would not do, I failed to highlight for students all the ways I could help them get back on track and the ways I would be able to provide support and assistance. I created an unnecessary impediment to students seeking assistance.

Furthermore, that impediment hindered some students more than others. An academically experienced student well versed in higher ed's "hidden curriculum" might let that statement roll right off their back and confidently proceed to seek assistance when they needed it. An inexperienced first-generation student or a student already feeling isolated and wondering if they really belong on campus at all, or a student who's missed a couple classes and is now caught in a destructive cycle of shame, avoidance, and denial, or a student with a chronic health condition, could interpret that statement as confirmation that something's wrong with them and they're on their own.[7] Professor Neuhaus certainly won't be interested in listening to them talk through their academic struggles and strategize for improvement!

With this policy, I intimated that no matter what their life circumstances are or how much they're learning in a class, if students miss a deadline or an assignment, that's just too bad. But a student's life circumstances matter very much to their academic success, and in order to best enable subject area learning for every student in our class, we need to first and foremost consider the historical and continued reality of systemic opportunity gaps in higher education for some groups of students when their success becomes dictated not by their ability to learn and demonstrate their learning but rather by their life circumstances.[8] An equity-minded pedagogical approach strives "to realize equal outcomes among all students" and "is informed by principles, practices, and historical understandings that aim to realize equal outcomes among all students, with particular attention to students of minoritized races and ethnicities."[9] Inequity—not ability nor willpower nor mindset nor any personal quality whatsoever—is the big scaly razor-toothed monster snafuing learning for so many college students.

When inequity interferes with learning, we have to see and name that alligator, avoiding a deficit model that labels and limits students by mistakenly defining lack of resources as lack of students' ability to learn.[10] For example, when a student's most basic physical needs—food and shelter—are insecure, their ability to learn, demonstrate their learning to the best of their ability, and even just remain enrolled in college is seriously compromised.[11] As a 2022 *Washington Post* article described, a lack of familial economic resources can turn even a $25 bus ticket into a major obstacle to a college student's success.[12] The pandemic era crises of 2020 onward only exacerbated the problem. According to the Urban Institute, "more than half of students at two-year colleges and over 40 percent of students at four-year colleges experienced housing insecurity in 2020, and 14 percent experienced homelessness . . ."[13] Research consistently shows that housing and food insecurity is more likely to constitute obstacles for student success when students come from historically minoritized groups, an inequity that became more marked during the pandemic.[14]

Housing and food insecurity is linked more frequently and persistently to certain racial identities and to disabilities, disproportionately draining these students' physical, cognitive, and psychological resources. Navigating ableism, racism, ethnocentrism, heterosexism, and other higher ed systemic biases creates obstacles and barriers for some students and not for others in terms of health, safety, and sense of belonging on campus. By the most crucial single measure of student success—graduating with a degree—racial disparities illustrate how systemic biases and discrimination create inequitable learning conditions. Data published by the U.S. Department of Education in 2022 showed that "nearly 68 percent of all White students graduated within six years. But only 45.7 percent of Black students had earned a bachelor's degree within six years. There was a gap of 22.2 percentage points in degree attainment between Blacks and Whites."[15] First-generation students also graduate at significantly lower rates, and, again, the COVID-19 pandemic appears to have directly exacerbated these inequitable educational conditions.[16]

These statistics won't concern you if you see your professorial job as keeping the maximum number of people shut out of the Hallowed Halls of Learning or if you're a proponent of "weed-out" classes (as if some of the students admitted to your institution are as disposable and unwanted as weeds in your Edenic educational garden). But most people taking the time to read a book about college teaching believe that a necessary part of our work as educators is to actively support and encourage *all* our students—to invite all of them into our subject matter rather than acting as subject gatekeepers.

It's helpful here to use an illustration created by the Robert Wood Johnson Foundation (RWJF) and reproduced in figure 1.[17]

In my old "Equal Opportunity Policy," I stated that learning activities and assessments would be administered in the same way for every single student. This is "equality" as defined in the RWJF illustration: "Everyone gets the same—regardless if it's needed or right for them." While an equal approach to all our assignments and course materials sounds good at first, it does not adequately consider students' various starting points and ambulatory needs before they "cross the street." An "equal" approach fills our class with curbs and poorly designated street crossings, which pose no problem for some students but make crossing the street unnecessarily difficult for others.

Addressing inequity does not mean creating different standards for some students. Just like in the illustration where everyone must travel across the street, everyone in our classes must meet the same learning goals. But we don't need to insist that all students follow precisely the same path in lockstep toward that goal if the path creates unnecessary obstacles for some. For instance, you're going to give students a reading assignment. Great! I'm a big fan of reading. I'm living that bookworm life. But if your reading assignment is in a very expensive textbook, right off the bat you've created an obstacle for low-income students who will not be able to easily access the book. So you state in the syllabus and several times in class that students can access emergency funds for school supplies available through Student Support Services, and you put a copy of the book on reserve at the library, which creates an additional step that some students must do to complete the assignments but technically now everyone has access.

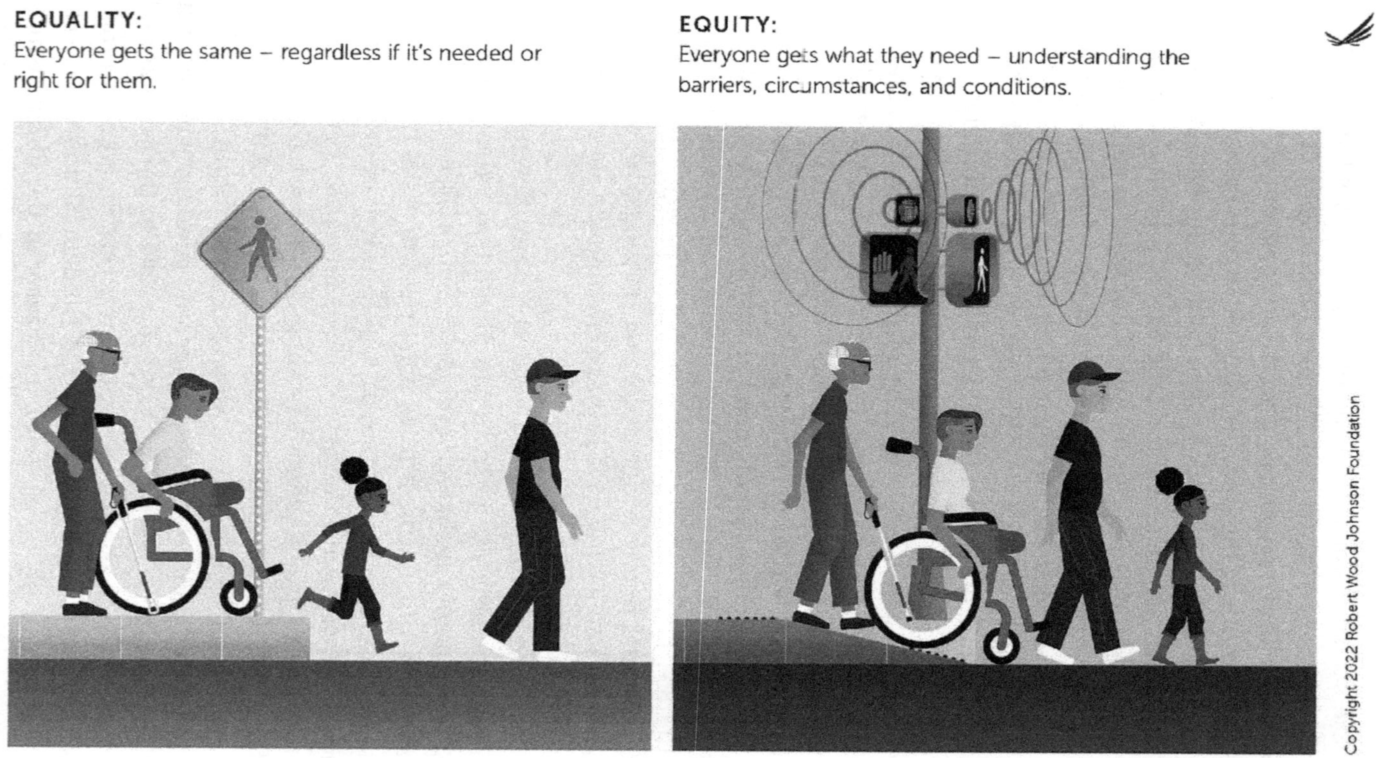
EQUALITY:
Everyone gets the same – regardless if it's needed or right for them.
EQUITY:
Everyone gets what they need – understanding the barriers, circumstances, and conditions.
Copyright 2022 Robert Wood Johnson Foundation

Figure 1. Equality vs. Equity

Uh, hold up, Professor Speed Racer. There's a visually impaired student in your class, and there is no audio version of the book. The student could use an e-reader device but only if there's an e-reader–enabled copy of the reading. Okay, so you email this student a PDF of the reading. Fixed? Not yet. Their e-reader doesn't do PDFs, and in any case the book is full of detailed, convoluted graphs and images that are difficult to summarize in words. No matter what your intentions were in assigning that book, you've increased the likelihood that this student will feel frustrated about a physical disability they have no control over, and as a bonus you've just made extra work for yourself while increasing the probability of a student perceiving you as unhelpful. Everyone must read the book—it's the same assignment for everyone—but while it's equal, it's not necessarily equitable. The visually impaired student is having to work more to clear a higher hurdle than the other students to achieve the same learning goal.

Or consider an in-class lecture. Everyone hears the exact same lecture, so it's equal, right? But then again, not everyone *can* hear, nor does everyone have the physical or linguistic capability to process spoken language at the same speed. That's assuming, of course, that everyone will be in perfect health, able to attend class the day of the lecture, and ready to maintain a high level of alertness and receptiveness to information conveyed in this way. LOL. What's more, taking effective notes during a lecture is a learned academic skill, meaning that students graduating from elite high schools with many AP classes under their belt arrive to your class having had a lot of training and practice for effective note-taking that students from less academically privileged backgrounds do not. When it's time to review for an exam, students from the latter group will have fewer notes and therefore fewer takeaways from the lecture to review, creating an equal but not equitable learning environment.

In contrast, equitable assignments and classroom activities would look like the well-marked street crossing with a modified curb in the RWJF illustration, defining "equity" as "Everyone gets what they need, understanding the barriers, circumstances, and conditions." That's our task as educators: understanding the barriers and getting students what they need so that they can successfully make their way across the street. In their landmark book on this topic titled *Inclusive Teaching: Strategies for Promoting Equity in the College Classroom*, Kelly Hogan and Viji Sathy explain that "equity is the goal we strive to reach, in which all learners start by having access to the same opportunities. But access is not enough. Equity requires naming and dismantling the systems, structures, and oppressive forces that act as barriers for some students more than others. When we work to remove barriers, more individuals can succeed. This is an ongoing process."[18]

"Naming" these "systems, structures, and oppressive forces" is the starting point. We begin by recognizing the numerous ways that it fouls up learning. But inequity also fouls up teaching, and that too must be addressed and clearly named.

Inequity Fouls Up Teaching

Discourse about college teaching commonly ignores or underplays the reality of scholars and instructors living in bodies with identity markers and physical limitations, in a world where every gathering of human beings in every institution is affected by stereotypes, assumptions, and biases regarding embodied identity and physical limitations. Additional factors such as economic precarity and workplace conditions such as class size and number of classes further create teaching conditions that are far from equitable.[19] Just as inequity creates obstacles and barriers for some students' learning and not others, inequity forces some educators to continually navigate barriers that other educators never encounter. Published advice and discourse about inclusive teaching has lagged behind in its attention to inequitable teaching realities, but students' gendered and racialized assumptions about academic expertise in the college classroom, and the obstacles those assumptions create for teaching, are extensively and thoroughly described in a vast number of articles and books across numerous disciplines.[20]

Obviously, it's not only students who bring assumptions about academic expertise and ability into the spaces of higher education: gendered and racialized stereotypes about who can and who cannot be a scholar and a professor proliferate across disciplines and all academic spaces, though some disciplines seem especially likely to spawn hostile higher ed workplaces. (I'm looking at you, STEM.)[21] In academia generally, women faculty of color are "presumed incompetent," in the words of the groundbreaking anthology of the same name edited by Gabriella Gutiérrez y Muhs.[22] Scholarly literature and first-person accounts extensively document the relentless discrimination facing Black, Indigenous, Latinx, and other people of color working in higher education.[23]

One particularly harmful way that inequitable teaching conditions negatively impact faculty is how many aspects of the tenure process fail to account for disparate teaching realities and other systemic inequities in academic work, such as disproportionate intersectional emotional labor and service demands.[24] Statistical data reflects this reality, as sociology professor and scholar of teaching and learning Chavella Pittman writes:

> Tenure-track and tenured faculty members at degree-granting institutions in the United States are disproportionately white. White faculty members are especially overrepresented at the higher ranks, making up 79 percent of full professors and 74 percent of associate professors, according to data from the National Center for Education Statistics. And while racial minorities are underrepresented at all faculty ranks, they are particularly underrepresented among full professors: only 4 percent of full professors are Black, 4 percent are Hispanic, and less than 1 percent are American Indian or Alaskan Native (assistant professors, by comparison, are 8 percent Black, 6 percent Hispanic, and less than 1 percent American Indian or Alaskan Native).[25]

These numbers connote the power of obstacles to tenure for faculty from historically marginalized groups. Tenure in fact goes to the very heart of disparate teaching and working realities in higher education, as TaLisa Carter and Miltonette Craig argue, noting that "Black faculty pursuing tenure is a political threat to white hegemony in the academy resulting in an increase of social control."[26]

Because of their embodied and social identities, many instructors stand on the edge of the higher ed ocean, already exhausted by microaggressions and ongoing systemic discrimination in every other academic experience.[27] That includes the sheer physical toll wrought on instructors' bodies by the ongoing stress and trauma of racism and sexism.[28] An additional physical taxation on an instructor's pedagogical batteries increases exponentially when navigating the ableism of higher education.[29] What happens when literally—not figuratively but literally, actually, for real—opening a door creates an obstacle for someone to literally—not figuratively but literally, actually, for real—enter the classroom or sit at a desk?[30]

Classroom and other academic spaces that are inaccessible in the most rudimentary way create greater pedagogical hurdles for instructors with physical disabilities or who are neurodivergent.[31] Rooms too crowded for a wheelchair or walker, inaccessible chairs and desks, elevators that don't work, teeny-weeny restrooms, "open plan" offices, nonexistent microphones, seizure-inducing lighting—the list of ways higher ed learning spaces can actively repel instructors with disabilities is truly endless. Even once you've gotten in the door, student biases about an instructor's physical disability create additional teaching labor—work required to interrupt those biases so students can proceed forward to learning the content.[32]

Similarly, when an instructor's gender fluidity or presumed or stated sexuality identity fails to conform to the highly limited and limiting heterosexual cisgendered male stereotype of "professor," additional obstacles to effective teaching and learning materialize.[33] Research further demonstrates that these obstacles manifest in different ways depending on the content and subject matter of a class. Instructors teaching classes related to social justice issues routinely face higher levels of student resistance and incivility.[34] One of the most persistent underlying obstacles to effective teaching is how gendered and racialized stereotypes about intellectual expertise cause students to question and distrust an instructor's abilities and authority. Instructors who don't fulfill that stereotype start every class hoisting a specific pedagogical burden that white, cisgendered, able-bodied men do not have to shoulder.

The most prevalent inequity facing college educators, cutting across all identity groups and institutions, is employment status and its impact on teaching conditions. The majority of people teaching college-level classes are working on a contingent (non-tenured or tenure track basis). Contingent positions account for 68 percent of all faculty in U.S. colleges and universities as of fall 2021, according to the National Center for Education Statistics.[35] Such faculty would be better referred to as VITAL (visiting, instructor, teaching assistant, adjunct, or lecturer),[36] yet the sheer numbers of contingent faculty have barely moved the needle in higher education when it comes to workplace equity. A two-tiered system of tenure track or non–tenure track employment conditions remains fully in place.[37] Contingent employment gives faculty little or no support for doing the things they are expected to be doing as scholars in academia—conducting research, pondering the results, disseminating new knowledge—let alone support for formal ongoing pedagogical learning. Although graduate student and adjunct instructors are working to organize and collectively bargain for wages and improved working conditions, vast inequities remain.[38]

Contingent faculty's low pay means that someone trying to earn a living will usually have to teach a large number of classes and a large number of students, often at more than one institution, leaving less time and energy for each individual student and each separate class. This is not to say that VITAL faculty cannot be effective educators and facilitate transformative student learning, but they face specific teaching realities not faced by college professors who are on the tenure track or already tenured.[39] Low pay and employment precarity hamper instructors' ability to engage in the pedagogical reflection, revision, and learning that most benefits our ability to facilitate student learning.[40] In terms of both time available for these activities but also in terms of the risk-reward balance inherent to improving teaching, contingent employment creates inequitable teaching conditions. Trying new techniques or redesigning assignments is far less viable or even desirable when those things mean a lot of new and extra prep, leading almost inevitably to mistakes that need correcting and possibly even student confusion, resistance, and pushback.[41] In a contingent employment context, the long-term rewards for such innovations are often not on the table.

Crucially, such student confusion, resistance, and pushback can negatively impact student course evaluations and student evaluations of teaching (SET)—an almost ubiquitous part of college teaching that are poorly implemented and poorly utilized on a routine basis when assessing teaching efficacy and make-or-break employment decisions in higher education. SET plays a highly significant role in negatively impacting employment and retention of instructors from structurally disadvantaged groups, instructors with visible disabilities, and indeed anyone who doesn't match the characteristics of the professorial stereotype.[42] Another serious aspect of how inequity fouls up teaching is the way that poorly designed and interpreted SET can deeply damage teaching self-efficacy. Derogatory and demeaning student comments, and statements from students that reinforce racial hierarchies, sexism, homophobia, transphobia, or ableism, can deplete an educator's willingness to make the extra effort—i.e., engage in pedagogical learning and reflection—that effective teaching demands. Such discourse can and does create exhausting additional mental, intellectual, and emotional obstacles for instructors who want to help students learn but have been attacked and degraded by anonymous student comments.[43]

One final and vivid example of how inequity can flare up in the college classroom involves the simple question shaping the very first interaction between students and between students and instructors: What's your name? "What's your name?" is never merely a request for information. It's a recognition of someone's subjectivity. Learning, correctly pronouncing, and routinely using our students' names is a teaching practice resoundingly proven to have a positive impact on student learning, no matter the class size or subject matter, on-site or asynchronously online.[44] However, names are also one of the things in the college classroom that can go wrong, and not knowing and incorrectly pronouncing names frequently fouls up teaching and learning.[45]

Learning and using each other's names gives us a snapshot of how systemic inequity is a gatekeeper that routinely and regularly polices who does and does not really "belong" in higher education. If some names are deemed "difficult to pronounce," then the presupposition is that some other names—more, ahem, *normal* names—are *easy* to pronounce. For students in the college context, a "normal" name is like an automatic entry pass to the campus community. When your name—a primary, defining characteristic of your personhood—trips right off the tongue of your professors, your right to belong there is literally reiterated. Of course you should be here, *Emma!* Obviously you belong in college, *James!* In contrast, what happens when the professor stumbles? Wait, say that again? How do you pronounce that, Alearyah, Demyan, Jonnell, Tayzara? Afraid of making a mistake, the instructor may well avoid saying the name at all, and, hey ho, there you go: the student is more often left out of classroom activities, feels less welcome and less like a full member of the learning community.

For instructors as well, a "normal" name reinforces academic authority and reinforces student biases about professors. Professor *Jones* is easy to talk to. Professor *Miller* seems like a good guy. "Wait, what the [redacted] is that professor's name again? Xie? Somasunderan? Zakrajseck? How do you even *say* that?" The normalization of certain names in the college setting is more than a mere blip on our pedagogical radar. Names and using names can have a real impact on students' first impressions and throughout the class. Furthermore, the norming of certain kinds of names isn't unique to students. I once saw a tenured senior professor introduce a visiting professor from India to the entire university with a jokey comment about how "difficult" it was to pronounce their Indian name. The subtext of that comment was "What a weird 'foreign' name you have! How will we—the people who *really* belong here—ever learn to say your name? Hahaha!"

Consider too the systemic inequities at work when the white, cisgendered, able-bodied professor says to students, "Hey, call me Michael, my dudes." Sure, no problem, *Michael*, because before you even opened your mouth in the very first class, students assumed you have academic expertise and teaching authority because you fulfill all their gendered, racialized, and other embodied expectations about what a professor "looks like."[46] Michael gets extra credit for fulfilling student preconceptions about what learning itself looks like because his only mode of teaching is lecturing nonstop with extra pomposity. Even when students don't actually learn much, they *think* they're learning because lecturing's what college professors are supposed do, right? That's what Super Teacher does on TV and in the movies. For those instructors who don't "look like" a professor, their credentialed title—"Professor," "Doctor," and so on—is an essential part of their name in the college classroom and a recognition of their full subjectivity in the educational environment.[47] Titles become particularly important if instructors are utilizing a variety of pedagogical techniques above and beyond the Professor-Never-Shuts-Their-Cakehole method of nonstop lecturing—a technique with which many students, despite their own lack of learning and engagement, are most comfortable, at least initially. For nonbinary and transgender students and instructors, chosen or even preferred names are so important that a name assigned at birth—the name subsequently changed to better reflect the person's sense of self—is termed a dead name.[48] Persistently being called one's dead name is an act of hostility and erasure.[49] While we might term it a microaggression, the impact is far from small because it's a denial of one's subjectivity.[50]

What's an upstanding educator to do? Let's face it: names *are* hard to learn, and names that are unfamiliar to us for any reason are even harder to learn. What if we offend someone? What if in trying to say someone's name we end up alienating them instead of making a connection? Also, because so many of us teaching college classes are smarty-pants scholars prone to perfectionism and afraid of looking foolish, it's tempting to give up and not even try. Large teaching loads, precarious employment status, and big classes add further inequitable burdens to the pedagogical labor of learning student names. Similarly, helping students learn, correctly pronounce, and use instructors' names and titles isn't easy either. Many students, especially first-generation students, may not understand why using an instructor's professional title is a sign of respect and a recognition of academic authority and expertise. But peevishly snapping "It's 'Doctor,' not 'Mrs.'" is not usually the best corrective. It can alienate students at a moment when you need to establish rapport and approachability, and I'm speaking here from sad personal peevish experience.

Learning, correctly pronouncing, and regularly using each other's names, pronouns, and titles in the college classroom isn't easy and it's not a perfectible activity. Things can go wrong. But all students and instructors in higher education should be able to exercise the subjectivity and dignity that comes with being recognized as an individual with an individual name and titles that they've earned. Learning, correctly pronouncing, and trying to use everyone's name, pronouns, and titles is a perfect case study in increasing equity in college teaching and learning. It illustrates the fact while systemic exclusions and historical marginalization and opportunity gaps exist and will cause damages that are outside our individual pedagogical choice and control, it nonetheless also matters what we do as educators to increase equity one class at a time, one name at a time.

Gear for Your Go-Bag

- Equity-minded course design and teaching practices begin with understanding that students' life circumstances—not their lack of willingness or ability to learn—often create unnecessary and inequitable obstacles to their academic success.
- As academics, we must recognize the multiple, intersectional ways that systemic racism, sexism, ableism, and other types of discrimination in higher education creates professional and pedagogical obstacles for many faculty.
- As academics, we must recognize how economic precarity and other inequities of VITAL teaching positions create professional and pedagogical obstacles for many faculty.
- Learning, using, and correctly pronouncing student names, and instructor names and titles, is one specific and meaningful way that we as individual college educators can make teaching and learning more equitable.

Chapter 2

REPAIR STRATEGIES FOR INEQUITY SNAFUS

What can you do when an inequity alligator's got you in its jaws and it's going to drag you under and devour you piece by bloody piece unless you can keep it from shaking you and rolling over? Inequity snafus are particularly scary and injurious because they are embedded in some of the most contentious, emotionally laden, and outright litigious issues anyone must deal with in any setting: namely, racism, sexism, and other types of discrimination and bias. A teaching or a learning mistake related to inequity thus often has the potential to explode a single misstep into atomic levels of destruction. So, when things go wrong, we need to be prepared.

We need to cultivate careful, ongoing awareness of the many ways inequity can foul up learning and teaching. We need to be ready to STIR—Stop, Think, Identify, and Repair. In this chapter, I give a short overview of how to identify inequity snafus. Then I examine two specific repair strategies: (1) Have some plans and scripts in place for what to say when things go wrong because of the inequitable teaching and learning conditions, and (2) apologize to students when we ourselves have caused a snafu entangled with inequities.

Identifying Inequity Snafus

First and foremost, it behooves us to cultivate awareness and build our inequity snafu-spotting skills as educators. Thinking about how an inequity misstep in a classroom or on campus can explode into a fiasco, some blatantly obvious examples come immediately to mind. Such as: A white professor uses the n-word in a lecture or when reading a text aloud. University police stop a prospective student of color who is taking a tour—or an enrolled student of color entering a dorm, or a graduate student of color using the library, or a professor of color headed home—and questions that person's right to be on campus. A professor refuses to make legally mandated accommodations for a student with a disability. A student posts a racist slur on social media.[1] *Whoomp*, there it is. Those are some worst-case inequity scenarios in college. When that level of things goes wrong, it doesn't take an instructor's careful individual discernment to spot the inequity, and the necessary redress is less about any one individual's pedagogical strategy and more about crisis management, mandatory meetings with human resources, or actions taken by the student misconduct committee.

I want to focus here on some of the steps we can take when things go wrong in the classroom in less obviously egregious but still critical ways related to inequity. These are the inequity snafus that are more common but also harder to identify than headline-making debacles. For example, let's return to the issue of learning and using everyone's name, pronouns, and titles. Right off the top of my head, I can list a bunch of name-related teaching and learning inequity snafus from my own teaching experience:

- Despite clearly and politely asking to be called "Professor Neuhaus," a student continues to call me "Jessamyn."
- White professor (me) twice mixes up the names of the only two Black students in a class of predominantly white students at our predominantly white institution (PWI).
- Despite clearly and politely asking to be called "Professor Neuhaus," student continues to call me "Mrs. Neuhaus."
- Cisgendered heterosexual professor who is a woman (me) learns names of students more easily and quickly when students are cisgendered men than when students are cisgendered women.

- White professor (me) gets flustered taking attendance during the first day of class and, in front of the entire class, asks a student of color about pronunciation of the student's *own name* with the poorly worded and instantly regretted phrase "Are you sure?"

Whoomp, there is it again: inequities cropping up, in more ordinary yet nonetheless troubling ways.

None of the above examples are instances of conscious and deliberate racism, sexism, exclusion, or discrimination. There are no white supremacists chanting Nazi slogans at the lectern. But what we do have here are mistakes made by people socialized in political and cultural systems of racial and gender hierarchies. Students persist in calling me by my first or my "married" name because I'm a postmenopausal-aged lady, and to many students in their late teens and early twenties I probably don't "look like" a professor; I look like their high school teacher. Or maybe their auntie, mom, or grandma. I learn men's names more quickly than women's names because, in a hierarchically gendered society, I've unconsciously learned to pay more attention to men than to women. In a racially hierarchical and often racially segregated society, it took a more concerted effort for me to learn and use the correct names for students of color in my predominantly white college institution.[2] As for the last example ("Are you sure?"), well, that was easily one of the most asinine mistakes I've ever made as a professor. I 100 percent knew better and 100 percent should have been able to stop those preposterous words from coming out of my treacherous mouth. Which just goes to show how sometimes, at the very moment that you're getting complacent about avoiding alligators, you feel the teeth sink into your leg and the water rush up over your head.

Name snafus exemplify what could be termed microaggressions, or even micro-assaults or microinvalidations.[3] There are virtually unlimited examples of ways that inequity can raise its ugly head in college teaching and learning in "micro" ways. Here are just a few examples I've seen or heard about from students or other faculty:

- A white student from rural upstate New York assumes a student of color must be "from the City."
- A student is asked by a professor or another student to speak for their entire social, ethnic, or racial group.
- A professor allows the use of a laptop computer only if student has a documented disability—and then out loud identifies that student as having a disability in front of the whole class.
- A professor compliments a non-native English speaker on being "articulate."
- A graduate education program is structured in a way that students must have access to their own cars to complete their student teaching.
- A student with one type of disability says in class that having a more severe disability would reduce his will to live.
- A professor with hearing loss is perceived as being less approachable.
- A VITAL faculty member is deliberately excluded from professional development opportunities.
- A professor does not acknowledge in any way a recent major campus or national event that is particularly troubling or even traumatizing for some students.
- A professor schedules an important exam on a religious holiday.
- A professor calls out a student in class for using an assistive note-taking device.

When we've consciously set out to detect them, these types of snafus will predictably start appearing regularly on our pedagogical radar, including when we've made the mistake ourselves, when it's occurred between students, or when we're on the receiving end.

When it comes to inequity in teaching and learning, things will frequently go wrong in "micro" ways like these. We need to be attentive to the fact that no matter how successfully we're implementing inclusive teaching techniques in our own individual

classes, student learning is being circumscribed by inequity snafus across our campuses. Every educator also needs to understand
and cultivate awareness of overt student incivility, class disruption, and outright hostility rooted in student biases about faculty.
If we're on the lookout for discrimination and systemic biases,
won't we start seeing them everywhere and all the time? Won't
we start second-guessing every interaction, every aspect of every
class design and teaching activity, and every word out of everyone's mouth? Kind of. But cultivating our attention in this way
does not have to be disempowering because it can increase our
knowledge and understanding, and we higher education peeps
are, as a group, incredibly good at absorbing and implementing
new knowledge and understanding. We can approach inequity
snafus as an equation where more information = more strategies
and solutions.

When things go wrong in our teaching and our students'
learning, asking ourselves, *Is inequity at work?* will increase our
ability to respond productively. Ignoring snafus rooted in inequity
is not an option because they undermine student learning and
they perpetuate inequitable teaching conditions.[4] As Chavella Pittman writes, "It's really important for all faculty to become better
at dealing with diversity related conflict, not only for their own
wellbeing and ability to teach in class but for students' ability to
learn."[5] The more we cultivate attention to these issues, the more
we can understand them, respond productively to them, and work
toward repairing them.

Inequities in the college classroom aren't a matter of *if* but a
matter of *when* and *how*. Whatever other factors might be creating obstacles to a student's college success, racial hierarchies
and other types of discrimination based on social and embodied
identities are likely to foul up learning. Faculty who are already
navigating intersectional biases about academic expertise and
authority are likely to encounter students being directly, overtly
disrespectful, demeaning, or disruptive. When we realize that
something has gone wrong between students, or between students and ourselves—something that can be traced to a stereotype, assumption, bias, or microaggression—we have to STIR:

Stop: Call a time-out and pause before doing or saying anything.

Think: Closely consider all aspects of what's happening and how it might be resulting from and/or perpetuating inequities.

Identify: Inquire, observe, listen, analyze, and try to figure out what happened.

Repair: Use follow-through and follow-up strategies to get back on track.

And one of our best follow-through and follow-up repair strategies for when things go wrong because of inequities is utilizing a carefully prepared remark or set of remarks.

Use a Script

Having these scripts ready overlaps with but is not quite the same thing as being ready to use certain classroom management techniques or specific pedagogical approaches to addressing incivility and class disruptions, which are a hugely important aspect of inequitable teaching conditions that I address in later chapters. But even when it's not a case of incivility or disruption, whenever inequity is interfering with teaching and learning, our words matter. And because of how personally and professionally taxing and complex educational inequities can be, and how quickly they can balloon into snafus, scripts can be especially helpful.

One individually empowering strategy for responding and repairing when biases and stereotypes foul up teaching and learning is having a set of ready remarks that we can use almost automatically. Knowing what types of educational inequities I'm likely to encounter each semester, I have a curated collection of scripted remarks to use after I've stopped, thought, and identified what is going on. For instance, I know what I'm going to say when:

- A student uses a term commonly used in the past, and stated in a historical primary source we're reading for class, but which is considered racially insensitive or discriminatory today.

- A faculty member consults with me about a student's biased comments on an evaluation form.
- A first-generation student needs support in navigating the hidden curriculum in higher education.
- An instructor expresses doubt that legally mandated academic accommodations are legitimately needed and complains about it being "unfair" to other students.

I don't mean that I can recite word for word a prepared monologue or that I doggedly stick to a specific scripted set of phrases in every such situation. Rather, I arrive at the potentially snafu-causing moment when inequities are at work with some useful phrasing, having thought through the best way to begin necessary repairs.

One common way that instructors from a range of disciplines in a wide variety of classes encounter inequities creating obstacles to learning is when a microaggression occurs between students. This can happen both on campus as well as in asynchronous online courses.

Stop: Halt the discussion or class activity or post to the online forum or activity.

Think: Reflect on what's occurring and run through some possible scripts.

Identify: Ask for information and clarification as needed, making sure what we think was said was said, and try to name what is happening.

Repair: Put words to what's occurred to get started on repairing.

For instance, Hogan and Sathy recommend this script for addressing a student's microaggression toward another student:

> *"Hang on a second, I'd like to take a moment to think about what just occurred. You may not have intended your statement to mean _____, but it may have been heard that way by others and felt hurtful because _____. These things are difficult but let's not ignore this just because it's difficult. Let's see if, together, we can rephrase this."*[6]

That pause, the stop in your STIR, is an invaluable tool for when things go wrong in class because of biases. It provides thinking time for everyone and, as Hogan and Sathy write, puts students "on alert that something transpired that requires attention."[7]

Clearly and deliberately addressing what has happened with a scripted comment like this does not mean putting one individual student in the spotlight to reckon, publicly and right that second, with their own ingrained biases and stereotypes. In fact, that could exacerbate the potential harms of the microaggression by wielding your power as the instructor in a way that would likely elicit a defensive stance on the student's part, which in turn shuts down their ability to address the issue with thought and to do better in the future. Furthermore, it places the student who may have been affected by the statement or action in the position of being solely a victim instead of an active participant in making the class better. Addressing it as something we can work on together empowers everyone in the room to consider how to best redress it. It reframes the repair work needed when inequity fouls up learning as not solely the purview of the instructor to utilize inclusive teaching practices, nor the responsibility of the student to overcome their own biases, but as an issue requiring the combined efforts of educators and students.

But all those nuances can't be in the mix if the words out of our mouth, or the sentences we typed into the forum don't make space for them. We need go-to "scripts" to have ready on our mental back burner instead of trying to come up with wording on the spot. In one such suggested script, human rights educator Loretta J. Ross argues that when students make an inequity snafu, rather than publicly criticizing and chastising the student or "calling them out," we can draw students into meaningful reflection and critical discussion for learning—i.e., calling them in. Ross recommends using phrases such as:

- ➤ *"I need to stop you there because something you said is not accurate."*
- ➤ *"Do you think you would say that if someone from that group were with us in the room?"*

➢ *"There's some history behind that expression you just used that you might not know about."*

➢ *"In this class, we hold each other accountable. So we need to talk about why that joke isn't funny."*[8]

The suggested examples here are just a starting point. Our scripted responses must be authentic to our teaching personas and a reflection of our own individual teaching context.

In addition, it's not enough to think briefly about them one or two times, as Chavella Pittman points out in her work on how to respond to micro- and macroaggressions in the classroom:

> Faculty are encouraged to edit these starter statements to fit their "voice," preferred tone, and pedagogy. The next step is to then practice, practice, and practice by saying them aloud. Of course, how faculty respond depends on the context of their institution, course, pedagogy, the incident itself, their identities, and other related factors. The point is that if faculty have an idea of what they might say and practice doing so, it should better equip and prepare them to act—more immediately—when troublesome classroom moments arise . . .[9]

Being prepared to act more immediately is the great advantage of using a script. For anyone who is constantly navigating inequitable teaching conditions, having a ready script for predictable snafus is a small but meaningful and important strategy for when things go wrong between students and faculty because of student behavior based on biases and stereotypes. I must add that preparing scripted responses should begin with knowing our campus processes and systems for addressing the most blatant violations, such as how harassment incidents are reported to the Title IX officer, campus police, or the human resources office. Also, chapter three discusses in more detail how to respond and repair when classroom disruptions and incivilities snafu learning and how these intersect with teaching inequities.

For all college teachers, there are numerous times when being ready to say or write some preprepared words can be an empowering pedagogical strategy for us at the individual and classroom level. I used to feel like a dork standing in my office before class, practicing certain sentences that I wanted to be ready to use. Until the day came—and the day always comes—when something went wrong and I knew just what to say. And sometimes what I'm ready to say is: "I'm sorry."

Apologize

Apologizing directly to students when you've made any kind of mistake can feel risky and, depending on your teaching context and positionality, may entail actual risk. Employment precarity and an instructor's embodied and social identities are some of the factors in the instructor-student power dynamic that can make apologizing tricky. But there's no way around the fact that increasing equity for students means that when we make a mistake as an individual instructor that can chip away at or undermine equity, an apology is in order. The good news is that these apologies do not have to be, and indeed should not be, elaborate or extensive. Short and simple is what's needed.[10]

For example, when we mess up someone's name, we need to apologize. And we will mess up someone's name. No matter how experienced we are, what modality we're teaching in, or our own intersectional identities, we will make this mistake. Here's how a STIR response and apology as a repair strategy could help if you, the instructor, egregiously flub a student name:

Stop: In class or in one-or-one conversation, instead of rushing onward, call a halt and say something like:
➤ *"Wait, hold on for a second."*
Think: Reflect on the snafu, remembering how names are linked closely to subjectivity and how much they matter. Consider options for what you can do next, and choose your words carefully.
Identify: Clearly summarize what just occurred, as in
➤ *"Wow, I just really messed up your name."*
Repair: To state the obvious, you can't go back in time and say the student's name correctly. What you can do in the

moment and in the short term is apologize. In the long term, you can make a strenuous effort to use the student's name correctly.

Repairing doesn't erase your mistake, but it is what's possible for you to do and to move forward, and in this case we need to apologize.

> *"I'm sorry. I know that names are important to us and I apologize for my error. I will work to do better in the future."*
> *"I want everyone in our class to feel welcome, and our names are an important part of that. I apologize for my mistake."*
> *"Thank you for correcting me on how to pronounce your name. I apologize for my error and appreciate your patience as I continue to work on connecting names and pronouns to faces in our class."*

A couple of sentences taking responsibility and making a commitment to doing better is all that's needed.

We want to avoid "non-apology apology" language such as "I'm sorry if your feelings were hurt" or the quintessential non-apology passive voice approach: "Mistakes were made." We especially have to avoid lambasting ourselves or phrasing our apology in a way that puts an additional burden on the student to forgive us. Do not make big performance of insisting that I, White Professor Foot-in-Mouth, am really a good person without a racist bone in my body! That problematic response not only makes you look like a complete tool but it can—and has—turned a single, relatively manageable name-related inequity-based snafu into a massive career-ending foul-up, like the Fordham professor who insisted in a lengthy email that because he was a longtime "ally," his mistake was a "simple, human error" having "nothing to do with race." As Chantel Sims, one of the misnamed students, stated after receiving his email: "It seemed a little excessive, like all you needed to do was say sorry, and it would have been fine."[11] Sims makes it clear that a short, simple apology is what's needed when we've stumbled.

Apologizing isn't easy. For most of us mere mortals, it's never fun to admit our failures, and we make ourselves vulnerable by admitting an error. As an educator, the context for apologizing to students is always shaped by those three big truths I described in the introduction to this book.

Truth #1: Teachers and learners are human beings who will make mistakes and mess up. Apologizing isn't admitting to an unacceptable level of failure. Rather, it's an inevitable reality of being a human person interacting with other human people.

Truth #2: Positionality matters. In some teaching contexts already shaped by inequities and systemic vulnerabilities with real emotional and economic consequences, a direct and unequivocal apology to a student may be asking too much of an instructor. I said "apology," not "self-immolation."

Truth #3: The Super Teacher myth sets an unrealistic standard for what "good" teaching looks like. Super Teachers never need to apologize for anything because they never do anything wrong! But in real-life teaching, we will all do something wrong and we will need to apologize.

That said, apologizing can be empowering too. I've modeled it in class and seen it pay off in student behavior with one another and with myself. Apologizing when you have caused something to go wrong can humanize higher education by addressing and repairing a teaching and learning failure in ways that have been proven effective in other professional and personal settings.[12] Meaningful apologies can defuse a mistake, even one potentially intertwined with inequities, before it builds into a snafu.

Gear for Your Go-Bag

- Being attentive to inequity snafus in our daily teaching contexts isn't easy because they can range from a minor stumble to a major problem , and they're entangled with potentially explosive issues and emotions. But recognizing when inequity fouls up learning and teaching allows us to take necessary action.

- When we realize that something has gone wrong between students or between students and ourselves because of biases or stereotypes, STIR provides a structure for responding.
- We can prepare for predictable inequity snafus by thinking ahead of time about the wording we want to use. Using a script can be especially empowering when navigating the loaded and fraught issues around inequity.
- Used judiciously and adapted to our individual teaching contexts, apologizing when we make a mistake can be a powerful and effective repair strategy and is particularly useful and necessary when we've mistakenly contributed to inequitable learning conditions.

Chapter 3

INCREASING EQUITY

Inequity alligators are always lurking. There are, however, ways to make water conditions far less hospitable to those toothy monsters. Increasing equity in the college classroom when and where we have the power to do so is the subject of entire libraries of works on educational reform, teaching advice, and scholarship. The examples in this chapter for equity-increasing strategies are just that: a small number of examples from a much larger body of work. They are just a few of the ways we can help to reduce inequity snafus in teaching and learning with course design, in-class activities, and interactions outside of class.

Plan for Learner Variability

Some of the most effective steps we can take to reduce systemic barriers and increase equity for learners occur during the class planning stages. (If you've been handed down from on high a set-in-stone syllabus, you have my sympathy: it's hard to teach in a syllabus straitjacket.) Specifically, in the course design stages we can prepare for learner variability when planning how students will access content and demonstrate their learning. I'm forced to point out that "learner variability" does not mean "learning styles," that awful neuromyth that actively impedes teaching and learning.[1] "Variability" simply refers to the embodied variety in any group of humans, including students, and their various and diverse personal and academic interests, family backgrounds, past educational experiences, hobbies, physical/health conditions, and so on.

I first heard the term "learner variability" when I began reading about Universal Design for Learning (UDL). Expanding on the architectural universal design approach ("design of products, environments, and communication to be usable by all people, to the greatest extent possible, without adaption or specialized design")[2] a UDL approach to education posits that designing for learner variability ahead of time—before instructors even know their students—is the most effective way to reduce individual accommodation needs. In other words, offering students choices in how to recognize, engage with, and report back the information that they learned increases the chances that instructors can connect with their students and their learning needs.[3]

An instructor who plans for learner variability will

- "Present information in multiple ways"
- "Differentiate the ways that students can express what they know"
- "Provide multiple methods of engaging with material"[4]

Beyond the minimal standard of legally mandated accessibility in higher education, UDL preemptively and proactively strives to remove barriers to learning for the widest number of people possible.

The following three ways of planning for learner variability are the three principles of UDL, as summarized by CAST (originally Center for Applied Special Technology), an organizational UDL proponent:

1. Provide multiple means of engagement:
   a. Options for recruiting student interest
   b. Options for sustaining student effort and persistence
   c. Options for student self-regulation
2. Provide multiple means of representation:
   a. Options for perception (display of information)
   b. Options for language and symbols
   c. Options for comprehension

3. Provide multiple means of action and expression:
   a. Options for physical action
   b. Options for expression and communication
   c. Options for executive function[5]

That's a lot of option providing, I know! Moreover, as psychology professor Kristen Gillespie-Lynch notes, "universal design is an iterative process" that requires constant adjustments and revisions.[6] At first glance, it can seem like too much, particularly for faculty with high class loads, big classes, and/or employment precarity.

Trying to plan for *every* learner variability can get overwhelming fast, but fortunately we can always increase equity in our classes by planning for *some* learner variability. In their pioneering book, *Reach Everyone, Teach Everyone: Universal Design for Learning in Higher Education*, Thomas J. Tobin and Kirsten T. Behling describe this as a "Plus-One": "Is there just one more way that you can help keep learners on task, just one more way that you could give them information, just one more way that they could demonstrate their skills?"[7] For example, at the course planning stages, we can Plus-One how we present information to students by ensuring all visual materials include captions and, ideally, a written transcript. This Plus-One class planning accounts for learner variability in several ways, removing barriers for students with hearing loss or students whose first language isn't English.[8] Also, a variety of instruction and activities—mix it up!—not only increases equity by taking into account diverse student academic interests but also increases student engagement generally.[9] Plus-One works with course materials too. Adding just one reading, film, etc., that increases representations also increases inclusivity.[10]

Providing options for how "students express what they know" is one of the best places to Plus-One our class planning. Adding even just one additional option for completing an assignment can increase equity and learning. For instance, if you are going to use a written exam, could you also give students the option of taking an oral exam? If you are assigning reading responses or class discussion reflections, could students choose to submit their assignment as written documents, audio recordings, or a video? Unless the stated learning outcome of a class is "write an academic research paper," almost any major research project in any discipline can be a Plus-One, giving students the option to demonstrate their completed research in another format.

Plus-One additions that help students develop self-regulation and executive function while increasing comprehension are also a vital way of increasing equity before class begins and seem to be more and more important for college students' success.[11] For example, when assigning a large project, in addition to work requirements and grading rubrics, consider giving students a project planner, a graphic organizer, and/or fill-in timelines.[12] Such additions contribute to what Kelly Hogan and Viji Sathy call "high structure" classes that increase equity in learning opportunities, accounting for a wide variety of educational background and experiences.[13] A few highly accomplished students may not necessarily require, in order to succeed, things such as a research progress log reflecting on their own learning as they meet benchmarks, self-assessment work, and identifying their own coping skills and strategies. But planning for learner variability in this way will not deter or negatively impact any student's learning.[14]

Increasing inclusivity often boils down to thinking about and treating students as unique individuals rather than lumping everyone together into a faceless, nameless entity called "Student." And I bet you know where to begin, because I've been harping on it repeatedly. Yup, it's names: learning, correctly pronouncing, and using names (and correct pronouns). It's an issue near and dear to my heart. According to family lore, even as a shy preschooler. I would determinedly correct anyone who shortened my name and called me "Jessie." "No," I would say gravely, "it's Jessamyn. Jess. Ah. Men." (Like "cinnamon" or "specimen.")

It's not easy to learn, correctly pronounce, and use student names. It takes time and effort but it's not *Mission: Impossible* and there are plenty of techniques and strategies for learning student names and helping students learn each other's names.

- Have everyone in class record their name, and pronouns if they wish, with a free app like Name Drop that generates a permanent URL for the recording or via the learning management system.

- Have students briefly describe the origin of their name or what they like about it and annotate your roster.
- On the first day, students interview each other in pairs and then introduce each other to the class with a memorable fact and then test their memories by having students try to identify as many people by name as possible.
- Don't forget good old-fashioned name tags and name tents.

The strategies are endless; they just take effort and time.[15] Even in very large classes, when learning everyone's name isn't feasible, there are proven positive educational benefits when students are provided with name tents to keep displayed on their desks, and the instructor tries to use names as much as possible.[16]

Another example of increasing equity by recognizing students as individuals during class is to ensure that no one student is asked to "speak for" or represent an entire social or embodied identity group. As in "Lots of heterosexual white women attended that rally. Jessamyn, you're a heterosexual white woman: What you think about that?" Conflating an individual student with a larger group erases their individual subjectivity and suggests they're being seen not as a person but as a nameless (there it is again!) part of a bigger entity outside themselves. At the same time, planning for learner individuality and variety in class means cultivating ongoing awareness of and sensitivity to the potential impact of traumatic outside events on individual students. When professors hold classes in the wake of major events that might be particularly troubling for some students and don't breathe a word about that event, students can feel directly excluded. Here are two scripts I use when something has occurred outside of class that might be important for me to acknowledge:

> ➤ *"Like many of you, I was troubled to hear yesterday about the racist and homophobic graffiti on campus. I know these events can take a toll on everyone's emotional and mental health, so I wanted to take a minute to remind you of these campus resources."*

> ➤ *"Before we start, I just wanted to say that it's hard to be in a classroom without thinking about the recent school shooting. It's horrifying, but it also makes me especially grateful to see you all and be able to work with you today. Thank you for being here."*

You don't need to make a long speech, but it's a recognition of the individual and shared humanity in the room.

Increasing equity for student learning as individual instructors is rooted in awareness of learner variability and individuality.[17] Considering the diversity of the people in the classroom or logging onto the learning management system (LMS), and proactively planning for that variability, is a meaningful way to increase equity in our own classrooms.

Plan for Learner Biases

I wish I didn't have to advise readers to plan for learner biases. I would much prefer to be advising you to join a Rebel Force fighting to topple the Empire, revolutionize the academy, and create a brand-new system of higher education where everyone from any background in every body enjoys just and equitable teaching conditions. As individual instructors in higher education, we have quite a bit of individual power to reduce academic inequities for students via specific, concrete ways in our own classes, but reducing inequities for ourselves and other college educators is not nearly as clear-cut, given how entrenched systems of discrimination shape higher education and academia. These are systems that we can and should loudly identify, protest, and work to change. But meanwhile, classes start on Monday, and every instructor stepping into a room with students or logging onto the course site will be navigating student biases and assumptions from day one, and many VITAL instructors will also be juggling massive course loads with no employment security. No amount of innovative course design and pre-course planning is going to eliminate those inequities, but there are a few ways we can plan time for contending with disparate teaching realities, including interrupting student biases in pedagogically effective ways.

I know that "plan for learner biases" is akin to applying a Barney Band-Aid to a hemorrhaging arterial wound. But I also know that there are spaces in higher education where we can sometimes wrest a bit of practical power in determining our day-to-day teaching work. For instance, we know that student biases about an instructor who doesn't "look like" a professor can flare up when a grade is at stake. So, when we're planning the schedule of assignments, and when and how to provide feedback and grades, we can take that into account and allocate more time in class to review grading rubrics or schedule small group or individual meetings to answer questions about upcoming grading.

Our individual and unique teaching contexts dictate how and where we can plan for inequitable teaching labor and make adjustments. In my experience working with faculty to design classes and to plan my own courses, I've found that simply cultivating more awareness of such unnamed but predictable—and to be clear, inequitably distributed and unjustly burdened—teaching-related labor encourages us to schedule and plan in ways that can at the very least try to better account for that labor. The point here is not only to plan for how students will demonstrate their learning but also account for the time, energy, and effort needed on our part to counteract student resistance to learning that may arise when they bring gendered, racialized, and other such assumptions to the college classroom.

One way to plan for inequitable teaching labor is to strategize ways to productively interrupt student biases and stereotypes, which means designing assignments, scheduling class activities, and so on while taking into account the time needed for the additional emotional and cognitive labor to counteract stereotypes and navigate intersectional discrimination as part of our teaching work. For example, in "How Blind Professors Win the First Day: Setting Ourselves Up for Success," Sheri Wells-Jensen, Emily K. Michael, and Mona Minkara explain that student stereotypes about disabilities will significantly shape students' first impressions of them as visually impaired instructors. They argue that meticulous preparation for the first day, including becoming familiar with the classroom and planning activities that convey their expertise, enthusiasm, and authority, can help reduce those biased reactions:

> We come to class knowing where things are, with our plans in place, and with our best academic clothes on, ready to roll. The point is not to exude authority for the sake of authority; the point is to show that we are at peace with ourselves and in control of our immediate environment and that we are comfortably in charge. We are clear that, whatever blindness-based panic might be brewing among the students, it is unfounded.[18]

This teaching preparation doesn't reduce inequity so much as increase the instructors' abilities to counter the biases that will flare up—in this case, students' "blindness-based panic."

Instructors like Wells-Jensen, Michael, and Minkara, whose embodied identity does not conform to the totally outdated yet perpetually powerful stereotype of what a professor "looks like," recommend a variety of first-day activities designed to reinforce their own subject area expertise and enthusiasm for student learning, including some types of self-disclosure, "telling students your belonging story," active learning, and an emphasis on inclusion for all.[19] Some other ways to plan for interrupting student biases correspond with class planning that benefits student learning more generally as well. For example, allotting time and choosing resources to share with students about the science of learning and effective study habits has the additional benefit of helping students understand how limited the Super Teacher stereotype really is. Emphasizing and defining diversity as an educational asset not only increases classroom inclusivity for students but may also help students see a diversity of instructors as an educational asset as well. Planning innovative assessment and grading structures such as student-faculty collaborative rubrics and self-assessments that build student autonomy and self-efficacy can proactively interrupt student biases about educators and education.[20]

When balancing expected teaching labor (class meetings, office hours, class prep) with unstated, inequitable, yet predictable additional teaching labor, cut yourself some slack. I mean it. Academia is chock-full of overachieving, overworking intellectuals driving themselves to excel and trying to meet some ridiculously outdated ableist, racist, and sexist gatekeeping standard of professoring.[21] We pour time and energy into college teaching until our batteries are really and truly drained—and we were doing that even before the pandemic.[22] So whenever and wherever you can, look for places in your scheduling to give yourself a break once in a while. Midterm is a high-stress time, for instance, so can you make the first class back after spring or fall break a low-prep review and planning session? If you know that you are going to get numerous requests for extra student-related service, and that students who are not in your class but are desperate to connect with professors who look like them are going to seek out your advice and support in large numbers because you are one of the all-too-few professors on campus who look like them, can you plan for office hour policies and structures that help you balance those needs with your other teaching work?

These strategies have in common the starting point of *planning* for pedagogically effective ways to increase learning while also interrupting intersectional stereotypes about academic authority. However, it's not just the responsibility of some professors from certain historically minoritized groups or those who embody certain identities to plan for interrupting students' biases: everyone, in every teaching context, should be paying attention to how they can contribute to increasing equity for all college instructors. For example, when we can choose class content, it should reflect the true diversity of experts who produced that scholarship. Striving to "decolonize the syllabus" is something that's often within our power to work toward decreasing inequities in academia while increasing student learning.[23]

The quintessential way that college instructors can both plan for student biases as well as increase equity in higher education is to ensure that we state and maintain clear and explicit standards of professional interpersonal academic conduct for students, including the consequences for when a student violates those standards. It is more likely that students will be overtly disrespectful to faculty from historically minoritized groups, and they will far more readily question the academic authority and intellectual expertise of anyone who doesn't "look like" a professor. White professors and cisgendered male professors therefore have a moral, ethical, and pedagogical responsibility to contribute to creating greater equity for all instructors by not silently accepting the privileges of students' racially and gender-based assumptions about professors and, further, by helping students understand the university and classroom codes of conduct. Everyone teaching a college class can include as part of their syllabus or in a class discussion what is meant by "respectful" class behavior. Specific examples of both respectful and disrespectful interactions with instructors will help. Everyone teaching any college class can make sure that students understand the negative consequences of engaging in disrespectful, uncivil, or aggressively hostile behaviors toward an instructor.

Reduce the Harms of Student Evaluations of Teaching[24]

Higher education just can't seem to quit bad student evaluation of teaching (SET) practices. It's like "Yup, evaluations reflect students' racial, gender, and other unconscious biases, but, oh, well, what're you gonna do?" 🔫 We are in crying need of widespread, systemic reform in how college teaching is documented and evaluated.[25] However, within the deep-seated, systemic, institutional SET practices that perpetuate inequities and damage faculty personally and professionally, there are three strategies that individual faculty can enact in most teaching contexts to mitigate those harms: (1) Solicit student *feedback* on teaching (SFT) frequently, asking questions students can productively answer, including identifying what is going well in class. The terminology matters because the commonly used phrasing "evaluation of teaching" suggests a comprehensive review based on the evaluator's expertise about skills being reviewed (and almost always refers exclusively to end-of-term, anonymous, standardized forms). In contrast, "feedback on teaching" suggests some, but not nearly all, information about teaching at one point in time, and not necessarily from an expert on the topic. It also helps expand our thinking about feedback beyond end-of-term, anonymous, standardized forms. (2) Frame all student feedback on teaching as formative. (3) Put student feedback on teaching into proportion when assessing teaching.

Solicit Student Feedback Frequently

For instructors who have repeatedly experienced racialized or other identity-based attacks via SET, individually seeking more frequent student feedback as an instructor or participating collectively in getting more department- or campus-wide feedback might sound like a bad idea. Create *more* opportunities for students to say discriminatory, demeaning things about me? Um, no, thanks! But proactively soliciting more regular student feedback and asking questions that students can productively answer—especially about what is going well—will mitigate the harms done by anonymous, standardized end-of-term SET surveys by accumulating a much bigger pool of student comments and feedback, reducing the disproportionate import of one single set of student surveys.

I recommend, at minimum, administering a short survey at the end of the first class, at the end of two weeks (in a semester), and at the midpoint of the term and/or shortly before the first major assessment activity or assignment. For instance, at the end of the first class or the first week, I usually ask questions such as:

> ➤ *What are you looking forward to in our class this semester?*
> ➤ *Which of the Student Learning Outcomes for our class sounds most interesting to you and why?*
> ➤ *Do you have any concerns or questions about our class at this point?*
> ➤ *Is there anything else you'd like me to know?*

At the two-week mark, I often ask questions such as:

> ➢ *What questions do you still have about your [upcoming assignment] due on [date]?*
> ➢ *In what ways are the other students in our class supporting your learning?*
> ➢ *What aspects of your work so far do you hope to improve or keep doing well?*
> ➢ *What aspects of our class do you most enjoy?*
> ➢ *Is there anything that is unclear or confusing to you about our class assignments, our in-class activities, or any of the feedback that I've given you about your work so far?*
> ➢ *Is there anything else you feel that I should know about our class meetings, LMS site, assignments, or student interactions?*

At midterm, there are many ways to productively solicit SFT.[26] I use a modified version of the Stop-Start-Continue format:[27]

> ➢ *Is there anything we as a learning community should stop doing/start doing/continue doing to help students learn and succeed in this class?*
> ➢ *Is there anything you should stop doing/start doing/continue doing to help yourself learn and succeed in this class?*
> ➢ *Is there anything I (Professor Neuhaus) should stop doing/ start doing/continue doing to help students learn and succeed in this class?*

As with the above version of Stop-Start-Continue, SFT should ask students to identify and reflect on their own roles, actions, and responsibilities as learners, encouraging metacognition, reducing the problematic overemphasis on "rating" professorial performance, and include questions that they as students can productively answer.

One of the best kinds of questions to ask students that they can productively answer is about what's going well. Promoting a class culture of feedback in which you and your students look for what's working in class, which will include the things that *you* are doing well, reduces the harms of standardized, anonymous, end-of-term SET. For example:

- Regular ask students in low-stakes (i.e., not associated with big portion of a grade) assignments or short in-class check-ins to identify specific things about the class that are helping them learn and succeed in class.
- Combine their feedback with your positive feedback for the class, such as weekly shout-outs that commend students for ways they've shown improvement, and students' reflections on their own improvement as well.
- Use your syllabus as a record and jot down after each class meeting a high point, such as a student question that demonstrated new insights or an observation you made about a particularly engaged small discussion group.

Things going well is as inevitable as things going wrong, but without being consistently attuned to them and collecting feedback on them throughout the class, end-of-term, anonymous, standardized SET will overshadow them.

There will be many aspects of your course design and teaching practices that work well and that students perceive as useful and helpful, but students might not, unless you ask them directly and specifically, clearly identify those things in their feedback. We need to regularly and proactively request feedback that speaks to our teaching strengths. Just like good feedback to students always points out what they're doing well and where they've made progress, good SFT identifies what an instructor has been doing well and, if applicable, where they've made changes or improvements during the class. Here are some sample questions along these lines, based on forms I've used in my previous classes:

➤ *What aspects of our class did you find enjoyable?*
➤ *List one aspect of our class that you found challenging but worth your time and energy to do.*

> ➢ *List one specific way that I supported your learning in this class.*
> ➢ *What academic skills did you build in this class?*
> ➢ *How will you use your new skills in your future classes?*
> ➢ *What are some things I should continue doing if I teach this class again?*

Admittedly, every once in a while a student will answer these types of questions as negatively as possible: "Nothing, I hated everything. She knows nothing and shouldn't be teaching." (And it's always "she," never "you," or even "the professor.") But these are the outlying comments, the ones that by and large should not be counted or weighed heavily in statistical analysis—or, to the extent it's emotionally and psychologically possible, in our own personal views of our teaching abilities.[28]

One way to avoid the "She did nothing right" answer is to phrase the question as multiple choice. For instance:

> ➢ *Which of the following aspects of my teaching practices helped you succeed this semester? Check all that apply.*
> ☐ *Starting and ending class on time*
> ☐ *Providing note-taking guides ahead of time*
> ☐ *Making available recorded lectures*
> ☐ *In-class work and help sessions*
> ☐ *Offering the option to revise and resubmit the research paper assignment*
> ☐ *Grading rubrics for major assignments*
> ☐ *Meeting with you outside of class for extra assistance*
> ☐ *My enthusiasm for the course content and for student success*

I can attest that seeing no boxes checked for this question is not as personally harmful and hurtful as "There was nothing good about this class." We don't need to manipulate students into singing our praises, but we do need to help students better name specific positive teaching practices that, as students—not to mention being tired and stressed-out students at the end of the semester—they have little practice or training in describing.

Frame Student Feedback as Formative

Even with increased opportunities for more nuanced feedback, there will also be limitations to what SFT can provide. Student feedback can never be a summative assessment of anyone's teaching abilities because, as participants in one class at one point in time in the instructor's teaching career, students do not have the information needed to make a summative assessment. For instance, students don't have access to information such as what types of professional teaching development the instructor has completed; what specific improvements the instructor has implemented in their course design and pedagogical practices over time; any SoTL research the instructor has completed; and in what ways the instructor has had to navigate student biases and stereotypes.

Framing SFT as formative means that one important criterion for interpreting student feedback is to ask: "Does this student's comment and/or response give me formative feedback for my teaching?" If the answer is "No," then it should not be viewed as a viable or useful part of assessing teaching. Unfortunately, instructors are almost always required as part of their employment reviews to address student comments or "ratings" from end-of-term, anonymous, standardized SET forms that do not meet this criterion. But when interpreting student feedback ourselves, and when responding to it as part of a broader assessment of our teaching, we can increase equity by systematically and meticulously defining student feedback on teaching as formative.

Take a student comment such as "This class was a waste of my time and money." Ouch. But read it again through the framing question "Does this student's comment and/or response give any formative feedback for teaching?" No, it really doesn't. If a statistically relevant number of students made this comment about a class taught by many different instructors across many semesters, it could be meaningful feedback about the course for the Curriculum Committee to consider. But there is no actionable feedback here for improving teaching. Framing all SFT as formative feedback won't eliminate the shot to the heart that hurtful student comments like this can inflict upon us. But it can serve as a kind of shield to at least reduce the harm caused to our teaching self-efficacy when we read a comment like this.

Put Student Feedback into Proportion

The authors of *Critical Teaching Behaviors: Defining, Documenting, and Discussing Good Teaching* point out that "while the intention behind SET may be in part to provide instructors formative feedback on their teaching practices, too often these results become the sole metric by which teaching effectiveness is assessed, prompting more anxiety and aversion than reflection and growth."[29] SETs should never be the "sole metric" for assessing teaching efficacy. We need multiple sources of information and documentation. As one group of researchers bluntly states: "Using one measure to make an important decision about a person's career is the cardinal sin of psychological and educational measurement."[30] The very worst thing we could do—the "cardinal sin"—when trying to measure or assess teaching efficacy would be to rely solely on SFT or SET. Everyone in higher education who has any role whatsoever in assessing teaching, and anyone who plays any part in using teaching assessments to make employment decisions, should insist that reviews or assessments of any instructor's teaching always include numerous types of feedback, reflection, and evidence of teaching effectiveness, with SFT given some but only limited weight.

Putting student feedback in proportion is not easy to do at the individual level. For instructors who have worked hard on their classes, pouring a lot of time and energy into teaching, a carelessly worded comment or deliberately cruel statement from even one student can become lodged in our brains for years, undermining our teaching self-efficacy and our desire to keep building our teaching skills. But, implemented routinely and regularly, the strategy of putting SFT in proportion can build up some protection against these harms. If we consistently remind ourselves about what types of questions students can answer and what questions they cannot answer, the outlying comments or rankings may be less permanently scarring. If we consistently document and give weight to what we've been doing well, it will help mitigate unproductive, biased, and harmful student comments.

Gear for Your Go-Bag

- We can increase equity for learners in our individual classes by planning for students' wide variety of identities, physical abilities, interests, and life circumstances.
- We can increase equity for learners in our individual classes by presenting information to students in multiple ways; offering options for students to demonstrate their learning; and providing a variety of means for students to access materials.
- Planning for learner variability can quickly become an overwhelming task, but adding just one thing—"Plus-One"—will increase equity.
- Knowing that learners have biases, stereotypes, and assumptions that contribute to inequitable teaching labor, we can to some extent prepare for and mitigate at least some of that labor ahead of time with course planning and clarity about classroom civility.
- To reduce the harms of anonymous, standardized, end-of-term student evaluations of teaching can do, we can solicit student feedback about teaching more frequently, making sure to routinely ask about what's going well and having students identify and reflect on their own responsibilities and actions in the class; frame student feedback as a formative only; and strive to make student feedback just one of multiple sources of information used to assess teaching efficacy.

PART II

DISCONNECTION

As soon as you realize that your chute is bad, signal to
a jumping companion whose chute has not yet opened
that you are having a malfunction. Wave your arms and
point to your chute.

—"How to Survive if Your Parachute Fails to Open,"
The Worst-Case Scenario Survival Handbook

Chapter 4

DISCONNECTION FOULS UP LEARNING AND TEACHING

Dante never mentioned it, but surely somewhere in the nine circles of Hell's infernal torment there are some wretched souls condemned to doing eternal busywork—the time-consuming, valueless, soul-sucking tasks that accomplish exactly nothing and yet for some reason must be done anyway. To my mind, Satan himself could not devise a more heinous instrument of torture than busywork. Unfortunately, busywork abounds in college classes. Way too many students perceive and experience far too many assignments, assessments, and course requirements as busywork, an ongoing problem that seemed to increase exponentially during the emergency remote instruction semesters of 2020–2021.[1]

When students cannot see or do not understand the relevance of an assignment or activity, let alone a subject area skill or an entire subject, it is extremely difficult to facilitate their authentic learning.[2] Did I say "students?" Because I meant "humans." One thing our brains are pretty good at doing is conserving our precious cognitive resources.[3] When we do not see the relevance and purpose of learning how to do a thing, it's hard to trick our smart brains into expending energy on learning how to do the thing: we must be able to make a direct and clear connection between our lives—what's truly important to us—and the stuff we're trying to learn how to do. When students see academic work as busywork, we're all in trouble, because disconnection creates a treacherous void between the student and the learning goal.[4]

A disconnection between students and learning goals creates predictable problems for instructors and for students. "Why should I have to learn this?" is a question teachers have been trying to answer lo these many ages, but it has taken on particular urgency in the midst of global and national health, political, environmental, and social crises happening in tandem with steeply rising college costs.[5] But a lack of connection between students and academic subjects is not the only dangerous disconnection causing things to go wrong in the college classroom.

Seemingly intensifying levels of disconnection between students and other students, and between individual students and the campus community at large—especially linked to pandemic aftershocks—also pose a threat to effective teaching and learning.[6] Disconnection will snafu learning, as leading scholar of teaching and learning James M. Lang writes: "Classrooms are thoroughly social settings, and our connection to the people around us—or lack of connection—can have a significant impact on the quality of our learning. When we feel comfortable and connected, we have plenty of brain space to devote to learning; when we feel isolated or threatened, valuable cognitive resources are being drained away in response to those feelings, and we will not learn as deeply or effectively."[7] Lack of meaningful interpersonal connections among college students is a significant snafu because a sense of belonging in the "thoroughly social setting" of the classroom is not an incidental perk of being in college but rather a basis of academic success.[8] Without it, students cannot learn "as deeply or effectively."

Obviously, helping students build connections with one another and feel a sense of belonging on campus cannot be the responsibility solely of individual instructors. The issues contributing to students' sense of disconnection are vast and systemic, causing trouble far beyond any one individual classroom.[9] But because disconnection fuels so many teaching and learning snafus, we have to give time and pay pedagogical attention to facilitating connection building in our classes and during our interactions with students. Students need to make connections with the material they are learning. They need to make connections with one another. And they need to make connections with us.

For faculty members, disconnection from our colleagues, from our institutions and disciplines, and from our students undercuts our teaching efficacy in serious ways. To my fellow introverts and all ambiverts, let me reassure you that disconnection and its attendant isolation, which can make our teaching labor feel overwhelming and futile, is not the same thing as enjoying some rejuvenating solitude in your glorious mind palace. Many of us teaching college have spent innumerable happy hours alone with our brilliant ideas and fascinating ruminations. It's fun to visit, but you can't live in your mind palace even though much of academic culture tacitly prizes and prioritizes the rarified solitude of that mental space. You can't live there because, in addition to being a professional know-it-all, er, I mean researcher and scholar most of us are also teachers.

You can't teach and you can't learn all by yourself because human beings are social animals and when we undertake difficult endeavors, we need support and connection with other human beings. We need connections to survive and thrive, to make sense of the world.[10] As unique individuals with unique life circumstances, students and educators need widely varying levels and types of connections. But when things go wrong, connections are one of the most important means we all have for figuring out what the problem is, for making adjustments or doing damage control, and for moving forward.

Think of all of us, professors and students, as individual parachutists leaping from the safety of the plane out into the exhilarating but emotionally, socially, intellectually, and financially risky sky space of new learning. Sometimes the jump goes flawlessly and you float down to earth beneath your own perfect parachute; new skills mastered, new ideas successfully grappled with, new abilities honed. But sometimes our chutes malfunction and the jump goes wrong. Your chute doesn't open. Or it has a hole in it. Or you forgot to put it on because you were up all night with the baby/have been working double shifts/were so anxious about the upcoming jump that you couldn't pay attention during the parachute safety protocol review. There is only one way you'll stop from crashing to the ground and pulverizing yourself: your fellow parachutist can share their chute. However, you have to get their attention and communicate. You have to say: "I need help." You have to "wave your arms and point to your chute," because when our chutes go bad, we need to connect with our jumping companion.

Disconnection undermines students' abilities to learn and succeed, and it enervates educators. Therefore connection building is not touchy-feely "Kumbaya"-ing. It's not irrelevant or tangential to our "real" work of teaching our subject areas. It's not all rainbows and unicorns, nor does it detract from the intellectual and academic endeavors we want students to achieve. Connections are fundamental to learning and to teaching. They are your lifesaving jumping companion when your chute doesn't open.

Disconnection Fouls Up Learning

Despite vast reams of peer-reviewed, rigorously researched, irrefutable evidence that the "knowledge transmission" model of teaching and learning is, at best, minimally effective, we in higher education just can't relinquish The Lecture.[11] I don't mean a carefully crafted interactive lecture that interleaves new information with previous learning and intersperses presentation with pauses for practice, structured review, supported note-taking, and other types of active learning.[12] I mean the nonstop barrage of verbiage delivered by one person while everyone else in the room sits silent, immobile, and inert—what Paulo Freire called education's "narration sickness," which grants subjectivity only to the (endlessly) talking Teacher and renders students listening objects only.[13] Or as another scholar of teaching and learning bluntly states: "Straight lecture is death."[14] Many students, even if they personally have experienced little authentic learning by listening to these lectures, still believe that lecturing is a college professor's main job. Many *professors* believe that lecturing is their main job, and even if traditional lecturing isn't usually very good at helping students learn how to do things, *their* lectures are different.[15]

Maybe they secretly envision themselves as the star in a cinematic version of the college classroom Super Teacher. Pop culture depictions of college professors engaged in teaching rarely show anything other than a (white, cisgendered, and able-bodied) guy standing in front of a cavernous lecture hall, brilliantly elucidating without once referring to notes or saying "um" while an auditorium full of students listens raptly to his flawless oration, even applauding at the best parts. There's nary a sleeping or scrolling student in sight because they're completely entranced and endlessly entertained. One of the many negative results of all this lecture lovin' is that both faculty and students don't pay enough attention to how students need structured opportunities in every class to build connections with each other. They don't have to all become BFFs but students do need to make some productive, reciprocal connections to other students in their classes.

Students learning new skills cannot go it all alone. A lack of meaningful connections to peers can really foul up learning and hinder academic success, and this is particularly true for first-generation and historically minoritized student groups.[16] Research clearly shows the inverse of this as well: increased connections via facilitated cohorts and groups contribute directly to these students' success.[17] Even if a professor could give the very best lecture in the history of all lectures—an entertaining, illuminating, and endlessly insightful lecture—and even if this (entirely unrealistic, give me a break, it's not gonna happen, okay?!) amazing lecture was completely rocking everyone's world and miraculously filling every listener's brain with new knowledge, how effective could that lecture be if the students in the class never spoke to or looked at one another, or, in an online asynchronous class, if they never interacted with each other in any way? Wouldn't students learn more from the lecture if they could compare and review notes afterward and while studying? Wouldn't students be more likely to be sitting there in the classroom in the first place if another student in class was helping them stay on track, like maybe meeting up to get coffee before class or just texting each other reminders and checking in when someone is absent? Wouldn't they be more likely to log onto their online course if they've gotten positive feedback on a discussion board from another student?

Yes. Duh. Obviously.

Or maybe not so obviously. Many students and faculty don't understand or haven't given much careful thought to how the connections students make with one another are necessary for learning. Similarly, the corollary fact that *dis*connection fouls up learning did not receive enough attention until physical isolation became a requirement for most students during the 2020–21 pivot to emergency remote learning. Awareness of sociality as a key component of learning suddenly took center stage in popular and academic discourse about education.[18] How can we teach effectively, asked millions of instructors, when we are not in the same room as our students?

Expert online instructors and scholars of online college teaching and learning knew long before COVID-19 that sociality, instructor presence, and building connections with other students is not dependent on physical proximity. Online educator and faculty developer Michelle Pacansky-Brock, for example, identified the imperative to, in her words, "humanize online learning" in the early 2010s.[19] As scholar of online teaching and learning Flower Darby wrote in 2019:

> Students need more than access to videos, text, and disembodied voices commentating on their work. They need the presence of their peers and instructor to help them learn. . . . [E]ven for experienced online learners and instructors, it's easy to forget that a name on the screen represents a human being who can benefit from your presence and benefit your learning with their presence. . . . To create community in online courses, then, we should help learners see both ourselves and one another as human beings behind those names.[20]

For educators well-versed in effective online teaching, helping "learners see both themselves and one another" as members of a class community was a well-established best practice. In their book about digital learning environments, scholars of teaching and learning Kevin Kelly and Todd Zakrajsek summarize this point, writing that, irrespective of the teaching modality, "making a meaningful connection with either a faculty member or fellow students is a powerful predictor of student success in higher education. This connection is essential."[21]

But the distancing and isolation of the pandemic created unprecedented levels of fear, loss, trauma, and upheaval, which in turn often thwarted even the most effective proven strategies for online class community building. Social distancing during a pandemic, and taking classes online because you have no other option during a global crisis, is not the same as choosing an online class voluntarily. Additionally, a huge number of faculty charged with creating and facilitating those online classes had no inkling of the scholarship and research about effective online connection building. In the wake of those crisis semesters, the lack of meaningful connections between students, between students and instructors, and between students and institutions continues to be a cause for concern in higher education. In spring of 2022, faculty at a variety of institutions reported a "stunning level of disengagement," which at least in part can be traced to many students' struggle to forge meaningful connections.[22]

The coronavirus may have snowballed social isolation and social anxiety among students, but this problematic trend was on the rise before 2020 and it is not unique to higher education. Researchers have increasingly identified loneliness as a public health problem for millions, with elderly and young adults particularly at risk.[23] More than reductionist hand-wringing—or, on the flip side, dismissing this issue as the "snowflaking" of American youth, who just need to toughen up—there is good reason to be concerned about the mental health, coping skills, and overall emotional resiliency of young adults in college.[24] Psychology and educational researcher Sarah Rose Cavanagh argues that calling it a mental health "crisis" may be an oversimplification, noting that "the destigmatization of experiences of anxiety and depression" may "lead to an overpathologizing of ordinary human suffering."[25] However, as Cavanagh goes on to emphasize, complex factors, such as disparate economic and political threats to a student's community, impact the mental health of young adults in varying ways. "Lack of security and the absence of support," she notes, "are driving up distress" for some students. But "no matter the nature and extent of the crisis," educators must facilitate learning environments where students need to undertake intellectually and emotionally difficult tasks in spaces where they feel safe to do so—what Cavanagh terms "compassionate challenge."[26]

Educators can't provide this compassionate challenge if they don't make some crucial connections with students. While peer-to-peer connections are vital, so too students' connections with instructors. For example, research has long shown that faculty approachability—students' perception that they can ask an instructor for assistance and clarifications—is an essential type of pedagogical connection.[27] When students don't feel able to approach a professor to ask a question or seek assistance, even a minor misstep can cascade into a major snafu. A student confused about one assignment becomes a student failing the assignment, who then becomes a student feeling ashamed, who then becomes a student stuck in avoidance, who then becomes . . . well, you get the picture. A professor's approachability can derail a student's learning by further deepening any sense of disconnection the student may be experiencing with any aspect of the course.

"May be experiencing" is a euphemism here because it's practically guaranteed that some or, alas, *many* students can't see even a tiny glimpse of the meaning and relevance of many types of academic subjects and skills. It's a bitter pill for many professors to swallow when we realize that a whole bunch of our students are arriving at our classrooms convinced that our scholarly subject is a big waste of their time. Or, perhaps even more problematically, a waste of their money. Viewing education as a transaction sets students and their instructors up for all kinds of snafus. Yet even the most high-minded, idealistic educators can themselves fall into transactional thinking mode, especially when continually having to prove that what they're teaching is worthwhile and proving to students that the time and effort required to learn these new skills in this subject is worthwhile. It is easy to default to "Because we said so" when students are implicitly demanding "Why should we have to learn this?" Often this appears in everyday discourse around general education in college. Just suck it up and take all these classes you feel are pointless, and then we'll let you start doing the things you're really interested in learning how to do.[28]

A disconnect between students and the subjects they're supposed to be learning about is not easy to bridge. The scholars and experts teaching college classes have long been deeply, intrinsically, motivated to learn the skills of their subject areas. Our scholarly passions may fuel our teaching, but they can also interfere with being able to clearly perceive, let alone productively address, the disconnections between students and our subjects. It can help to remember that some of the best scholars you know probably didn't excel at every single aspect of their own schooling. I was a mediocre high school student myself, well below mediocre in mathematics, and an outright flunker of gym class. I was a mediocre student *except* when it came to reading, writing, researching, and formatting footnotes. My intrinsic motivation to learn how to do those things made me an outstanding student in those teachers' classes, whereas my gym teacher believed that my poor performance in his class was a result of my "bad attitude" and stubborn refusal to learn.[29] I know he did, because he told me so.

Was I disconnected from the academic purpose of playing dodgeball and increasing my "tumbling" skills? Um, *disconnected*? More like plummeting right out of the sky with a completely shredded parachute and not a single jumping companion in sight. "Tumbling" on a gym mat was never, and I mean never, going to be relevant to my life. Too many students feel the same way about the subjects and skills we're asking them to learn, and it will foul up their learning big-time.

Disconnection Fouls Up Teaching

When an individual faculty member consults with me about a teaching dilemma, one of the first things I often say is: "Yes, many instructors are seeing this same issue in their classes too." Whatever pedagogical problem they're puzzling over, it may well be popping up all over campus, across disciplines and programs, and even across the nation. But how would they know that? College teaching is tacitly defined and frequently experienced as a solitary endeavor—just you and your subject area expertise out there, taking on teaching and learning all alone, one syllabus at a time. Many department meetings rarely include even a cursory discussion about teaching, let alone strategizing for effective teaching based on research and evidence about what works for facilitating student learning in our discipline.

While teaching and learning centers have made inroads on college campuses, professional teaching development in higher education is still overwhelmingly optional and seriously undervalued. In addition to the entrenched academic culture of teaching as an individual undertaking, intersectional teaching inequities and employment disparities further distance and isolate faculty members from one another, even when they are in the same department, teaching the same classes, and encountering some of the same challenges. Disconnection is the norm, not the exception. In many ways, the typical working conditions for teaching in higher education can actively create disconnection between faculty members, between faculty and the institution, and between faculty and students.

One of the most glaring disconnections for faculty that fouls up teaching is the persistent, normalized distance between the individual people who are teaching, which prevents regular conversations about teaching practices. Many faculty members in most teaching contexts do not have regular opportunities to have conversations about teaching and learning, let alone observe each other teaching or strategize together about ways to improve teaching. In addition, becoming distanced and disconnected from colleagues and students is almost inevitable in teaching contexts that are inherently precarious, inequitable, and exhausting. Professional burnout looms large in these contexts.[30] In her book about burnout in academia, faculty developer and communications researcher Rebecca Pope-Rurak identifies a lack of meaningful connections with institutions, professional organizations, and colleagues as a key component of the "chronic or unrelenting stress associated with one's work" that causes burnout.[31]

Burnout and disconnections increase when workloads become unmanageable, and unmanageable workloads were rampant in higher education even before pandemic-era conditions created a host of brand new demands on faculty and staff. When the coronavirus pandemic broke out, everyone—even the most privileged tenured faculty member—had to reexamine and in most cases majorly adjust everything they'd ever done as a college teacher. They had to adapt every aspect of their course design and teaching practices to the polysynchronous and Zoom-y reality of higher education in 2020–21, all while surviving a global crisis.[32] That is an unmanageable workload for anyone's brain, no matter how deeply committed and connected one feels to teaching and to students. But even before the COVID-19 pandemic, inequitable, invisible, and unpaid labor plagued higher education. The entire peer review system for scholarly publication is based on the unpaid intellectual labor of both authors as well as peer reviewers and editors. Women are statistically doing more than their fair share of academic service at colleges and universities, and all faculty of color assume a greater percentage of the emotional labor intrinsic to teaching and learning, including advising, mentoring, and in numerous additional ways providing support for students in need.

Such working conditions can render the whole process of pedagogical learning untenable. Teaching effectively is an ongoing process of accruing new knowledge, trying new things, assessing the result, reflecting on what worked well and what didn't, revising your pedagogical practices, and repeat. Employment precarity, an unmanageable workload, and systemic biases deeply undermine any one faculty member's energy and ability to engage in ongoing pedagogical development, which requires at a minimum some time and cognitive resources. It also requires at least a small community of practice—other people who want to be effective teachers with whom you can brainstorm, share strategies, and go to when you're stumped by a teaching problem. Building one's pedagogical community of practice with other educators is no easy task for most college instructors, for all the disconnection reasons described above but also because academia in general is legendary for its ability to generate toxic workplaces. Every workplace has the potential to perpetuate human misery, but there is something exceptionally awful about the dysfunction and rampant pettiness of bad academic work environments. In some cases, academic departments have even deployed the very concept of "collegiality" to perpetuate discrimination and exclusion.[33]

A lack of connections to colleagues can foul up our teaching, but even more directly hindering our teaching efficacy is a lack of connection to students. Feeling disconnected from students, Pope-Ruark writes, is a big red flag for people who have previously enjoyed the challenges and rewards of teaching. It was an early sign of her own burnout and, in some of the faculty interviews she cites, being able to retain a sense of connectedness with students appeared to be the only thing that held professional burnout at bay.[34] It is a key component of effective teaching practices. When disconnection causes us to depersonalize students and we can't see students as individuals, we cannot effectively assess what we need to do in order to facilitate their learning.

The disconnect that occurs when we're not teaching the students we have, but rather the students we imagine we have or would choose for ourselves or even the students we had last semester, can be especially problematic. Being uninformed about who our students are is a source of disconnection between faculty and the people in their classes. Again, this disconnect is not about instructors' willful ignorance or ill intent, although of course that can be a factor. More frequently, the lack of knowledge about who our students are can be traced back to teaching inequities and a lack of time, energy, and meaningful support for teaching. Paying close attention to changing student needs, recognizing what we have to change or adapt, and then doing so is a heavy lift—cognitively, time-wise, and even emotionally. Inequitable teaching conditions greatly exacerbate this potential disconnect, and for faculty who must constantly counteract student biases and stereotypes about professors, connecting with students can pose additional types of work and increased amounts of pedagogical energy and reflection.

Finally, being disconnected from teaching and students can be caused, in disturbingly increasing ways, by outside politicized pressures. Political and cultural conflicts in the United States have always claimed local sites of aggression and battles, including public schools and universities. In the 2020s, politically

motivated prohibitions on subjects, books, even words and terminology—not to mention vital offices, programs, and student
support services—is cutting a ruinous swath through higher education. It's hard to imagine a more damaging final straw breaking
the proverbial backs of college educators than a politician dictat-
ing, by law, what can't be included on your syllabus—particularly
when the things that can't be included on your syllabus are precisely the things that you know *should* be included because you,
the expert, know a lot more about your subject than Senator Blow-
hard. What a surefire way to snafu teaching and learning.

Gear for Your Go-Bag

- When students can't make meaningful connections
  between their own lives and interests and the material and skills being taught, it creates obstacles to their
  learning.
- When students don't make meaningful connections to
  other students or to instructors, it creates obstacles to
  their success.
- When faculty members can't make meaningful and
  supportive connections to their colleagues and peers or
  can't make meaningful, professionally appropriate and
  educational connections with students, it creates obstacles to their teaching efficacy.

Chapter 5

REPAIR STRATEGIES FOR DISCONNECTION SNAFUS

Disconnections can creep into teaching and learning slowly, like a tiny tear in the seam of your parachute unraveling thread by thread. Or they can rip through your parachute in a heartbeat, shredding it like Wolverine's adamantium claws slicing through a bad guy. Disconnection snafus can be difficult to spot or they can be glaringly obvious, so STIR is especially handy when connections fray. Whether they're overt or murky, stopping and thinking can help us identify a disconnection. Repairing disconnections is challenging and ongoing work because, whether they're overt or murky, there's no simple quick fix for a disconnection snafu. The two specific strategies—conveying care and making revisions—that I explore in this chapter can give us some tools to help students and help ourselves when our chutes malfunction and we need to reconnect.

Identifying Disconnection Snafus

Anyone who's been a college teacher for more than a couple of weeks knows that feeling when you're standing in the classroom or you're on the LMS and a student is drifting away. Sometimes they're quietly sliding out the proverbial door or sometimes they just suddenly disappear. Sometimes it's just one student or sometimes it's a whole class that's slipping through your fingers. You're losing them. Yet, as vividly familiar as this feeling may be, clearly identifying students' disconnection can be difficult.

Disconnection snafus are hard to see and name because they can look like and take on the qualities of some of the most frustrating, migraine-inducing student behaviors. Behaviors like displaying blatant boredom in class, frequently missing deadlines, or skipping class are often entangled with a student's disconnection from their peers, from the course, from the institution, and from you. Even some of the student behaviors that are so blisteringly bad they scorch the student's whole academic earth—things like deliberate cheating, flagrant incivility, or hostility and conflict—can sometimes be rooted in disconnection.

Moreover, the life circumstances contributing to that kind of student disconnect are often outside of our control. A student struggling with trauma, for example, may be doing things such as missing class that may make a faculty member assume the student doesn't care about doing well. A student who dozes off during class may seem utterly disengaged but they may simply not be able to get enough sleep because they work long hours at their wage job to support or help support their family. Systemic discrimination, stereotype threat, and bias incidents may be undermining a student's ability to participate in any class modality.[1] Then there's all the reasons that students may not be connecting with the point and purpose of learning the skills and content in your class. Again, this can take the form of discouraging and even disrespectful behaviors, i.e., sighing, eye-rolling, snickering, and snoring.

Unable to see the relevance of the class material and learning outcomes frequently translates into a deep disconnection that we may be able to mitigate but must first recognize it as such. That's not easy to do when we're working our professorial butts off to facilitate student learning in our beloved scholarly field, and students are metaphorically and sometimes literally responding with a big loud yawn. Disconnection displaying itself as boredom is a particularly hurtful teaching and learning snafu because it's a direct shot to our academic egos to see a glazed look of profound indifference on a student's face (and it's hurtful to students because "boredom" renders them passive actors in their own education). Such student disconnections may even contribute to teaching burnout. Suddenly or gradually or something in between, we can become aware that we are angry, sad, burned out, or just plain exhausted. We know we're underpaid, over-worked, constantly navigating systemic biases, and/or perform-ing uncompensated labor, but we may not recognize as quickly the telltale signs of disconnection creating a sucking void in our teaching lives. As with students, our life circumstances can slowly or suddenly disintegrate connections to teaching. A trauma, ill-ness, or economic calamity happening to us or someone we love can completely sap the energy we need to build and maintain con-nections to students, peers, and our teaching work.

Because lack of connection can look like a lot of things, some-times it takes very careful discernment and reflection to recog-nize when disconnection is contributing to teaching and learning snafus. Consequently, the stop and think steps of STIR can be especially useful for identifying and repairing disconnection and stopping the runaway train of ego-blame-shame that can take over in those moments when disconnection is spurring an especially egregious behavior or fueling a conflagration threatening to burn out all your teaching energy. We need to pause, think, and seri-ously consider: Could disconnection be a factor here? Could there be a damaging gap between this student and their peers, class content, the institution itself, or me? Could there be a damaging disconnect growing between myself and my students, peers, or the institution itself? Could disconnection be causing this snafu?

One place where weak or weakening connections can foul up a student's learning in the classroom is peer-to-peer networks fray-ing the edges of their learning environment. Sometimes it could be obvious, like a group project that despite all the planning, role assignment, agreement making, and regular check-ins from you, has one or more members who just can't show up for collabora-tive efforts. Sometimes personalities clash in any group of stu-dents or sometimes it manifests as classroom cliques. A class of hundreds won't be the same as a small seminar in terms of the specific ways students can connect with one another, and what connections mean to students can vary depending on the overall student population. For example, a friend of mine teaches at Utah State University, where most students in their late teens and early twenties are Morman, married, and starting families. In contrast to many other student populations, his students have very strong connections with other students based on their shared religious practices. Identifying disconnection snafus among those students will take some specific kinds of discerning that would not be helpful with other kinds of student populations.

As in the case of identifying inequity snafus, the more concertedly and habitually we cultivate our *attention* to disconnection as a possible cause of things going wrong, the more we will *find* disconnection causing things to go wrong. But so too will we be able to increase our ability to effectively implement strategies for identifying, addressing, and repairing those disconnections. There are limits on what we as individual instructors can do about systemic issues or a student's individual life circumstances that may be contributing to disconnection. But there are two strategies that instructors in almost every teaching context can use to repair disconnection: First, convey care for students, and second, make revisions when necessary.

Convey Care

Congrats! You've got a head start on this because I happen to know for a fact that you very much care about student learning, success, and connections. You would not be reading or listening to this book if you didn't. So, this strategy is less about creating a brand-new teaching technique out of thin air and more about building on what you're already doing, with the goal of having a freshly honed utensil in your go-bag: clearly conveying care when students are getting disconnected from each other and disconnected from you.

"Care" is a loaded word, with gendered and anti-intellectual overtones. But conveying care as an educator doesn't necessarily demand exorbitant emotional labor, nor engaging in insincere emoting or unprofessional boundary crossing. It does require that students hear us say or see us express very clearly that we value every student's learning and success and that we are working to facilitate those things.[2] Conveying care is really just about ensuring that we acknowledge and express, as the facilitators and leaders of class learning communities, consideration and concern for the academic success and well-being of the other humans in our learning community.

Maybe that sounds overly simplistic—like, why *wouldn't* you be able to treat the other humans around you as human beings?—until you take into account the power differentials and the socio-economic and cultural systems crisscrossing school settings. It sounds simple until you consider how many aspects of higher education, such as contingent labor conditions for faculty and pervasive inequities for students, staff, and faculty, can reduce the whole endeavor of teaching and learning to a financially fraught and dehumanizing Thunderdome. In this context, conveying care for students becomes more complicated. However, I want to emphasize, as I did in my previous book about teaching as an eggheaded off-the-charts introvert, that we can convey pedagogical care for students in a variety of ways—ways that are fully congruent with our own personalities and employment conditions.[3] Conveying care doesn't mean pretending to be someone we're not or playing a role with students that makes us uncomfortable. It doesn't mean you have to work yourself to a compassion-fatigued frazzle.

With a lot of practice and after years of teaching, I've gotten comfortable with conveying care for students, and it comes easily to me . . . when things are going as planned. It gets harder when things go wrong. Getting embroiled in a snafu makes it harder to convey care because there are so many other things pulling at my ego, emotions, and energy. It gets even more challenging to convey care when so many things that cause disconnection can look like something else and, moreover, may well look like something that is exasperating or disconcerting.

For example, when a student has begun missing assignments, it's easy to get frustrated fast, especially when I've carefully built in many nudges, reminders, and alerts that all appear to be achieving exactly zilch. Pretty soon I'm feeling ready to chalk this up to the student's lack of personal responsibility or poor time management. Or, more compassionately, to unknown outside factors such as serious health or family problems. But in either case it's easy to decide that I've done what I can and, oh well, you win a few, you lose a few. If my classes are very large, I've got even more limited time and capacity to deal with a single student's struggles. Without advocating for getting hung up on that one student or suggesting that we devote every waking moment to student outreach, I do think that it's worthwhile to consider conveying care as a strategic response.

Viewing this snafu—missing assignments—as weakening connections can help us STIR the situation and identify it, which may offer us some chance for repair.

Stop: Before reaching the point of no return (writing the student off), could this be a disconnection snafu and could conveying care be helpful?

Think: Are there connections that could be strengthened to help the student get back on track? Connections to the material, to other students, or to you as the class facilitator which you could increase?

Identify: Get more information by reaching out to the student in person or via email.

Repair: Conveying care could look or sound like this:

> ➤ *I'm concerned that you haven't been able to turn in the last two assignments. I hope you're okay and I'd like to help you get back on track because I know you want to do well in this class. Here's how to get back on track:* [Explain how to submit late work or take advantage of an upcoming opportunity to meet a deadline or whatever specific concrete step the student can take to improve.] *Let me know what I can do to support and assist you: Email me or drop in or Zoom in to my Assignment Support Session this week* [name/time/place].

To reduce labor on your end, for large classes especially, this kind of message could be automatically generated in your LMS and it can be as useful in an asynchronous online class as a traditional on-site in-person class.

Conveying care for students this way strengthens connections between you and the student. It's no professorial pixie dust, magicking away all problems and guaranteeing the student will in fact be able to get back on track. It does, however, change the conversation—the conversation in your head and the actual conversation with the student. It puts care—academic care for a student's learning—rather than the student's misstep at the center of this issue. Something's gone wrong, yes, but by conveying care we can perhaps help the student take action and avoid spiraling into guilt and avoidance.

It also reframes the issue for us. For people who want to be effective teachers, first thinking of how disconnection might be playing a role when a student begins to fall behind or appear disengaged, and then enacting a strategy to convey care, is more pedagogically empowering—and less professionally and emotionally enervating—than angrily/tiredly/resignedly/passive-aggressively letting the student flounder without responding. But I have to admit that, for me, conveying care as a strategy when things go wrong has sometimes been a fake-it-till-you-make-it deal. There are plenty of times when my very first (defensive, insecure, and academic-ego-fueled) response to student disconnection issues has been "Whatever. I don't care if you don't." The beauty of a "convey care" strategy is when I say out loud or write something like "I know you want to do well" or "I want every student to succeed," it shifts my perspective immediately. Enacted as a pedagogical strategy almost automatically when things are going wrong, *conveying* care invariably helps me see the situation a little more clearly and to remember that in point of fact, I do care. I care a lot.

Peer-to-peer disconnections in a class can also be productively addressed and repaired by conveying care. Let's say that in-class discussions have been really dragging, with very few comments or students not listening or responding to each other. They seem super-disconnected. What would a STIR approach and conveying care look like?

Stop: Literally stop the discussion, saying something like:
➢ *"Wait. We need to take a beat right now."*
Think: What connections aren't coming together at this moment? Let the silence get noticeable, signaling the

import of what's happening and indicating that you are thinking carefully.

Identify: Conveying care, you can say:

> ➤ *"I'm concerned about how this discussion is going. Or, rather, not going. I know how important it is that this class meeting be a good use of our time. I want everyone to benefit from discussion."*

Repair: Halt content discussion for the day and do connection building instead. Brainstorm ways to get more voices into the discussion or do a writing reflection on the skills discussion helps build or how discussion connects to the class learning outcomes, or ask everyone to write a note of encouragement to their peers, collect them, and redistribute the notes in the next class.

It's less about the specifics of the repair and more about the message we can convey—that is, letting students know we noticed something's not going quite right, we care about it, and we can work together to make it better. Again, "care" in this context means employing an effective teaching strategy. The class discussion is not achieving its intended goal; it is not generating the learning opportunities it's supposed to be generating. Chastising or belittling students or railing about their lack of participation will get you nowhere fast (except maybe TikTok famous in a "Professor Completely Loses It" video). But conveying care can be a more effective intervention.

Conveying care includes facilitating student connections to other resources on campus. I am especially pleased to suggest this strategy to those among the professoriate whose first understandable reaction to statistics about student anxiety, depression, and mental health issues is an alarmed protest that we are not trained counselors, social workers, or diagnosticians. Fortunately, conveying care can be, again, a professional and pedagogical strategy that helps students without requiring us to be someone we're not. By conveying care, we can foster stronger connections between students and the people who *are* trained counselors and student support experts. Listing campus resources such as the accessibility resources office, tutoring services, counseling center, and emergency food shelf on your syllabus is an excellent start.

Further, we can destigmatize and normalize utilizing those campus resources on our syllabus along with providing basic contact information. The Student Experience Project suggests statements like the following:

> ➤ *"This campus provides extensive academic supports for students, and these supports are there to let students achieve the academic success they are truly capable of. I've provided a list of academic support offices below."*
>
> ➤ *"Everyone needs a support system to maintain good mental health. Many students benefit from using our campus counseling services to help manage issues related to personal growth, self-confidence, anxiety, depression, eating disorders, academic difficulties, and career indecision. Counseling services are available for all students at the Student Health Center."*
>
> ➤ *"Many students have visible or invisible disabilities, and the college offers accommodations that allow them to achieve their full potential. The Accessibility Resources Office collaborates with all academic departments to arrange appropriate accommodations for students with disabilities without compromising the academic integrity of the curriculum."*[4]

Scholar of teaching and learning Liz Norell regularly reminds her students that these are prepaid services, included in students' tuition and fees, and encourages students to take advantage of what already they've paid to use. Communicating messages such as this in our syllabi, normalizing getting assistance by connecting students with support and resources, is a way to convey care in all our interactions with students.

Ideally, conveying care by encouraging students to access resources should be accompanied by just a bit more of an assist. For example, when recommending any type of campus resource to students, Kelley Pickreign, an academic advisor at SUNY Plattsburgh, always then asks, *"Do you know how to get there?"* and *"Is there someone who can go with you?"* This extends to recommending that students access a service, information, an appointment, or really anything at all via the university website, followed by: *"Can I show you where to find that? Let's look on your phone."* This is an extra step for conveying care, and it may not be possible every time, in every teaching context. Educators' concern for students' mental health and their physical health and safety may lead to compassion fatigue.[5] But conveying care as a pedagogical strategy when things go wrong can, while building connections, also actually provide professors with a bit of buffer between the students' deeply personal, sometimes overwhelming needs and our professorial role.

For example, gender studies scholar Akanksha Misra uses a simple student check-in question that conveys care at the midpoint of her classes at SUNY Plattsburgh: *"How are you feeling about our class?"* Importantly, there is always a follow-up question: *"Why are you feeling this way?"* In most cases, when a student reports that they're feeling negatively about the class in some way, the follow-up question reveals reasons that have little to do with the class itself. Students are stressed, tired, overworked, or discouraged about other classes; they are struggling with financial worries, roommate problems, family situations, too many hours on the job, health problems, and so on. Misra finds this feedback helps her gain some relieving perspective on the variety of issues contributing to students' class engagement, while at the same time clearly conveying her care for students experiencing those issues. We can thread the needle on conveying care with this type of feedback by making a small adjustment, like telling everyone that because of how behind many people are feeling, we're going to drop a reading assignment and instead use class time to get caught up on something.

"But I have to focus on teaching my subject," faculty say. "We're not counselors or social workers." Yet, one of the most persistent ways things go wrong in the college classroom has less to do with individual student life circumstances and everything to do with teaching our subjects: specifically, how little students seem to give a hoot about our subjects. We've all seen, on the faces or in the lackluster responses to an online assignment, evidence of students' obvious lack of interest and disengagement. "Disengagement" is a dryly clinical term for things like student boredom that spread like a horrible virus and makes you seriously question all the life choices that led you to standing in a room, your head absolutely crammed with knowledge that every other person in the room appears to believe is profoundly uninteresting.

Instead of shrugging it off or ignoring it when students look like they're about to pass out from sheer unadulterated boredom, or when their assignments are so limp and listless they're DOA to the LMS, we can STIR it up.

Stop: Could there be a disconnect interfering with student learning?

Think: Where can I intervene, taking into account the role of intrinsic motivation and all the life circumstances shaping a student's interaction with the classwork?

Identify: Express care for the student as a human being, then concern for them as a student. As in: *"I noticed you've been a little checked out and your work is not quite hitting the mark. I just wanted to see if you're doing okay."*

Repair: Ask if you can help: *"Can I support or assist you with anything right now?"*

See how this changes the tenor of the whole exchange from chastising (Shape up or ship out!) to caring (Hey, are you okay?), and moves smoothly into repair (Maybe I can help). This approach rarely translates into additional work for me—an important consideration, especially if you have large classes. Rather, in most instances, students respond with gratitude that I noticed them and add that there is an outside issue dragging their attention or putting them off their game. In other words, it's not actually about me or my teaching or their work in the class. But by conveying care, hopefully there can be an improvement.

My last example of how to convey care is (ominous pause) email (cue Darth Vader theme). Every professional I know, including every college instructor, is buried in email. It can feel like a never-ending pile of busywork. But it really matters how we communicate with students via email—or any type of text-based exchange. I hear the cry of protest already: Students never read their email, though! Sometimes that's true. But it's also true that students will vividly remember emails from their professor that convey anything perceived as belittling or cruel. A brusque email to a student, or typed message via any communication app, dashed off with even mild annoyance can have an outside negative impact on students.[6] Faculty might routinely lament students' poor email etiquette, but, in my experience, poor email techniques for communicating with students abound among college instructors as well.

There are a couple of good strategies for conveying care with students via email without spending every waking moment of your life writing emails. For instance, we can establish email hours and communicate them clearly to students:

> ➤ *"At these times during the week, I will check and answer your*
> *messages. I may be able to respond at other times, but I will*
> *for sure always respond during this time on these days."*

We can also get in the habit of certain easy verbal cues in our email, such as opening with:

> ➤ *"Thank you for reaching out"* or *"Thank you for your*
> *message."*

And closing with a question to ensure understanding or follow through:

> ➤ *"Does that sound doable?" "Is there anything else I can do to*
> *assist you with this?"*

Email is one of the best places to STIR. "Stop and think" should be engraved on every computer monitor and email-enabled screen for every professor everywhere, because on occasion, no matter how pedagogically skilled and deeply caring they are, professors receive awful email messages from students. Messages ranging from the merely thoughtless or poorly stated ("I was absent. Did I miss anything?") to TMI ("Dude, I was too wasted to do the assignment") to professionally threatening ("I am going to contact the dean about this grade unless you change it") to biased ("You are not as qualified to teach this class as that other guy in the department [the one who looks like the professors on TV and lectures all the time].")

STIR has frequently helped me stop and think when I get an awful email from a student, and, somewhat counterintuitively, conveying care is the most effective strategy I've found for responding. Here's what it looks like:

Stop: Do not hit "Reply" yet. Or reply but only as a pause, as in *"I will get back to you about this by the end of the week."*

Think: Send your heightened emotions to the cool-down corner and let your big brain take a turn. What are the circumstances here that you need to address and what are things that you can let go? What's the snafu, exactly, and if disconnection is in the mix, can it be repaired?

Identify: Consider conveying care for student learning and success, even in the wake of an awful email. I have a go-to first sentence I use in fraught email situations:

➤ *"Thank you for your email and for sharing your concerns/ views/this information with me."*

Immediately, I've changed the terms of the exchange by showing that I care about this student's perspective and experience. I don't need to debase myself or in any way later validate the concern/views/information as justifiable or actionable. I'm only identifying it in a productive way, not an inflammatory one.

Repair: If a positive and productive response is possible given all the variables in the situation, try to move the whole thing out of the cyberspace cloud, off the screen, and into human-to-human conversation, on the phone or in person:

➤ *"I'd like to discuss this with you. Can we make a phone appointment or talk this week after class?"*

Important caveat: This doesn't apply if you're being physically threatened or harassed by a student via email. That's not a pedagogy problem; it's a time for drawing on whatever resources are available to keep you safe. Also, no promises that having this conversation with a student will be an easy or conflict-free fix. But I can promise that inscribing your caustic or even mildly exasperated comments onto an eternally readable and rereadable email will increase the snafu, not reduce it.

Conveying care, whether in email, in person, or in a recorded message, is a valuable pedagogical strategy. But it is also an important tool for taking care of the connections we need for ourselves, and I'm not referring only to connections with students. Sarah Rose Cavanagh points out that taking care of *yourself* is "the first thing you can do to maximize your daily effectiveness in the classroom."[7] I'm well aware that "self-care" has been so overused as to become almost meaningless, depicted as, say, getting a facial when the whole damn world is on fire, or taking a bubble bath when white supremacy and the death of democracy has got you feeling a little bummed. But as scholar of teaching and learning Cate Denial argues in her work on the pedagogy of kindness, self-kindness is not a facile panacea but a meaningful act of affirmation and empowerment.[8]

Refusing to be isolated from other teachers is one way to exercise authentic self-care, especially when things go wrong. When your parachute malfunctions, you must wave your arms and signal that you need help, and that's not easy to do in academia in any situation, let alone teaching—you know, that closed-door thing you're supposed to be able to do all on your own. So asking for assistance as a teacher in higher education is a radical act of self-care. It means prioritizing not only your pedagogical efficacy but also your own well-being. It means saying out loud, "There's a hole in my knowledge parachute," and no academic trained up in the ways of Petty Scholarly Fault-Finding and Backbiting does this lightly. Admitting that there's a hole in our parachute and getting help means we need to find jumping companions—at our teaching and learning centers, in our departments, in online communities. It means finding them and connecting with them before we jump out of the plane.

Make Revisions

I can't remember where it's from originally, but the best piece of advice I've ever heard about how to write well is "Learn to love revisions." It's a maxim I frequently pass on to students when teaching writing, and it's an even more important adage at a time when generative AI is reshaping what "writing" even means. Revising your written work, I tell students who are facing a long and daunting list of changes to the first drafts of their research papers, is not easy but it's how we project our own unique voices out into the world, and how we make our ideas as strong and powerful as they can possibly be. I believe this with my whole heart. In the classroom, helping students build their writing skills, I just naturally wax lyrical about the revision process, nerding out about the rewards of reworking, rethinking, and redoing our writing projects.

Many accomplished authors could counter this rosy view of revisions with their writing horror stories: the fruitless hours at the keyboard; the frustration of deleting, then putting back, then deleting again all those words; becoming trapped in a loop of endless tinkering that leads to unfinished projects, broken contracts, and broken dreams. "Learn to love revisions" may sound glib, given the intellectual and emotional risks, long labor, and sometimes sheer drudgery of revising our writing. It may sound glib as applied to teaching practices as well, but, like any good writing project, effective teaching practices never stop with a first draft. Being ready, willing, and able to make revisions is a necessary skill and an effective strategy for when things go wrong.

Easier said than done. Revising class activities, assignments, course design, and teaching practices can be hampered by any number of obstacles. Time needed to reflect on, design, and make careful revisions often far exceeds an instructor's available time to make revisions. Employment precarity and lack of compensation for extra teaching work makes revising courses and teaching practices unmanageable for many faculty. Departmental, program, or institutional pressures create constraints on what can be revised, while red tape and bureaucracy create roadblocks to revision.

Student biases can increase the possibility that they'll misinterpret an instructor's revisions as a sign of pedagogical weakness.
Isolation and lack of support from colleagues or a pedagogical
community of practice adds to the labor of revisions, not to mention the emotional and psychological toll of changing things that
we really, really thought would work.

It can be helpful, in day-to-day teaching, to view revisions as
work we do bit by bit, in bite-size chunks. Making any major,
sweeping, evidence-based revisions and changes to classes and
curricula is an important but long-term goal. It should be undertaken in stages and hopefully in collaboration with colleagues, and
with the support and resources necessary to sustain us for the long
haul. Making some smaller revisions—changes that don't entail
big investments of prep or grading time—is a lot more manageable
in most teaching contexts and an important strategy for repairing
common disconnections. Take, for example, students being unable
to identify the point and purpose of an assignment/unit/the whole
darn subject and the purpose of spending their valuable time and
cognitive resources on doing it. What revisions could we make to
our course activities or assignments when this disconnect appears
to be growing? Like when too many students aren't turning assignments, when their work is lackluster at best, when they stagger in
and out of the classroom as if they're on their very last legs and you
and your beloved content are getting on their very last nerve?

I usually look for a way to cut down content "coverage" and
replace it with a low-stakes but required relevance-building
activity,[9] such as throwing out a lecture and doing a low-stakes but
required class activity such as "List three things you've learned
how to do better in this class so far and how it's making you a
better student or citizen of the world or employee or writer or
thinker." Bonus points for doing this theatrically, like "I had a
lecture planned but I'm throwing it away because today we need
something different!" while dramatically hurling your lecture
notes to the floor.

Here are some other low-prep suggestions for strengthening
connections:

- Remove one of your planned units or topics and replace it with a topic or skill that the class decides together would be of greater interest.
- Offer an extra-credit opportunity with any assignment if students will explain its significance and relevance as if talking to someone who hasn't taken the class or done the assignment.
- Have a "What Matters to Me and to Us" or "Learning Shoutout" day where you and the students list on the board or big Post-it notes significant takeaways so far, what matters about what they're learning, and how other students, their own actions, and class activities are helping them advance toward their important goals and the class learning goals.
- Take a few minutes reviewing in class, or in a low-stakes assignment, the class learning goals, including having students identify how these connect to their own individual goals.
- Post a short video message from a former student who successfully completed the class about why such and such was important to their progress.
- Bring in new real-world case studies and examples

Revisiting the end goal—and emphasizing the ability to students to meet that goal—is another way to strengthen connections. When my students are working on a major assignment, they sometimes lose track of how each step of the process builds on the previous one. At that point I forgo introducing new content and increase workshopping time, setting a specific goal of building connections. I might say:

> ➤ *"Review the work you've done so far on the Big Project and my feedback on your last assignment. Then, in small groups, sketch out timelines for the next two steps and share what's worked to help keep you on track."*

This does double duty for building connections because it focuses on connection to content and connection to other students in class.

It takes effort for me to stop, think, identify, and repair connections that, in the end, have little to do with how much I know about my subject (which, just to be clear, is so much: I'm supersmart) and a lot more to do with my willingness and ability to help students connect to the relevance of the content, to one another, and to me. It has a lot more to do with how effectively I can convey care and nimbly revise.

Gear for Your Go-Bag

- Disconnection can manifest in many different and sometimes frustrating student behaviors.
- Conveying care to students by clearly stating and showing that their academic success and well-being matters to us—and that we're willing and able to assist them in appropriate ways—goes a long way toward strengthening connections.
- Conveying care includes choosing your words carefully, including all written communication.
- When conveying care, don't neglect self-care and making connections with other educators.
- Being able to make revisions and adjustments to assignments, classroom activities, and course design can be an empowering and effective repair strategy. Although major revisions are periodically necessary as part of our ongoing work as educators, even small changes and adjustments can help repair disconnections.

Chapter 6

INCREASING CONNECTIONS

It seemed to happen overnight, or maybe so slowly that it was imperceptible, but one day about a decade into my teaching career I looked around a room filled with students waiting for our class to begin and it suddenly hit me: it was eerily silent. Every student was noiselessly scrolling and staring at the tiny screen they were holding. Every. Single. Student. In that moment I felt a real sense of loss on behalf of my students. For us Olds who taught on-site classes before smartphones took over the world between 2010 and 2015, it's hard not to lament the dear departed days when most students entered the classroom and made eye contact and spoke to one another instead of silently, fixedly staring at the hypnotic glow and addictive beeping and pinging of their devices.

Commentators and scholars regularly point to smartphones and social medias as the source of social ills for youth,[1] but that's a serious oversimplification. Current research suggests that social media and smartphones play complicated and sometimes contradictory roles in twenty-first-century sociality and culture, and, anyway, there's no putting the wireless tech toothpaste back in the tube.[2] Yet the fact is that many students seem to have lost a uniquely precious sliver of time—the few minutes before an on-site in-person class begins—for making connections with their college peers and with the professor.

Those inimitable minutes are one of the places we can facilitate connection building, and we need to do so when we are teaching in the physical classroom. However, there are numerous other ways to facilitate stronger connections in all modalities. In this chapter, I outline four strategies for sustainably increasing connections for students and for us: helping students recognize the relevance of their learning; structuring student interactions; getting good at small talk; and talking about teaching.

Prioritize Recognizing Relevance

What's the point and purpose of what we're working on in this class? Students need to recognize the relevance of course material and assignments to make meaningful connections, and we need to help them do so. Sometimes I present it to students this way:

> ➢ *"At the end of this course, you will be able to convincingly answer the question for yourself: 'Why should I learn how to do this?'"*

When I began trying to help my U.S. history students answer this question, I discovered that many of them had never been asked in an educational setting to consider in a real way the value or meaning of the curriculum for their own unique lives. They thought I was fishing for formulaic answers or quizzing them—that the only correct answer to the question "Why should you learn this?" was why I, the professor, thought they should learn it.

I soon began to repeatedly and with a lot of emphasis tell students that when it comes to this part of their learning, I'm not interested in what Generic Student thinks. I'm not looking for standard answers to standardized exam questions. I want them to identify for themselves, and I want to know as the facilitator, what this content means in their own unique lives. What are the connections they can see between these past events they're learning about and the events in their own lives right now? Students need opportunities and incentives, via our course design, to actively identify connections between the stuff they're learning how to do in the class and what is important and meaningful to them. Ideally, we can build on those connections to help students identify what researchers have identified as "a sense of purpose, and especially self-transcendent purpose"—the ways that their own individual learning can "make a difference to the world."[3] Research on goal setting generally and in the classroom specifically shows that when students have the opportunity to identify their own goals and make a public commitment to meeting those goals, they are more likely to succeed in the class, even when those goals do not directly intersect with the course contentment.[4] Before the class even begins then, we can help students frame the work they're going to do in the class as a way to take at least one or two meaningful steps toward achieving their own individual and unique academic, personal, and professional goals.

Another way to help students make this type of meaningful connection to the material is to build some choice and options into the course. Not only is student choice a means for increasing inclusivity and accessibility but it also encourages students to engage with course content in ways that matter to them. Ask yourself if there is a way to give students some options in how they demonstrate their new learning and their completed research. Advocates of the un-essay, for example, report that students being able to present their research in nontraditional ways increases students' motivation.[5] Infusing even a little bit of "Choose your own adventure" or "Select from a menu" energy into your course design and syllabus can be one way to create opportunities for students to identify and build connections between the course learning outcomes and what they love, what matters to them, and where they want to spend their time, energy, and cognitive resources.[6]

It's an open secret among college faculty that many of those aforementioned learning outcomes—the standardized, mandated course student learning outcomes (SLOs) that we are required to put on the syllabus—stink. Many of them are written in ways that seem calculated to deliberately create disconnections between students and the subject. Jargon-filled, passively voiced, abstruse, and objectively boring, bad course learning objectives, outcomes, and goals are a surefire way to automate disconnection snafus between students and subjects. Lots of times, the intention, the actual goal, of SLOs is a good one, but it's buried beneath extraneous verbiage or is so abstract that it's almost impossible to discern. And don't get me started on SLOs that make basic errors like stating a class activity, not an actual learning goal, or listing content covered rather than learned skills and abilities. This is one of those higher ed realities that really should not exist anymore. There is a huge, robust, evidence-based body of research on this topic, and it should not be hard to translate such clear and conclusive scholarship of teaching and learning into writing good learning outcomes.[7] Until institutions catch up, there are three things we can as individual instructors can do to repair this disconnect. First, create clearer and better additional outcomes for our classes (sneaky!), and, second (less sneaky), translate poorly written SLOs into language that will be more likely to spark student curiosity.[8] Third, we can make space in the syllabus for students to create and pursue at least one of their own individual learning goals in the class, identifying exactly what will make learning in the course most meaningful for them.[9]

Using low-stakes but required reflection assignments on their progress toward achieving SLOs can be a win-win-win way to help students recognize the relevance of what they're learning while increasing students' metacognition skills.[10] I say "win-win-win" because it increases relevance and student learning without a huge addition to our workload. For instance, we can have students do three "Learning Reflection" assignments at the beginning, middle, and end of the class for a small percentage of their grade, earned by simply completing the assignment. I usually give students the option to submit their learning reflection via a written document, PDF, slide, or recording, answering one or two questions about their own learning.

At the beginning of the class, learning reflection questions could include:

➤ *"Of the three student learning outcomes (SLOs) for this course, which are you most interested in achieving and why?"*
➤ *"This class is required for all [fill in the blank] majors. What specific skills and abilities do you think this class is going to help you build, and why does every [fill in the blank] graduate need these skills?"*

> ➤ *"How do think that successfully achieving the SLOs for this class is going to help you land your dream job after graduation?"*
> ➤ *"What previous experiences have you had learning about this subject? What was the worst experience? What was the best?"*

At the midpoint of the semester, students can reflect on questions such as:

> ➤ *"What are you most proud of learning in our class so far and why?"*
> ➤ *"As you've worked toward achieving the SLOs for this class, what have you found most surprising?"*
> ➤ *"How would you describe what you're learning in this class to a friend or relative?"*

Similarly, at the end of the class, you could ask:

> ➤ *"What can you do better now than you could back at the start of this class?"*
> ➤ *"What three specific skills are going you take with you from this class to your other classes?"*
> ➤ *"How are you going to apply what you've learned to your professional and/or personal goals in the next six months? In the next year?"*
> ➤ *"Look back at your first learning reflection. In what three specific ways have you achieved the goals you set out for yourself?"*

Giving students the opportunity to practice their metacognition skills is good for their learning while also helping them actively identify the relevance of the work they're doing toward achieving their own unique academic, professional, and life goals. Bonus: These are not the kinds of questions a chatbot could easily answer. Thwarting AI while also encouraging metacognition and increasing relevance without a big increase in teaching labor? Add another win to these assignments.

Prioritizing relevance is also a way to help us as the instructors strengthen our own sense of connection to students and to the content. Unless you're some kind of pod person or evil robot posing as a human professor, churning out student-widgets who can repeat a list of facts they will forget immediately is not your goal. So, students being able to articulate and demonstrate some authentic connections to learning the material, based on their understanding of what it relevant to them, taps into what, for many people teaching college classes, is our whole reason for being there in the first place: our deep interest in a scholarly field, subject, and skill. We can increase relevance for ourselves in our teaching when we can begin course design and learning assessment by asking ourselves questions such as: What do I truly adore about this subject? Adore so much that I've made it my life's work? And how can I build my class around this in a way that will invite students to share, even just a little bit, in doing this kind of thinking/creating/calculating/researching?

Structure Student Interactions

Raise your hand if you disliked "group work" when you were a student. Yup, that's a lot of you. Raise your hand if you assign "group work" now that you're a professor. Uh-oh, that's a lot of hands, considering how many of you have painful memories of being the conscientious student who ended up doing all the work while the other group members did nothing. A lot has changed in higher education in the past few decades, but students still report that they dislike group work for these same reasons, with an added layer of widespread social anxiety.[11] So the answer must be: Never assign group work. JK! You *should* assign group work because it can be a highly effective way for students to increase their skills and knowledge while building connections with one another. It just requires a lot of careful structure, guidance, and frequent checks from you.[12]

Structuring student interactions formally, as in group projects, and during informal, ungraded class activities as well increases student connections and is a core component of student-centered classrooms. SoTL frequently throws around the term "student-centered," but it's far from easy to implement in real-life teaching. Most college curricula are content-driven—the "cover-age" model—which puts the expert instructor (not the student) at the center of class meetings. I mean, just take a gander at typical classroom architecture and seating, which customarily arranges students into rows facing forward so they can all gaze at—you guessed it—the solitary expert standing at the front of the room yakety-yakking. On-site meeting spaces designated for learning often, quite literally, preclude the possibility of student-centered rather than yammering-professor-centered classes.

Beyond planning for how to circumvent this actual material obstacle, in order to be effective, activities for student-centered class meetings have to be carefully planned, reviewed, and revised as needed. But a student-centered classroom is well worth our effort.[13] It jibes with what we know about learning in general and also directly, positively influences students' abilities to make connections and, specifically, to make connections with one another. Creating and providing structure for regular small-group activities and discussions in almost any size class is essential for strengthening student connections. It's not enough to say: "Now discuss." It's not enough even to say: "Turn to your neighbor and practice X, Y, or Z." We must design, plan for, and facilitate *structured* student interactions in class.

Kelly Hogan and Viji Sathy point out that structuring things like discussions or other active learning classroom activities are vital for facilitating equitable learning environments.[14] Engaging in academic discussion in a classroom is something that feels natural to me and probably to you, dear reader, because we have years of high-level training and lived experience that make us expert academic discussants. But most of our students are not highly skilled at this. Stephen Brookfield and Stephen Preskill point out that, for reasons ranging from the way that class discussions can "reproduce differences of race, class, and gender that exist in wider society" to how "supposedly democratic discussions are often a thin veneer for maintaining traditional teacher power," we "cannot expect that students are ready and willing to engage in discussion, much less able to do so."[15]

To productively engage in discussions, then, whether on campus and in person or via asynchronous LMS sites, students need structure.[16] To prepare for a discussion in person, structure might mean everyone submitting a discussion question before class; in-class prep time for thinking and brainstorming before discussion; and identifying specific learning goals for the discussion. Structuring the discussion itself could include assigning students to random small groups and including a meet-and-greet (yes, names again!); assigning rotating roles such as recorder, timekeeper, reporter, vibe checker, and so on; and in-class time for note review and summarizing. Providing those directions not just once, verbally, but on-screen or in a handout increases inclusivity.[17] Another way to increase inclusivity and help students benefit from discussion is structuring ways for students to demonstrate their learning after discussion has concluded, such as required discussion reflection assignments; review of discussion main points in the following class; and identifying "highs and lows," new understanding, and new questions in discussion follow-up assignments. Online discussion forum structures that can boost connections include ensuring that students introduce themselves, possibly with a video; giving students a choice of smaller group topics in which to engage; and incentivizing meaningful replies to each other's posts.[18]

We can counteract disconnection by facilitating student interactions in low-stakes but required and supported ways that help them talk to each other. Experienced educators know that these types of small-group activities help students make productive connections to one another, but students may not be cognizant of why these are a good use of their time. To increase their understanding of the ways this particular kind of connection is valuable, I often have students complete a short, low-stakes, but required personal learning network (PLN) assignment at the beginning of the term.[19] First, they list ten people and resources that have helped them learn and succeed academically in the past, such as teachers, textbooks, family members, coaches, teammates, friends, Wikipedia, film documentaries, tutors, and so on, and then identify one or two things they're really good at doing that they would be willing to help other students do well too. Then I compile and share their responses, explaining that this class is an opportunity to add people to your PLN and to other students' success as well. Assignments like this increase inclusivity while strengthening connection in the class by showing how students' diverse past experiences and skills are an educational asset in any class.[20]

Another way to structure student interactions is creating and facilitating regular in-class meetings of small student groups charged with helping each other remember what's due when and staying on track. You can call them "accountability groups" or "class buddies" or "success clusters" or whatever catchy name you come up with. We create them by randomly choosing students and then—this is the key part—regularly, routinely, repeatedly (ideally, in almost every class meeting) giving those small groups five minutes in class to meet and discuss upcoming assignments and deadlines and then formulate questions for the instructor as needed. We can encourage them to set up their own chat or text group, emphasizing that the groups will help everyone stay on track. Checking in regularly with these groups to ensure they're helping each other can be an easy (easy to complete and easy to grade) assignment whereby they're identifying the benefits of building connections with their peers and reflecting on their own contributions to helping others as well.

This is the type of assignment that physics professor and scholar of learning Melissa Eblen-Zayas recommends for encouraging students to identify learning assists."[21] A basketball player who passes the ball to another player who immediately make a basket is recognized as providing the assist because without the first player making the pass, the second play would not have scored. Similarly, we should recognize and celebrate students who have made a direct positive impact on another student's learning. A couple times a semester we can ask students to complete a short assignment explaining how someone in class helped them make progress toward a learning goal, remember a deadline, understand something better, or overcome an obstacle. In the words of James Lang, we want to "leverage peer learning power."[22]

If we want to encourage students to see connecting with other students as valuable, we need to ask them to reflect on and identify why these are valuable to them. Just saying, "It's valuable! Trust me!" won't work. I tried that and it didn't work. I just got a lot of student comments in the anonymous end of the semester evaluations along the lines of "You're the teacher, so why are we spending time in class talking to each other?" I realized that I had to better structure and facilitate student interactions, including requiring students to identify for themselves how these interactions were helping them make progress, in order for them to reap the benefits of stronger connections to their peers.

Get Good at Small Talk

In an old screenshot meme from the animated TV show *Steven Universe,* our young hero is closely reading a book. We see on the first page, "Step One: Think of what you want to say." He turns the page to "Step Two: Say it." Finally, we see the cover of this cutting-edge guidebook: *How to Talk to People.* The joke is premised on the assumption that talking to people does not require a lot of preparation in advance, but, in fact, some of the more socially awkward among us really could benefit from doing a little homework. I've used this meme in my professional presentations as a lighthearted illustration of my advice to introverted bookworms like me that we need to consciously prepare for the social interacting part of teaching. Casual social interaction—small talk—is an invaluable professional and personal skill. It's on us as classroom facilitators to get good at small talk and help our students do the same.

Frankly, that's asking a lot of us as college instructors. A significant portion of us aren't especially smooth operators in the social arena, preferring long hours of secluded study to small talk with strangers or acquaintances. In addition, some studies suggest that college professors are more likely to be neurodivergent than other professional groups.[23] Ableism in academia and reluctance to be labeled as neurodivergent may make small talk an even more complex undertaking for neurospicy professors.[24] Depending on all the additional pressures and demands on our time and energy defined by factors such as employment status, how our brains are wired, and our embodied and social identities, adding "how to talk to people" to the curriculum—for no additional compensation and without time and support for learning how to effectively do this as educators—may sound like an unreasonable, unobtainable goal. Most of us aren't being trained or paid to teach students how to talk to people.

As unfair as it can feel, and as much as it personally pains me as someone who is persistently terrible at casually striking up conversations, effectively engaging in small talk with students goes directly to the connections we need to make as social animals engaged in teaching and learning. Lord knows, it's always hard to leave my gorgeously appointed mind palace for the hurly burly world of, um, the world, where there are people. People who need to talk to other people, including me. But you know what? It was my crazy-in-love eternal fascination with my subject, that thing I was mooning about up in the mind palace in the first place, that drove me to start paying more attention to small talk. Because I adore the subject area skills my classes help students build, I've accepted that "how to talk to people" is a necessary tool for my own teaching efficacy.

Unstructured, non-content-related conversations are a not-so-secret weapon in the fight against disconnection.[25] As Sarah Rose Cavanagh notes, "'small talk' conversations are not just small but are building blocks to forming authentic relationships, which students report are a great source of motivation and learning."[26] The ten minutes or so before a class begins is small talk prime time and you have to do it. Yes, even if you have only a few minutes because you are rushing from another class. Yes, even if it is a very large class and you'll only be able to speak with a few students. Yes, even if you need to turn on the computer, review your notes, set up your slides, and erase the board covered in writing left behind by the inconsiderate professor in the previous class. Even when we're on the verge of burnout or suffering from racial battle fatigue[27] or coping with toxic colleagues or all the above, even in a class of hundreds, we can usually take a few minutes to talk informally with students. We need to be ready to chat lightly and pleasantly about not much of anything with students before class begins.[28]

That's never been easy for me and it's even harder today, because in order to casually shoot the breeze with a student before class, it's a near certainty that the student will have to first look up from their phone. You'll have to get their attention. Not gonna lie: it can be a little awkward getting started. The increased difficulty of exchanging a few pleasantries in the Age of the Smartphone has made other interactions with students outside of class meetings even more important. So too has increased numbers of online or mixed-modality classes added import to providing time and space for casual interactions among members of a learning community.

Take, for example, office hours. In SoTL and higher ed commentary, it's become a bit of a truism that office hours are not something we can or should expect students to know how to utilize. Increasingly, college faculty are rebranding office hours to more clearly convey to students the point and purpose of this allocated time. They invite students to "drop-in student assistance hours" or, alliteratively, "meet with me Mondays" and "talk to me Tuesdays."[29] These rhetorical strategies are a good start, but getting students in the door (or to stop in at the library or campus coffee shop or other alternative "student help hours" locations) or in the Zoom room or logged on the LMS is just the first step. Now the real work begins, in my introverted opinion: the interactions between us, faculty and students, that build productive and meaningful connections. Invariably, these interactions must begin with small talk.

For me, making small talk with students once they've arrived in my office can be fairly daunting. If I've been quietly doing anything in solitude, it takes a real effort for me to gracefully exit that mental space and begin engaging with others. I'm also self-conscious, knowing that this is an important opportunity to make a connection. One of my automatic coping mechanisms in this situation is to start nervous talking. And talking and talking. The students are generally polite and listen respectfully as I prattle on and on. This is not a good way to assist them or to build a meaningful professional connection. It's talking, maybe even small talking, but it's not *good* small talk. It reminds me of that study showing that patients can easily forget well over half of what is said to them during a visit to the doctor.[30] Students who've been on the receiving end of my nervous blathering probably retain far less than 50 percent of the loquaciousness I dumped on them.

To counter this tendency, I try to prepare for good small talk outside of class by planning to maximize connection-building opportunities during office hours without blabbing too much. For instance, in my tenured fifties I've embraced the mom-ish overtones of using food as an academic love language and code for "I care about your well-being." So I usually offer a snack to anyone who walks in my door. Some professors keep a basket of small fidget toys or office supplies to give away. A professor I know has decorated her office with pennants from the universities where she earned degrees, and students meeting with her for the first time often refer to them right away, making them a great conversational icebreaker and a subtle but effective way of visually reminding students of her academic expertise in a STEM field, a not-insignificant point, since advice about how to invite students to partake in office hours rarely addresses disparate teaching realities.[31]

Hogan and Sathy recommend these non-content-related conversation starters when meeting with students:

> ➤ *"What was one of your favorite courses last semester or in high school, and why?"*
> ➤ *"How did you decide to come to [insert school name]?"*
> ➤ *"Where is home for you?"*
> ➤ *"What kinds of things do you like doing in your spare time?"*[32]

When my office hours approach, I prepare myself for remembering to use my words carefully and say things as clearly as possible to convey what I want to convey. Things like:

> ➤ *"How can I help you?"*
> ➤ *"What are your most important goals for this class?"*

followed by:

> ➤ *"Let's talk about what you can do to meet those goals."*
> ➤ *"What obstacles have you encountered that have made it hard for you to succeed in the past?"*
> ➤ *"Let's strategize ways to overcome those kinds of obstacles."*

concluding with:

> ➤ *"I want you to do well in this class."*

If this sounds kind of loony to you and you're wondering why anyone would need to plan so much for simple conversations, congratulations on your remarkable social suavity, you smooth talker. For the rest of us, intentionally preparing for productive interactions, during which small talk isn't small, is essential for building connections with students outside of the classroom.

Building connections with students outside the classroom, getting good at small talk, is a student-centered teaching practice. Remembering this has helped me reduce my own nervous chatter and also shed new light on the benefits of attending college events outside of class. One particularly conducive locale for increasing peer-to-peer, student-to-institution, and student-to-faculty connections is college extracurriculars. For young adults living on campus, activities such as clubs, student government, athletics, Greek life, and the performing arts are valuable means for increasing connections. I know this applies to a small percentage of students today, when the "traditional" college experience of young adults living on campus is more the exception than the norm among people pursuing postsecondary education.[33] But I think these types of connections are still worth our attention because they can be a powerful means of helping students feel like a valued member of a campus community, which is a directly positive factor in successfully completing their degrees.[34] As classroom educators, we can support and encourage these connections, and attending extracurricular events can also increase our own sense of connectedness to the institution.

Time and again I've heard colleagues giving short shrift to extracurriculars, pitting these activities, and sports in particular, against academics. Time and again I've heard students say how much they value and appreciate it when faculty members support their activities, such as clubs and sports. Can you spot the disconnect? I once facilitated a series of Zoom roundtables, "What Your Students Want You to Know," with different student groups, such as international students, athletes, and students associated with student support services and the DEI office. One thing stood out among every student group: students wanted faculty and staff to know that they really appreciated seeing them at extracurricular events. It was remarkable how consistently we heard this from a variety of students. Attending a game or going to a play is additional unpaid time given over to work-related activities, and not everyone can do this regularly, but showing up to support student endeavors outside of class is connection-building gold.

Best of all for this awkward introvert, and one of the biggest motivators for giving up some of my treasured free time during the evenings and on weekends to attend an event, is that it gives me something to talk about with students. And it's an exemplar of the axiom that small talk is never small. "Great game/play/concert/club event yesterday" is a small talk conversation starter that says so much more than "great game/play/concert/club event." It conveys to students that we value and support their connections to other students on this campus; that we value what they value about being a student here.

Talk About Teaching

Making small talk will always be effortful for me, but talking about teaching with other people who care about teaching—that's my jam. It's hands down my favorite part of running a teaching center. It also happens to be one of the most powerful means we have as faculty members to reduce the disconnections that sap our energy and foul up our teaching. Being able to cultivate connections with other educators is a means for sharing insights about teaching and learning and for cultivating a reflective, metacognitive approach to our own teaching practices.[35] As educational developers Klara Bolander Laksov and Cormac McGrath write, reflection is essential to pedagogical learning and "central to deliberate reflection is the continuous evaluation of actions through an open dialogue with equal partners and significant others."[36]

Talking about teaching with other educators who share important aspects of your teaching context can help counteract academic workplace toxicity, hostility, dysfunction, and invalidations. Counseling and psychology professor Harriet Schwartz summarizes the importance of professional networks when things go wrong:

> Much of the work of our profession is done in isolation from our colleagues. Collegial relationships can take a back seat to our daily work and goal pursuit. However, we are wise to engage in the mutuality and richness of good collegial connections. These relationships not only help keep us steady amidst routine ups and down but also become even more important in times of disillusionment.[37]

Similarly, in "Teaching Up: Bringing My Blackness into the Classroom," Celeste Atkins offers this advice to readers, gleaned from her doctoral research interviewing sociology faculty who identify as Black or African American: "Find your people. Create a network of support, of individuals who understand or are willing to learn about the specific barriers and microaggressions you face. Create a safe space to vent, get your feelings validated, and possibly share ideas."[38] Conversely, notes scholar of higher education Candace Hall, "when faculty, particularly Black faculty, are recruited into spaces where there is little or no possibility of creating community, their wellbeing is likely impacted."[39]

For all faculty, honest, supportive conversations about teaching creates a necessary sense of community. In her argument for feminist facilitation of professional development, scholar of teaching and learning Niya Bond describes how the Online Learning and Teaching Community of Practice she co-facilitates created this type of "both-and space" during the pandemic pivot semesters, serving as "a place where they could come to re-energize their teaching during COVID as well as one that provided a nice escape from postsecondary pressures."[40] Many instructors plug into a community of practice with other educators they've never met in the physical world, meeting and sharing teaching ideas and resources in social media spaces.[41] A pedagogical community of practice is no less real and meaningful in the virtual space as face-to-face, in person, and sometimes even more so, like when you teach at a small institution and live in an isolated rural area. (Go look up Plattsburgh, New York, on a map.) I've also increased my connections with other scholars by reading and engaging in SoTL. There is nothing quite as affirming and reassuring as seeing there on the page, in print, a description of a specific strategy that you know you'll be able to use tomorrow in class and, by golly, it's going to work.

The pedagogical community of practice I found on the social media site then known as Twitter saved my bacon during the emergency pivot pandemic semesters. Pretty much every day the unprecedented demands on me as an educator were shared and discussed by my tweeps. When I felt overwhelmed, which was always, it helped to read ten or twenty tweets from other professors who were also overwhelmed. I got specific ideas for my online classes, but even more importantly I was reminded every day that I was not alone. I was far from alone. Knowing you're not alone in the worst of times—that's a connection everyone urgently needs.[42]

Conclusion: "The Best Part Was the Social Environment"

Connections are everything in education. Before the pandemic pivot semesters, when I started reading everything I could about how to teach online, I didn't truly comprehend this fact. The SoTL about effective online teaching made this fact so abundantly clear: without human connections, students can't learn, and faculty can't teach, to the best of their abilities. Online teaching practitioners and researchers have spent years identifying how to ensure that this irreplaceable aspect of human education can be facilitated in a digital environment, as Michelle Pacansky-Brock summarizes: "Relationships are at the core of meaningful college experiences."[43] It's ironic that I, a bona fide scholar of teaching and learning and a socially awkward introvert, had to sit totally alone in my office, spending months staring at a computer screen, in order to fully realize the importance of people-ing in effective teaching practices.

When on-campus classes restarted, relationships, community, and connections were uppermost in my mind. I saw this imperative in action after the fall of 2021 when debriefing with SUNY Plattsburgh professor of supply chain economics Wanda Carroll about her first-year seminar, Amelioration: Your Impact on Community. The class focused on building student self-efficacy, particularly students' ability to create new connections with other students, the campus, and the local Plattsburgh community. It featured collaborative projects, such as growing their own plants and learning how to knit under the tutelage of a "grandparent generation" instructor. It was wildly successful in meeting its official learning goals, but one of the key takeaways for me was what happened unofficially when the senior citizens who were volunteering to teach knitting attended Wanda's on-site class for a few weeks.

"First of all, they were always a half an hour early," Wanda told me, perhaps because punctuality is easier for someone who is retired and probably because these senior citizens valued the rare opportunity in our age-segregated culture and society to interact with the students, all of whom were recent high school graduates and eighteen to nineteen years old. "The seniors would come in, sit down, and start knitting," said Wanda. "And they started talking to each other and to the students instead of looking at their phones, right?" I asked. "Yes! Exactly!" Wanda and I stared at each other as we both realized that the intergenerational learning that happened in those moments was as much about social interaction as it was about knitting. She had anticipated the power of community building by bringing together these students and senior citizens but hadn't anticipated how skillfully the pre-smartphone generation could lead the young adults in learning how to casually interact with people sitting beside them whom they didn't know very well. Small talk, in this case, was one of the keys to increasing connections, which in turn, was a vital part of student learning and success in the class.

In addition to the "grandparent" knitting mentors who skill-fully struck up conversations with students and helped facilitate connections to the other people in the room, the variety of class activities for the different units made class attendance more mean-ingful for students and linked student learning to the broader community. Student comments at the end of the class indicated that increasing such connections were the most successful part of the course: "The first day I walked into class and saw balls of yarn all over the tables and our grandparents sitting in the corner of the room, I was intimidated; I didn't know what I walked into. The idea was to learn a new life skill and give back at the same time. [We] donated tons of blankets [to the local hospital] with the help of our grandparents and the combination of all our work in the class, and that was the biggest accomplishment of all." "I learned a lot about resilience and pushing through when my projects didn't turn out as planned. The lesson that I learned from this is patience: I had to learn that I'm not going to be great at something right away and that it would take some time for me to improve on it." "The best part is the social environment. I bonded with many of the people around me and that was the most enjoyable part of this experience."[44]

This first-year seminar specifically set out to help students make connections: between classroom and community ("The idea was to learn a new life skill and give back at the same time"); between students in the room ("The best part is the social envi-ronment, I bonded with many of the people around me . . .") and between content and students' own values, goals, and future aca-demic success ("I'm not going to be great at something right away and it would take some time for me to improve on it"). Most of us can't enlist a group of surrogate grandparents to help us facilitate increased connections in class, but we can, as Wanda's class did, ensure that our on-site class meetings or our LMS activities con-sistently offer student-centered activities and structured opportu-nities for interactions and help students identify ways the course content applies to their own lives.

We can give students the means for putting on their parachute and the structure they need to learn how to leap. We can provide an incentive to make the jump with assignments and activities. We can prep our own parachutes carefully. But, most importantly, we need to build connections before we take that leap.

Gear for Your Go-Bag

- Course design and classroom practices that help students identify the relevance of course material and learning goals to their own lives increases connections.
- Planning, structuring, and supporting productive interactions among students increases connections.
- Casual conversations and exchanges between instructors and students strengthens connections.
- Building a professional, supportive network of other educators strengthens connections.

PART III

DISTRUST

Make sure both vehicles are moving at the same speed.

> —"How to Leap from a Motorcycle to a Car,"
> *The Worst-Case Scenario Survival Handbook*

Chapter 7

DISTRUST FOULS UP LEARNING AND TEACHING

In 2016, Jesse Stommel, writing professor and cofounder of the Hybrid Pedagogy website, tweeted a #4WordPedagogy that blew minds on college campuses everywhere: "Start by trusting students."[1] Stommel's statement directly addressed the power dynamics in schooling systems that most disturbed him, linking him to critical pedagogy scholars such as Henry Giroux, bell hooks, Howard Zinn, and others who trace their deconstruction of traditional educational models back to Paulo Freire's *Pedagogy of the Oppressed*. It became a sort of litmus test for college teaching: Did you or did you not trust students?

When I first read Stommel's tweet in 2019, I hesitated to plant my pedagogical flag on this battleground. After about two decades in the college classroom and becoming a scholar of teaching and learning in my own right, my pedagogical practices[2] put me squarely in the student-trusting, empower-students-to-throw-off-school-shackles camp. But on the other hand I knew that my positionality and privileges as a tenured, able-bodied, neurotypical, white, cisgendered humanities professor with a reasonable teaching load and relatively small class sizes played a big role in how my teaching practices had evolved over time. I also knew how painful and infuriating it felt when it appeared that a student was taking advantage of me or trying to manipulate me. I rarely feel that way anymore but I have a lot of empathy for instructors who do and who might well respond to Stommel's arguably scolding statement with defensiveness and dismissiveness.

But while I was waffling, the coronavirus was spreading, and in March 2020 the COVID-19 pandemic shut down almost every college campus. We "went remote." At a stunningly poor time to be making this move, the spring 2020 semester was the beginning of my professional shift from being a full-time professor of history to becoming the full-time director of SUNY Plattsburgh's Center for Teaching Excellence. Everything I'd planned to do during the spring 2020 semester to support instructors and to encourage effective teaching on campus had to be entirely scrapped and replaced with . . . well, who knew what? Because it was—there's no other word to use for it—an unprecedented event in higher education. It had never happened before that millions of students and faculty who fully planned to be sitting in classrooms together—faculty who had been teaching and students who had been learning in this modality for their entire lives—shifted overnight to online instruction.

In the subsequent emergency shift to virtual space, one of the most discussed concerns among faculty across the country centered on testing. Or, more specifically, how to administer high-stakes timed tests to students when they weren't in the same room as you or even the same campus, state, or country. The amount of hand-wringing and lamenting over the (temporary) loss of this single means of assessing student learning, and the shockingly bad (intrusive, anxiety-amplifying, racist) "proctoring" solutions that certain ed tech companies provided—and which disproportionately negatively impacted some student groups more than others—surprised me.[3] This is what people were most worried about? Was this the best we could do? This was what we, the learned professoriate, possessors of some of the biggest, smartest brains in the world, were going to prioritize? In response to a deadly global pandemic, our uppermost concern was going to be . . . policing students more closely than ever before to ensure they didn't cheat on a timed test? Really? I'm exaggerating, because many professors at a variety of institutions, especially experienced online instructors, loudly and publicly advocated for a different approach during the pandemic pivot semesters, calling for assessments that could help us measure student learning without policing their every eye blink (literally) via creepy invasive monitoring and to do things to try to reduce instead of add to students' traumatic stress of living through a terrifying health, social, and economic crisis.[4]

But some of the same concerns that kept me from blithely advising faculty to "start by trusting students" remained unchanged or even amplified during the pandemic. Without job security and an adequate salary, for example, how could we in good faith demand that a professor revamp all assignments and activities? They weren't going to get overtime pay, that's for sure. What about departments and universities implementing teaching-related mandates without, oh, I don't know, ever conferring with the people doing the teaching about what would be most helpful? And, as always, what about positionality and the intersecting systemic biases facing some faculty? Because of stereotypes about academic authority and knowledge, both student trust as well as administrative and colleagues' trust—trust in a professor's expertise and skills as a scholar and as an educator—is not uniformly granted to instructors. Doesn't trust have to be mutual to be meaningful?

To some extent, the pandemic simply brought more to light pitfalls of distrust already pockmarking the higher ed landscape. Distrust extends deep into every corner of traditional education systems, undermining everyone's efforts to teach effectively and learn authentically, and rooted in the sense of betrayal and futility that can arise when things go wrong in school. Pick at a scab of distrust in the college classroom, and often what wells to the surface is a past negative experience as a student or as an educator.

Imagine you're vrooming happily down the freeway of teaching and learning on the mighty motorcycle of your intellect, gassed up with all your hopes and dreams for achieving academic success. Suddenly there's a weird knock in your engine and you're losing speed and about to crash over the railing. Wait, you're saved! There's a car speeding up beside you and all you have to do is leap from your motorcycle to the car. It will be the most dangerous, terrifying leap of our lives, and our only chance for survival is going to be if we can trust the car to be where we need it to be. Both vehicles must be "moving at the same speed." When snafus snarl our gears, we have to be able to leap off the damaged motorcycle and into the car.

Distrust Fouls Up Learning

When a big assignment is coming due, or an important exam looms, the Angel of Death suddenly swoops down and culls a shockingly high percentage of students' grandparents, cousins, and close family friends, creating crises that must be met with extensions and makeup tests. At least, this is how it might appear to a skeptical faculty member, faced with what seems to them like all-too-convenient excuses for poor student work, bad time management, or just plain laziness. So the professor demands proof of death—a funeral program, say—before they make any changes to the course requirements.

Fast-forward to the next time something in the student's life goes horribly awry—maybe even literally a life-and-death issue—and the student assumes that their professors will need proof, so they proactively email a photo of the death certificate or the hospital bill to all their instructors, some of whom will hurriedly say: "You don't need to show me this: of course I believe you, and it's no problem to make up the work/take the test another day." But then again, some of their other professors will only make alterations to due dates or assignments if the student provides medical records. (Note: This is not merely an ill-considered teaching practice; it's illegal. Students have a legal right to privacy regarding all medical information and/or documentation of medical treatment.) There may also be at least one professor who says something to the effect of "Oh no, too bad, so sad, guess you'll just have to retake this class next semester because I won't give anyone 'special treatment' for any reason whatsoever."

Nothing illustrates the extent of distrust that can occur between individual faculty and students quite like the "You must authenticate your suffering" process. The wide variety of ways a professor might respond to and be willing to provide some flexibility to students coping with a crisis complicates it further. The pandemic forced numerous instructors and institutions to examine this issue in a new light, at least for a while. The reality of students' life circumstances—and how those circumstances could impact students' ability to succeed academically—became unignorable. Even the most skeptical professor was probably less likely to dismiss a student's account of a death in the family as a made-up excuse when a deadly disease was sweeping around the entire world. For a brief time, then, creating more trust between instructors and students was on the table, up for reevaluation. But instead of making big changes, higher education institutions during this potentially transformative time became utterly determined to "return to normal."[5] Unfortunately, "normal" includes a deeply entrenched distrust that fouls up student learning in significant ways.

The lack of trust that fouls up learning does not begin in college. A great many students experience K–12 classrooms as places where compliance with rules and rigid standards is highly valued and the meaningful exploration of their own ideas, interests, and unique talents is less prized or even actively discouraged. This is not a criticism of K–12 teachers as individuals but rather a critique of schooling systems, which on the whole measure student learning and success in limited and limiting ways. Most educational institutions define student excellence through a highly circumscribed set of behaviors, including testing and measuring knowledge and skills in a very narrowly defined kind of way. This means that most students, by the time they reach college, cannot fully trust that the point and purpose of taking a class is to learn how to do things. For many, their educational experiences show them that the most important reason for being in any class is to receive the grade defined by the institution as sufficient for allowing the student to continue their education.

The transactional nature of schooling systems is a major source of distrust that fouls up learning. Students often perceive increasing their own knowledge or improving their abilities as secondary to checking the box, jumping through the hoop, and "getting" the grade. When school becomes a zero-sum grading game—you must earn this grade or you will fail completely—students will distrust anything that seems superfluous to that final summative assessment. Learning how to do anything skillfully is a long, effortful process of trying to do the thing, not doing it very well, getting formative feedback over time with ongoing assistance for improving, and then applying that feedback via repeated, spaced practice. But that reality does not align with a schooling system that prizes the final product far more than the process.[6] Too often students will deeply distrust anything that seems, in their view, unrelated to the only thing that's ever really mattered in school, i.e., their final grades.[7]

Student distrust of the point and purpose of learning itself in school creates conditions for problematic actions like cheating and other types of academic dishonesty. Again, in a zero-sum game, you have the option to win or to lose. Nothing in between. If you're disconnected and distrustful of the purpose of learning in a school setting—if the process of learning itself seems removed from the ultimate goal—there is little incentive to make the huge effort to honestly demonstrate your skills, but there is a powerful rationale for doing whatever action will result in the sufficient grade—particularly when the financial cost of failing a class is so enormous, to cite one overriding example.[8] In most cases, when students plagiarize or buy essays or find the exam answers on Chegg or via AI or cheat in some way we can't even begin to imagine yet, they aren't doing it because they're deceitful sociopaths or because they're pampered entitled snowflakes who want something for nothing. They're not doing it because they want to make your life miserable. They are violating your trust because they don't trust the system and the power structure in which you are trying to help them learn things. They don't trust that their learning matters enough to risk a lower grade by engaging in an honest assessment of their knowledge and skills.

Student distrust of the educational processes interferes with their underlying, basic trust of you, the individual professor. When a student does something that at first seems truly counterproductive to their academic success in your class, it may be because they're making decisions and taking actions based on what they've encountered and experienced in their past class-rooms with previous professors. For instance, if they skipped the extra review sessions you offered before the exam, one reason could be that the last review session they attended did not actu-ally offer much concrete support or opportunities for practicing the skills they needed for the exam. Are they extremely hesitant to make a comment or ask a question in class? Perhaps they're still smarting from a dismissive response they got from a differ-ent instructor. Keep in mind that a handful of highly privileged, usually tenured faculty face no consequences for ineffective or even objectively bad teaching, and students' negative experiences with these faculty may have a disproportionately large impact on their learning and success.

Students' negative experiences with individual instructors can be further exacerbated by systemic biases and discrimination both within school settings as well as every aspect of their life out-side of school. For example, if a student with a learning disability had a professor last semester who made a comment in front of the whole class that "outed" the student as needing accommoda-tions, that student may (understandably) try to avoid that experi-ence again and simply not request the accommodations to which they're entitled. That will mean they struggle unnecessarily and may become hostile and resentful, and you won't have the faintest clue about the underlying problem.

All students, no matter their backgrounds, life circumstances, and social and embodied identities, must develop trust in their own ability to engage in learning. So much of traditional school-ing disempowers students as active participants in their own edu-cation that they frequently arrive to college distrusting any activity or approach that isn't the top-down information transmission model. Many students believe, with good reason, that their main objective in any class is doing "what the teacher wants." Without more trust in their own power to achieve their own learning, stu-dents may develop a bad case of academic entitlement: the mis-taken idea that sole responsibility for learning resides not with the learner but with the teacher.[9] Many a conscientious professor who's worked their tail off to create active learning, student-centered classroom experiences has been subsequently gutted by students complaining that they had to "teach themselves."[10]

Student distrust comes in many such disguises. Resistance to active learning, cheating on an exam, failure to seek assistance—no matter what else might be contributing to these situations, distrust is frequently part of what's going on and what is fouling up student learning. But no matter their roots and the complexities of the causes, student behaviors like this can snafu teaching as well as learning.

Distrust Fouls Up Teaching

If you had told me in January 2020 that in the very near future, to do my job and to advance in my profession, I was going to have to watch my own face talking and interacting with other faces on-screen on a daily basis, I would have told you to get bent. That would have sounded completely unthinkable to me as a self-conscious, camera-shy introvert. Little did I know that in a matter of weeks this nightmare scenario would become reality. There were alternatives, other roads we might have taken, because when the pandemic necessitated an emergency pivot to online instruction, experienced online educators spoke up and pointed out that effective online classes happened in virtual spaces "asynchronously"—that is, no video conferencing required. Unfortunately, higher education decision-makers ignored experienced online educators' professional and scholarly advice. People who had never designed or taught or even once thought about online classes decided that Zoom—a branded webcam conferencing platform not intended for education—would be the default modality for college classes during lockdown. What could go wrong?

Thus began the Webcam Wars. Online classes became equated with Zoom video meetings, and almost immediately professors across the land began insisting that students attending these meetings would have to be on camera, webcam turned on.[11] Notably, nobody could even say for sure what it meant to meaningfully participate in a videoconferencing class meeting during a global pandemic. Also notably, student access to webcams, microphones, and a physical space conducive to videoconferencing depended greatly on each student's individual circumstances and economic resources, including how being viewed on camera made extra demands on students and faculty in economically precarious living situations or from historically minoritized racial groups.[12] Perhaps most notably, within just a few months it became clear that some aspects of Zooming—namely, maintaining continual eye contact while interacting with others—was decidedly taxing and unnatural to how humans human, engendering a whole new type of exhaustion referred to as "Zoom fatigue."[13]

Yet, from the very start of the pandemic, college professors bewailed "teaching to a bunch of blank screens." "I can't 'read the room' like I can when I'm teaching in a classroom," complained the professoriate, a group that in my personal experience is frequently unable to read the room in any type of gathering. What many of them really meant was that they were used to being the absolute center of attention in the classroom, and they equated "looking at the professor" with learning. Here's a news flash: staring at the professor and listening passively while said professor expounds does not equate learning.[14] The whole thing vividly illustrated how many people, no matter what they said or believed they were doing in the classroom, were most comfortable with professor-centered, not student-centered, teaching.

The Webcam Wars revealed in stark detail the extent and power of higher education's instructor-centered panopticon. Always subject to authority's scrutiny, the ultimate goal of panopticon architecture and its subsequent system of power is self-surveillance and self-policing of one's behavior.[15] Strict cameras-on-at-all-times policies assume that if the student doesn't have their camera on, allowing the professor to monitor students and scrutinize them for inattention, students cannot be trusted to pay attention—"attention" in this case being defined mostly as following the unspoken command to sit quietly and keep one's eyes fixed on the professor, who never, ever stops talking. Leaving aside for the moment this problematic definition of attention, the prisonlike aspect of panopticon cameras, and the question of what "attention" even means during emergency remote instruction, what I want to point out here is how basic distrust fouls up teaching.

In any modality, our pedagogical energies and abilities can be drained when we distrust students' willingness and ability to do all the things they could and should be doing in that moment. Instead of focusing on how best to facilitate learning, our big brains get caught up with scrutinizing student behavior. When this distrust is shaping our teaching labor, our job seems less about the fascinating things we enjoy doing most in our discipline and more about monitoring students. For most of us, that's not the type of teaching we want to do, yet it's so easy to get trapped here. When students are often less than thrilled to be in your class in the first place, feeling disconnected, and distrustful themselves and of the educational system, it's difficult to trust that, even though their cameras are off, they're doing what you see as important and worthwhile.

Distrust can, in an instant, foul up our best-laid plans for classroom activities or an interactive lecture, when it appears that students are checked out, uninterested, and deeply reluctant to actively engage in their own learning. There are some important, real reasons for this well beyond any one student's willpower or ability. But because when we care about student learning, and students do not appear to be learning and do not appear to even begin to appreciate the opportunities we're working so hard to provide for their learning, it hurts. For even the most intellectual eggheaded professors, an obviously bored or outright contemptuous student in class can cause us aggravation and frustration and generate distrust.

It's especially easy to get entangled in distrust when student behavior conveys disregard for one's expertise. Overt disrespect, when it springs from racist, sexist, ableist, and other stereotypes about expertise, from even a couple students at one point in time, can sow seeds of distrust that can foul up many future classes and student interactions. Microaggressions, microinvalidations, and direct questioning of an instructor's knowledge will repeatedly call into question to what extent a professor can trust their students. Indeed, all types of student disruptions in class, and antagonistic interactions at any point or place with students, are almost guaranteed to create distrust. When things go wrong in the college classroom because of student disruptions—an inadequate term for behaviors ranging from mildly rude to deeply discomforting to physically endangering—other students' learning will be fouled up and teaching will be fouled up, creating some of the biggest, most damaging types of distrust.

This specific snafu may well have been what came to your mind the first time you read the subtitle for *Snafu Edu*. "Things going wrong in the college classroom" frequently means an inappropriate disruption, unproductive and unprofessional exchange, or even hostile confrontations with students. Anecdotally, they're on the rise, but the SoTL/teaching advice is a bit scanty about what causes these moments and what we can do about them.[16] It has been especially inadequate at addressing the fact that teaching inequities and student biases frequently figure into inappropriate, confrontational, or disrespectful interactions. SoTL has given short shrift to how damaging these moments can be to any instructor's willingness and ability to extend trust to students. Even when the discourse around teaching and learning addresses disruptions, it's often depicted as a singular event that can be counteracted with some specific direct actions, but in reality the impact of these events extends far beyond the immediate situation.

I know faculty members who exert themselves to grant deep understanding, grace, and support to students yet find themselves on the receiving end of the exact opposite from a student, and it's gutting. Like when an instructor has a family or medical emergency and a student responds callously or skeptically, particularly in anonymous, end-of-term SET comments. "I know she said there was death in her family or whatever but she posted grades three days late, that's unacceptable." "She missed a meeting with me because she supposedly had the flu and it was super inconvenient for me to reschedule." In short, sometimes a faculty member has very good reasons for feeling distrustful of students, based on their previous classroom experiences and interactions.

We cannot simply condemn professors for not trusting students when students have, at times, very concretely broken all levels of trust with that professor. A lot of teaching advice I've read in recent years pays close attention to the power of an instructor's words and actions to negatively impact a student's sense of belonging in college, which is all to the good. Fewer scholars and commentators have truly grappled with how a student's words and actions can negatively impact instructors' sense of belonging in the higher ed classroom. Instead of simply censuring and chastising professors for not trusting students, I want to frame this problem through the snafu lens. Because this is very much a "situation normal." We can expect disruptions and incivilities to erupt at times in the college classroom. If we don't "look like" a professor, we can even more reliably predict such moments, and they will erode our energy for and ability to cultivate trust with students. Our distrust then may obscure some things we need to see as clearly as possible.

For instance, student behaviors that can appear to be signifying disengagement, or disregard for their own learning and success, can be indications of mental or physical health problems. A student falling asleep in class is one example of a behavior that can seem incredibly disrespectful and distracting to us and to other students, but falling asleep in public, in a brightly lit room, when you're not supposed to be sleeping, isn't physiologically easy. What kinds of life circumstances are exhausting this student? If distrust doesn't overtake our perception of the problem, what might we see and how might we help?

Falling asleep in class barely registers, however, as a trust-eroding classroom behavior compared to the behemoth that is wireless technology distractions. Like webcams in a Zoom class, how students use (and misuse) phones and laptops during class regularly imperils faculty's ability to trust students. I will unpack this complicated distrust snafu in the next chapter, but I do want to note here that faculty distrust triggered by technology reached a level I'd never seen before, in matter of mere weeks in November 2022, when the generative AI tool ChatGPT (Chat Generative Pre-trained Transformer) launched.[17] Faculty's overriding, most frequently voiced concern was that generative AI offered students a new, impossible-to-detect-or-thwart means for cheating.[18] The distrust of students exhibited by many professors in response to ChatGPT was a striking example of the broader distrust that drives faculty to implement more and more layers of monitoring the process of assessing learning and less and less attention to students as individuals and what they could be learning.

On the other hand, concerns about ChatGPT must be understood in historical context, using a more nuanced way of defining faculty distrust. At first, I was quick to attribute faculty freak-outs about ChatGPT to an unwillingness to reflect on and revise assignments and assessments. I thought to myself that if a student could easily purchase a paper or generate a paper with an AI tool that fulfills the assignment, then something must be amiss with that tedious, cookie-cutter, un-scaffolded, unimaginative assignment. I almost immediately had to check myself, though, when a colleague reminded me that by the end of 2022 most professors who care about student learning and want to be effective teachers had just spent almost three solid years scrambling to revise assignments, assessments, and pedagogical practices, attempting to cope with constantly changing world-altering events and unprecedented stressors. For many educators, ChatGPT seemed like the cherry on a crap sundae of higher ed working conditions in the pandemic era. In this context, distrust around how students might utilize yet another impactful technology cannot be discounted as just a few fusty old professorial dinosaurs who simply refuse to change with the teaching and learning times. (Online teaching expert and scholar Flower Darby likened the impact of generative AI on teaching and learning assessments to how the internet itself reshaped teaching and learning. Remember back when some of us thought that Wikipedia was going to bring about an educational apocalypse?)[19]

Rather, the distrust stirred up so strongly by new questions around AI reflected much more long-standing and widespread teaching conditions that undermine faculty's ability to trust students. We learned experts with vast knowledge of and usually passion for our scholarly subject routinely teach class after class after class filled with people who know little about and usually don't care much about our scholarly subject. A basic, vital starting point for easily building trust—a shared value for the work we're doing—is not present in much of college teaching. In this way, students and professors frequently can't get their cars and motorcycles to synch up at the same speed. Often, we're either racing in opposite directions or busted up in a head-on collision.

I've been focusing on navigating the trust freeway between students and faculty, but I also need to at least mention some of the other times and places in higher education where distrust fouls up teaching. One of the most significant is how problematic teaching evaluation practices create distrust in institutions, departments, teaching and learning centers, administrators, and individual colleagues. There's little space in many evaluation systems for the kind of constructive, informed, expert feedback and support about teaching efficacy that would be most beneficial to pedagogical learning and reflection. Instead, summative judgments about teaching ability and efficacy, made by people not well-versed in current SoTL and/or who do not adequately account for teaching inequities, play an outsize role in assessing teaching efficacy. Such distrust is multilayered: evaluative bodies don't trust instructors' ability to always keep learning how to teach effectively, while instructors know their teaching efficacy will not be evaluated in trustworthy ways.

To a lesser but still noteworthy extent, distrust can spring up when teaching and learning experts and advisors forgo constructive feedback for quick condemnation, i.e., "You're doing it wrong." For example, as productive and supportive as most of my social media interactions with other educators have been, I've also seen a few highly judgmental pileups on a professor who posted a poorly worded or emotionally charged take on a teaching issue. The closed-classroom-door culture in higher education, combined with the academic proclivity to pounce on and eviscerate anyone who intimates they aren't 100 percent sure about how to do something perfectly, can inhibit honest reflection and conversation about teaching. That's a lack of trust.

Like inequity and disconnections, distrust will cause snafus for every learner and every educator at one time or another. Like inequity and disconnections, we need to try to clearly identify it when it's causing something to go wrong in the college classroom and be ready to STIR and repair.

Gear for Your Go-Bag

- Students may have good reasons for being distrustful in the college classroom. Previous negative educational experiences contribute to student distrust and create obstacles to learning.
- Student distrust can manifest in troubling and destructive ways, such as academic dishonesty or classroom incivility.
- Faculty may have good reasons for being distrustful in the college classroom. Previous negative teaching experiences navigating student biases or overt, deliberate student disrespect and incivility contribute to faculty distrust.
- Academic structures and systems outside the classroom, especially lack of support for engaging in pedagogical learning, and shoddy methods of evaluating teaching efficacy, also contribute to creating faculty distrust.

Chapter 8

REPAIR STRATEGIES FOR DISTRUST SNAFUS

One attention-getting technique in TV and film for conveying to audiences a sense of extreme, jarring discomfort and confusion is having characters talk unintelligibly with no captions to translate, like when a member of Star Fleet is making first contact but the Universal Translator is broken. As a director of a university teaching center, I sometimes experience a disquieting sense of different groups on campus speaking completely different languages. Students, faculty, staff, and administrators can talk about teaching and learning in ways that seem alien to one another, discussing the same issue in radically different ways.

This is an ideal breeding ground for distrust, when nobody is on the same page or even speaking the same language. Trust can be fragile in higher education, and distrust can easily take hold in the classroom and be difficult to uproot. But we can learn to better identify the moments when distrust is laying down a spike strip on the teaching and learning highway. When distrust shreds our plans and sends the car and the motorcycle careening off in wildly different directions, we can STIR and repair. We can work to defuse distrust and to rebuild trust.

Identifying Distrust Snafus

One of the worst mistakes I ever made in the classroom started with distrust. In an intro-level in-person class of around forty students, I was trying to maintain a strict "no phones allowed" policy.

I believed this approach would help students stay more engaged and minimize distractions. I didn't think through all the ramifications of such a policy until I "caught" a student sneaking a look at their phone and told them in front of the whole class to put it away. As it turned out, this student had a medical condition and the "phone" in question was in fact a medical device that they needed to check. They had been trying to do it discreetly and there I was drawing everyone's attention to it. Like a jackass. I apologized to the student but the damage was done. Distrust had fouled up my teaching in a major way, and I had to take a hard look at what other ways distrust—and, oh yeah, ableism—were shaping my teaching practices.[1]

What exactly is going on and what exactly do we see when we see a student doing phone stuff instead of the tasks they're supposed to be tackling that day in class? It's all too easy to perceive this solely as students being disrespectful to us and to the other students and wasting their own expensive, important, on-site class time. But what's really happening is complicated. "Addiction" isn't really the right word, but the power of apps to draw our attention cannot be underestimated. Also, scrolling could be their coping mechanism for emotion regulation in stressful situations. Then there are all the other ways students might be deeply disconnected from academic work, as discussed in part two, which can make what's happening in class far less engaging than what's on their screen.

There are no quick, easy solutions to the challenge of facilitating a classroom environment where students cultivate their own ability to stop looking at their #@!$ phones all the #@!$ time, and distrust is the problematic starting point for faculty who feel they must maintain a policing policy for phones in the classroom. It cannot help but create moments of disruption and encourage incivility when we try to be a classroom phone cop, which, as my own sad story shows, can go very wrong. At a minimum, it puts distrust at the center of every class meeting. The phone problem can get so overwhelming that we feel we have no choice but to give up entirely and pretend it's not a problem. Avoidance behavior as a *not*-coping mechanism—it's not just for students! Things go wrong when we pay too little or too much confrontational attention to this issue, and trust is at the heart of it. Identifying it as a distrust issue is a necessary first step. The "Stop" and "Think" parts of STIR are a helpful way to begin to better understand the role of distrust in this common scenario.

Detecting distrust's role in a snafu can change the whole conversation about what exactly is going wrong. Missteps, from minor detours to major mistakes, perpetuated by both faculty and students, that can explode into snafus look very different when framed as moments of weakening trust. For example, let's say a student frequently leaves our classroom for no apparent reason. My kneejerk reaction would be to wonder why, for crying out loud, can't they just go to the bathroom before class starts?!? This reaction is mostly a cover for my feeling disrespected when I'm working hard to make the class meeting engaging and useful for them. But STIR helps me spot the distrust snafu. Stop: Don't just react to what's going on because some important trust is on the line here, and I'm beginning to distrust this student.

Think: Could there be some other reason the student keeps exiting the classroom? Perhaps a medical condition such as a UTI or a colostomy bag or a sensory disorder being triggered by the overhead lights or a panic attack? Are they having trouble coping with college life in general, making it harder for them to focus or even complete basic executive functioning time management tasks such as going to the bathroom before class begins? Or maybe they're not aware that I care if they're in class or not. Maybe they are experiencing inequities and disconnections as a student that make it hard for them to perceive that I and their classmates value their presence in the room.

Of course, it's possible that they don't respect me and are actively deciding that the class is too boring to tolerate, and are hoping to disrupt everyone's learning by clattering in and out of the room as often as possible. But I'm going to err on the side of trust. At the "think" stage of STIR, I'm going to keep an open mind, with an eye out for distrust, and let all the many other possibilities come to my mind before I address this in any way. I need to think about all the reasons for this behavior, recognizing that it's negatively impacting how much I trust the student. Moving away from seeing a problem as solely a direct affront to our work as faculty and more as a problem of systemic distrust removes some of the emotional labor required to address and repair it. It can also enable us to better identify when our actions have contributed to distrust. Like when we cold-call a student, not realizing that the student has a speech impediment that makes them highly anxious about talking in class, or we fall behind and cannot give feedback in a timely way before the next assignment is due, or we accidentally call a student by the wrong name or pronoun.

Spotting distrust snafus and employing STIR are especially valuable ways to navigate and mitigate one of the most common means by which something can go wrong in teaching and learning: conflicts and disputes about grades. Things frequently go wrong with grades because the stakes are sky high and extremely concrete: financial aid, academic honors, and even enrollment itself are all tied to grades. The stakes are also astronomically high personally, psychologically, and emotionally. Grades are often the most crucial factor in a student's sense of their own academic agency, ability, and even self-worth. In this context, then, when "good" grades equal success and "bad" grades equal failure, students and faculty cannot help but be caught sometimes in grading-related snafus that can escalate quickly when distrust is lurking.

The number of specific ways these snafus manifest is countless but all revolve around the consequences of a letter or point grade. Student-faculty trust can disappear when students are upset, confused, scared, and angry about those consequences. Students can feel betrayed and treated unfairly. But so too can faculty feel betrayed when they've made their very best effort to build trust, assess work fairly with constructive formative feedback and with a lot of hard, careful work based on their subject expertise, provided a final grade, and then are still met with student complaints, begging, or demands for a higher grade.

Distrust + grading snafus = particularly piercing damage to faculty when it becomes the pretext for charges of poor teaching or even wrongdoing. Recently, one of the most skillful, equity-minded, caring educators I know had to contend with a formal student complaint that centered around a grade dispute. The dispute reflected the student's ongoing distrust of faculty and of academic systems in general, which persisted even when working with a faculty member who is objectively trustworthy. Not incidentally, this faculty member is a woman, and the accusation came from a student exhausted and anxious after years of COVID social distancing, traumatic stress, and facing some systemic biases themselves. Even when this professor had done everything they could in order to build trust, the student was just not capable of returning that trust when grades were at stake.

Because grades are so fraught, they are consistently a place where trust can break down. Perhaps the ultimate grade-related snafus occur around cheating and plagiarism. Here again, grades loom large over academic dishonesty issues like the terrible all-seeing evil eye of Sauron wreaking havoc over Middle-earth. When students calculate that cheating is their best option, one of their main justifications is that the negative consequence of earning a poor grade is so huge that any actions taken to reduce such danger is defensible and worth the risk. Like a match to gasoline, discovering students cheating or reading a plagiarized writing assignment can in an instant burn down all the trust with a faculty member. Academic dishonesty can seem to faculty—we professional academics who care more about academic standards than anyone else in the entire world—like a betrayal not only of our individual trust as educators but also of every value we hold dear as scholars and researchers. That's not a little hiccup in our teaching lives. It's a five-alarm fire reducing our whole pedagogical house, including our ability to build trust with students, to a smoldering ruin. Being able to Stop and Think before doing anything else, and being able to identify where distrust is causing the foul-up, may keep that fire from spreading.

Similarly, disruptive student behavior and incivility pose a major threat to trust in the classroom. Particularly in classes facilitated by a professor from a historically minoritized group, students can deliberately violate basic norms of respect and civility, and trust will of course fly right out the window. Examples of such behavior described in the SoTL include when white students "scold" a professor of color or ostentatiously storm out of the classroom; loudly questioning the basic teaching competence of a professor with disabilities; aggressively disputing the professor's judgment or authority in class or in conversations with other faculty; asking to be placed in another class with the department member who "looks like" a professor before the course even starts; or rejecting key parts of course content because of assumptions and biases about the professor's embodied and social identities.[2] Recognizing distrust as a part of many disruptive classroom situations like these can be empowering and useful—but only within limits. As previously discussed, situations that demean or physically threaten anyone in the classroom or violate university policies are not a teaching and learning snafu; they're a workplace safety issue.[3]

Identifying common distrust snafus can give us more to work with. While nothing can make trust-busting snafus like these less time-consuming and energy draining, understanding the role distrust plays can lessen the sting when things go wrong. Knowing that student distrust is systemic and widespread and can manifest in various ways shaped by students' unique life circumstances and previous educational experiences, we can STIR. For me, the first step—Stop—has been the most important part of becoming more skilled at responding to distrust snafus, including grading disputes. In this case, Stop requires ongoing awareness of and attention to the ways distrust can manifest, including some that have less to do with me personally and my own individual teaching and more about the educational systems within which students must work. Recognizing the wider problem of trust helps me take grade disputes and plagiarism cases a bit less personally and a bit more in stride. The internal pause, to situate the issue in the context of trust before I even think about what I'm going to do, always helps me reduce my own knee-jerk reactions. Putting a name to it—uh-oh, here's a potential distrust snafu—can empower us to address and repair it more effectively by strategically defusing distrust and rebuilding trust.

Defuse

I chose the word "defuse" very deliberately for this first repair strategy, because distrust snafus have the power to explode in the classroom like a land mine carving out a pit of destruction at the heart of teaching and learning. We need to employ defusing strategies during distrust snafus as skillfully as the action movie hero snipping the right wire and defusing the ticking time bomb. Distrust can cause emotions to roil, ill-advised words to be spoken, and mistakes to be made or mistakes that have already been made to be made much worse. A defusing strategy, employed as part of STIR, can keep those kinds of escalations from detonating.

When I began to realize that I didn't have to (and shouldn't) address a student's complaint or grievance about a grade in the heat of the moment, it truly changed my teaching life. Instead of immediately shooting off a curt email or snapping back a sharp reply in a conversation—actions practically guaranteed to further escalate a tense and distrustful moment—I learned to write or say these powerful words:

> ➤ *"Thank you for bringing this to my attention. I appreciate that you want to do well in our class. I'd like to think about it more and I will get back to you by the end of the week."*

This response is an effective defusing strategy because (1) it acknowledges that we've heard what the student is saying without being defensive, (2) it makes a commitment to addressing the complaint/grievance soon, and at the same time (3) it gives both me and the student a short time-out to calm down and regroup so that the issue can be productively discussed. It's in keeping with recommendations made by Sarah Rose Cavanagh, who notes that when responding to what psychologists identify as student "reactance," we should use "language that is low in threat or demands, expressing empathy and interpersonal similarity" and immediacy cues that convey respectful polite attention.[4]

Defusing distrust is also a valuable strategy for addressing and repairing in-class snafus arising from disruptions or disrespectful words or behaviors aimed at the instructor. But in contrast to one-on-one interactions and communications, defusing class-room disruptions, face-to-face or online, requires our immediate action. When the whole class is a witness, defusing distrust needs to be rapidly employed. For instance, one common in-person classroom disruption is side conversations, i.e., talking out of turn or over someone else. Once or twice is understandable and not a big deal, but habitually talking out of turn can chip away at our trust in students as well as students' trust in our ability to effectively facilitate a productive discussion or class meeting.

A STIR strategy for defusing distrust, including identifying the source of the distrust and repairing the breach in the moment of the event, looks like this:

Stop: Call the class to a halt. Our instinct might be to ignore the side conversation or pretend it's not happening, but if we don't address it, distrust will spread.

Think: Where is distrust springing up and what's the necessary next step for addressing it and for defusing its power to negatively impact the classroom environment?

Identify: Do this for everyone by stating something like

➢ *"Before we go on, I need to address an issue I'm seeing right now."*

Repair: Reduce the potential conflict and defuse distrust by saying something like:

➢ *"It's hard for me to hear and for others to listen when there are continual side conversations. Talking over someone else makes it difficult to listen to each other and is disrespectful to our learning community. Let's work on making sure everyone has a chance to speak and to be heard clearly."*

Disruptions like side conversations are normal, so very, very normal. Approaching them with a strategy for defusing distrust foremost in mind can enable us to avoid getting stuck in the moment and reduce the potential of distrust to interfere with teaching and learning while reinforcing our efficacy as facilitator. It can prevent small mistakes from becoming snafus.

When a student is doing something that in some way undercuts my trust, I can address it with defusing uppermost in mind.

To take my earlier example, after I've stopped and thought about it, I can approach a student who's always leaving the room to see if there's a way to figure out together how to improve the situation. I might simply ask how they're doing and then say something like:

> ➤ *"I noticed you've been having to leave the room a lot and I hope everything is okay. I'm concerned you might be missing out on things we're doing and I value what you contribute when you're in the room. If it's health-related, that is totally, 100 percent a private issue and not something you need to discuss with me at all, but is there anything else going on that I can help you with?"*

Foregrounding and assuming trust may prevent distrust from growing and allow us to figure out a way to make this classroom situation better. (There are some long-term repairs to consider here as well. Have I made sure that students understand the value and purpose of being in the room during our in-person class meetings? Do students need a regular phone and bathroom break?) As scholars of teaching and learning Aeron Haynie and Stephanie Spong advise when responding to a student's disruptive behavior: "Begin by asking questions to see if there is something that you are unaware of."[5] Seeking further information helps both the faculty member and the student gain a better understanding of the disruption and begin to defuse distrust.

Defusing distrust with students is especially vital when we have made a mistake. Apologizing is a repair strategy in and of itself, as I discussed in chapter two, when inequities are fouling up teaching and learning, but it's also an effective defusing strategy when we break trust with students. Like most people, I don't like being in the wrong, and for a long time apologizing to students for anything felt too much like admitting I didn't know how to teach effectively. But the more teaching experience I gained, the more tools I gathered in my teaching tool kit and, not incidentally, the further along the tenure track I progressed, the easier it got to say to students: "Well, I goofed. My bad."

For example, I've lost count of the number of times I messed up the deadline setting on an assignment drop box in the LMS.

It's easy to type in the wrong day or time, and I've done it repeatedly. But I'm ready to defuse distrust when—not if but when—I make a blatant error, and I can correct it with minimal emotional flare-up or hostility.

> **Student:** Professor Neuhaus, there's a mistake in the drop box: it closed at 3 a.m. instead of 3 p.m.
> **Professor Neuhaus:** *Thank you for letting me know and I'll fix it ASAP. I apologize for my mistake.*
> **Student:** Thanks!
> **Professor Neuhaus:** You got it.

It really goes down like this. Yes, I made a mistake and one that negatively impacted students. But in the follow-through, I was able to defuse it by apologizing and correcting it (and maybe build some solidarity as students and faculty together sharing our mutual frustrations with the nitpicking intricacies of the LMS). Sometimes an apology is just what we need to get our cars and motorcycles going at the same speed and to take the leap.

Rebuild

Defusing distrust is often a matter of a quick action: a few words, a time-out, a short interaction. Rebuilding trust is a longer process, sometimes requiring some serious soul-searching. The interaction that demonstrated this most vividly to me—and forever emblazoned the power of STIR into my teaching consciousness—began with a missed assignment. In the spring of 2019, a student approached me after a class meeting and told me that he had turned in an assignment that was marked as not being turned in. His tone was somewhat aggressive, putting me on the defensive immediately. It was a low-stakes completion grade, not a point or letter grade, so he only needed to turn it in to get credit. He said he had done it. I said he hadn't.

Side note: The first big thing going wrong here was at that I required students to turn in printed hard copies of their written assignments. The LMS drop box for submitting assignment electronically was *right there*, but I'm a slow adopter of new technology and had not yet learned how to work it even though I totally knew that drop boxes made it so much easier to view previous assignments and feedback, increasing efficacy of scaffolding assignments, and it doesn't cost students anything for printing or paper. But I'm ashamed to say that I just wouldn't take the time to learn how to set up a drop box. In fact, I learned how to use the LMS assignment drop boxes only when world-altering events forced me to, teaching online for the first time during the pandemic lockdown. Of the many ways that remote emergency instruction expanded my views on education and gave me startling new insights to my own teaching practices, this is one of the most important: at long last, I got over myself and learned how set up a drop box.

Using electronic submissions with their time stamps and automatically enforced deadlines render the specifics of this interaction null and void, but the point is that this interaction, related to grades and assignments, was making me distrustful of the student. In that moment I luckily had the wherewithal to *stop*. And I had just the scripted response to do so:

> ➤ *"Thank you for bringing this up with me. I appreciate that you want to do well. Let me think about it and I'll get back to you after our next class."*

The stress odometer ticking upward between us fell back to normal with these words. Then I went back to my office and thought about it. I mean, *really* thought about it. (I also had a snack and a rest. Never underestimate the ways that hunger and fatigue can mess you up.)

To identify and repair this problem, what was most important? What mattered? I eventually decided that in this case the damage to any trust I had with this student by not accepting their assignment outweighed the possibility that he was pulling a fast one on me. This was a student who'd been right on the edge of doing poorly in the class—who'd been having trouble for a while. I decided that, because distrust was shaping this whole interaction and interfering with my teaching and his learning, rebuilding trust by accepting the assignment would benefit us both.

I told him in the next class that I had thought about what he'd said and decided I would accept his assignment for credit. The student's face brightened with relief and he expressed gratitude, not obsequiously or snidely, but like a human being to another human being. With this action, I actively rebuilt trust. It's not so much that I chose to believe the student was telling me the truth about the specific assignment, because I don't know that he was. But I chose to rethink my previous decision about the assignment and, in fact, my whole teaching approach to this type of issue when I decided to prioritize rebuilding trust with that student above all the other factors.

I continue to prioritize rebuilding trust with my students, even when things are going deeply wrong, like when I suspect a student of academic dishonesty. Unless I have irrefutable, undeniable, clear-cut, no-reasonable-doubt evidence that the student cheated, and I've done everything humanly possible in the way of course design and assessment mechanisms to minimize the possibility of cheating, I focus on the repair strategy of rebuilding trust with the student. Since I became more aware of how much distrust can snafu teaching and learning and how to STIR, I've become much more invested in rebuilding trust with students when I address potential academic dishonesty or any other grade-related issue.

Rebuilding trust with students is my go-to for when they've made a mistake, but it's just as useful when we, the faculty, mess up and betray a student's trust. It needn't be a hugely dramatic breakdown of trust either. Let's say you've gotten behind on grading and, whoops, the next assignment is due but you still haven't handed back the previous one. This is a super-duper extra-normal mistake that absolutely need not turn ruinous but could chip away at students' trust. Not getting assignments back in a timely way is one of the most common and understandable frustrations that students express about instructors. How could we STIR and repair by rebuilding trust?

Stop: Stop trying to ignore it or live in denial. Stop kidding yourself. Stop promising yourself that you're going to do all your grading tonight after the kids go to bed knowing full well that the only thing you're doing tonight after the kids go to bed is watching TV and eating too many Cheez-Its.

Think: Looking at the syllabus, the calendar, and deep into your psyche, something's gotta give.

Identify: You will need to change the deadline for the next assignment or even eliminate the next assignment and revise the grading scale.

Repair: With a focus on rebuilding trust, send a message to students and announce in class:

> ➢ *"I apologize for being unable to grade your last assignments more quickly. These are the steps I'm taking to get back on track."*

Rebuilding trust as a STIR repair strategy when we miss a scheduled meeting, make a mistake in the grade calculation, forget to open the quiz on the LMS, etc., can nip distrust in the bud.

Defusing distrust and rebuilding trust are actionable strategies when things go wrong: they give us something we can do when distrust is interfering with students' abilities to learn and our abilities to teach. But ideally, as in the case of inequity and disconnection, distrust can be proactively minimalized with course planning and teaching practices. Like increasing equity and increasing connection, increasing trust is in many ways easier and far more rewarding than mitigating and reducing mistrust snafus after they happen.

Gear for Your Go-Bag

- Distrust snafus are some of the most challenging ways things can go wrong, arising around fraught issues such as grading disputes and classroom incivilities.

- We can strive to consciously and deliberately defuse highly charged distrust snafus with STIR and with responses that prioritize maintaining trust.
- When a distrust foul-up has damaged teaching and learning, we can strive to rebuild trust with STIR and enact strategies that consciously create conditions for rebuilding trust.

Chapter 9

INCREASING TRUST

In a recent study on the concept of trust and what individual college instructors can do to generate trust in the classroom, researchers identified what they termed "teacher-initiated trust moves" and suggested a conceptual framework of four distinct but also overlapping areas of trust moves:

Cognition: Does the teacher show knowledge, skill and competence?

Affect: Does the teacher show interpersonal care and concern?

Identity: Does the teacher show sensitivity to their own and/or others' identities?

Values: Does the teacher show they are acting on principle?[1]

The ways and means—the "trust moves"—we use to increase trust build on and intersect with what we can to do increase equity and increase connections, as discussed in parts one and two. These practices help us sync up our motorcycles and rescue cars and build trust.

Proactive strategies such as planning for learner variability and getting good at small talk also increase trust between faculty and students. Encouraging students to identify their own most important goals and facilitating connections to the course material help students trust their own academic abilities. The overlap is significant between increasing equity, increasing connections, and increasing trust, and the converse—inequities and disconnection—regularly generate distrust. This chapter details three specific ways to increase trust with students: being continuously welcoming; cultivating clarity; and enlisting students as partners. I also describe how faculty can consciously build trust in ourselves by nurturing our teaching self-efficacy.

Be Continuously Welcoming

Most students will decide in the first five minutes of the first class whether they like you and will like the class, and that opinion probably won't change very much from the first day to the last day of class.[2] No pressure or anything! There is an increasing body of scholarship and advice for facilitating an engaging first day of a college class. (Sorry, but "read the syllabus" is not a good plan.)[3] Because high-wattage extroverted professorial performance is not part of my teaching persona, on the first day of class I don't try to wow students with the force of my personality or strut around the classroom like it's a stage; that would just embarrass everyone. Instead, I approach it as an opportunity for academic hospitality, and this applies as much to an asynchronous online class as a traditional on-site class. I set out to invite students into the classroom, the course, and my discipline. I want to convey my enthusiasm for the topic and encourage them to join me in nerding out about my topic—to show how very interesting, engaging, and important studying this thing can be. I want to ensure that they feel like they belong.

Everything that I say, plan, and do on the first day of class is aimed at making students feel welcome. I make sure the course number and title of the class are very prominently displayed on the board or screen, or as the first thing they see on the LMS site. I greet students as they enter the room or log on by saying, "*Welcome to* [name of class]*!*" For on-campus classes, I have upbeat music playing quietly. I have handouts, name tents and tags, and markers for writing, laid out on the desks. And I've got an "elevator pitch" when class starts. It's not a show-stopping oration full of flare and razzle-dazzle, but the first words students hear me say to the whole class focus on welcome:

"I'm Professor Neuhaus. Welcome! I'm so glad to be here and I'm so glad you are here. The most important thing you need to know about me is that I love teaching. I know how hard you've worked to be in this room right now and I'm confident that, with my support and with the support of everyone in this class, you are going to learn and succeed this semester. We're going to work together to help you achieve your goals, because you are an important member of this unique learning community."

These first words are my way of actively putting out the welcome mat to my class instead of just passively unlocking the door and waiting for students to walk in.

We can put out the welcome mat well before the course begins. One effective way to welcome students is in a short, carefully crafted, but informal (not highly produced or edited) "Welcome to our class" message delivered via a video, email message, voice recording—or all three. A welcome video can demonstrate your enthusiasm for teaching and desire to have students succeed in the class and convey approachability. It can also demonstrate your enthusiasm for the topic, kindling a little curiosity about it in the students. Introducing ourselves with a few personal details, to whatever extent feels natural and comfortable to us, can set the stage for further introductions and positive interactions.[4]

Welcoming, invitational language can be reiterated throughout the syllabus as well.

Our choice of language, tone, and policy statements in a syllabus influence student perceptions of being welcomed by the professor and included as a member of the class learning community.[5] Things like moving away from the "contract" to an "invitational" syllabus and facilitating active engagement with it (for example, by using annotation, or a "liquid" syllabus) can help students— and faculty, for that matter—reframe the syllabus as a more equitable and engaging document.[6] It can, quite plainly, demonstrate to students that they belong, as scholar of equity-minded teaching and learning Mays Imad does with the first line of her syllabus: "Welcome brilliant minds! I am so glad you decided to register for [name of class]. This course is going to be amazing because you're part of this awesome learning community."[7]

But the syllabus, no matter how welcoming in tone, is obviously only a starting point. As SoTL researchers Peter Felten and Leo Lambert, referencing work by Dave Scobey, argue, our ability to be not merely welcoming but *relentlessly* welcoming is key to creating trust.[8] By continuously welcoming students, we frame our classes and academic spaces as places where students belong and where their presence matters. Instead of serving as gatekeepers, we're hospitable guides, throwing open the door and saying "Please come in" like the world's best, brainiest hostess at the learning party of the century. I say "Welcome!" all the time: "*Welcome, everybody. I'm glad to see you*" at the start of every class; "*Welcome, come on in*" when a student stands at my office door; "Welcome!" when a student enters class after it has begun—or, if this might cause self-conscious awkwardness, I give them a quick smile and a nod.

That last one was the hardest for me, being a real stickler for starting on time. But here's the beauty of providing a continuous welcome: not only does it increase students' trust in us but it also increases our trust in students. When a student enters late and I welcome them, I've very clearly told them that I want them to be there. But, just as importantly, I've reminded myself that I'm glad the student is here, I'm the students' academic Hostess with the Mostest, and just as I would welcome a late guest to my party, I'm going to welcome this student. If habitual tardiness starts to feel disruptive, I'll talk with the student and ask for more information, but the first and most immediate response is "I'm glad you are here because your presence matters."

Being continually welcoming can be as or even more important later in the class than it is in the beginning. Like when a student who has been falling behind or missing a lot of classes or struggling in some other way and has been avoiding even meeting your eye in class, let alone answering your messages, or coming to office hours, sends you a short email saying something frustrating like "I missed some stuff. Cool if I just turn it all in now?" More than ever, I've got to remember that I am hell-bent on being continually welcoming. So however I choose to respond to this message, my starting point is continuous, relentless welcome: I *want* the student to be here.

I'm not suggesting we plaster a fixed smile on our face and conduct our classes and office hours like a servile Stepford wife at a cocktail party or engage in performative speech or actions that feel inauthentic to us. But we can increase trust in meaningful ways—and decrease distrust foul-ups—when we strive to be continuously welcoming.

Cultivate Clarity

I used to submit my final class grades with a pit in my stomach and a lump in my throat, anxiously anticipating one or two emotional, sometimes outright demeaning and disrespectful, email messages from students unhappy about their grades. By hugely upping my transparency with students about grades and checking much more frequently that students understand how I will be calculating and assigning grades, I've almost totally eliminated those emails. But grades remain a flashpoint where distrust fouls up teaching and learning, and things can go wrong. As educational scholars Cathy Davidson and Christina Katopodis succinctly put it: "Grades cause problems."[9]

Assessing student learning—i.e., determining to what degree students have made progress toward and achieved the learning goals of a class—is one of the hardest things we do as educators. What makes it even more difficult is that these assessments are frequently assigned points or rankings in a letter system that has far-reaching and potentially highly negative academic, financial, intellectual, and emotional consequences for students. As a result, the phrase "assessing student learning" is not how a typical student will describe what happens in a college class. What they say instead is "being graded." When grades are at stake, it's very difficult to get students to unlearn their distrust and increase trust in us as facilitators of their education; to not see us as a fickle and hard-to-please God of Grades, granting As, Bs, Cs, Ds, or Fs for unknowable reasons. Consequently, when we're planning classes, before we dive into the nitty-gritty details of assignments or rubrics or all the specific means by which students will demonstrate their knowledge, we must give precedence to transparency and clarity.

We must plan exactly how to best communicate with and help students understand how grades work in our classes. Advocates of transparency in teaching and learning (TILT) argue that increasing equity with course design and classroom practices begins with ensuring that our students thoroughly grasp the purpose and relevance of all aspects of every class and how each assignment and activity will help them learn.[10] For most student and most college instructors in most teaching contexts, I believe that true transparency must begin with the grades themselves. We can increase trust with students by ensuring that we've made it absolutely crystal clear precisely how we will determine the number and/or letter grade that appears on their college transcript at the end of the class. Achieving that clarity requires extensive planning and numerous, various, and repeated types of communication. Our syllabus is important but it's only the very beginning of cultivating clarity. I used to make the mistake of thinking that because my carefully crafted syllabus outlined assignment points and grading scales, I'd made my grading practices clear and "transparent." Uh, no. Not even close!

I drastically underestimated how much information about grading and assessments students taking four or more classes must remember day-to-day, week-to-week, month-to-month. For a long time I overestimated students' ability to extrapolate from certain syllabus phrases or statements and failed to consider the diversity of students' previous academic experiences about grades, which influence their understanding of grading. When I said in the syllabus, "This assignment accounts for 30% of your grade," I assumed they would read it as "This is important, so don't wait to start it until the night before it's due." That . . . didn't happen. I also underestimated how much distrust many students brought with them regarding grades and how previous negative experiences could generate a fog of fear, even hostility, obscuring their understanding of how grades would be determined in my class.

There's no quick fix for clearing that fog, but one relatively simple step to take even before class begins is to plan for and schedule ongoing communication with students about grades. I don't just mean providing a grading rubric, although rubrics can be useful.[11] I mean things like scheduled email or LMS reminders that summarize how an upcoming assignment will be graded; maintaining an open forum or drop box in the LMS to answer questions about grades; and devoting time in class to going step-by-step through the grading rubric for an upcoming assignment. Though not possible in every teaching context—teaching load, class size, and employment status determine feasibility—incorporating individual grading conferences at least twice a semester into your course schedule is a tried-and-true strategy for cultivating clarity around grading. A grading conference includes reviewing assignments together with a student, discussing your feedback, planning with the student how they will apply your feedback, and possibly having students contribute to their grades through self-assessments.[12]

What matters is planning for the time and the ongoing effort it will require to clearly communicate with students about grading. That includes fully accounting for the vast amount of grading-related baggage everyone is bringing with them, which in turn increases the time and different types of communication needed to make grading practices clear and transparent to students. The syllabus isn't enough. Saying it in class isn't enough. When it comes to how grades are calculated, we need to discuss, explain, and check for understanding in as many ways and as many times as possible:

- Communicate about grades in the syllabus.
- Talk about grades in class.
- Have students review rubrics or grading info in small groups and report to group with questions and points for clarification.
- Send emails and LMS reminders.
- Facilitate Q & A sessions in class, via Zoom, and in asynchronous forums about grades.
- Provide time for in-class grading rubric reviews.

- Record video and voice memo messages about grades to post and send.
- Collect midterm surveys, self-reflections, or other types of low-stakes but required assignments to check that students know what grade they currently have and understand how it was calculated.
- Do regular "muddiest point" check-ins with students.

The "muddiest point" activity is usually a quick check for an individual student's content understanding, and it is administered as a class exit ticket activity. I'm suggesting that it could also be used to check understanding about grades. For example: "*Before you leave class today, please write on the index card one thing that's not quite clear to you on the grading rubric.*" Or "*Take a minute to jot down a question you have about how the project is going to graded. I'll answer everyone's questions on our discussion board and in class next week.*" Write grading info in foot-high letters on a sandwich board and parade around class wearing it and ringing a bell like ye old town crier—anything you can think of to make sure students understand their grades. Because grades are so fraught, any type of assessment and feedback strategy we are using can cause trust-related snafus, and thus repeated, crystal clear communication about those strategies must be a course design priority. It's even more important if you are employing any nontraditional grading practices, because students are likely to feel unmoored, disconcerted, and even distrustful when first encountering nontraditional grading.

Understandably, crystal clear communication about grading tends to sink to the bottom of faculty's priority list. I say understandably because almost every college instructor on the face of the earth has gotten trapped in grading-related conflicts with students. Across all types of teaching contexts, grades are one of the most persistent ways things can go wrong in the college classroom. Negative interactions with students about grades with instructors from historically minoritized groups are complicated by racism, sexism, ableism, heterosexism, and other biases. Acceding that more, not less, communication with students about grades will reduce snafus is a bigger lift in some teaching contexts than others.

Cultivating clarity around grades will increase trust but it's not the only aspect of course design essential for increasing trust. Highly consequential class policies—the ones that are going to have the most direct impact on students' grades and ability to succeed in the class—are another area that requires as much clarity as possible. For example, the late-assignment policy. Cultivating clarity about what we and what students will do when students miss a deadline can go a very long way toward increasing trust and minimizing distrust snafus. Students missing deadlines has been a big personal challenge for me as an educator. At the risk of sounding like an insufferable goody-goody, I almost never miss a deadline. That's a great professional and personal skill to have but it interfered for a very long time with my teaching efficacy. I just could not understand or empathize with students missing deadlines, which I'd very clearly stated on the syllabus from the first day of the class. As a result, my late-assignment policy was rigid and punitive for many years.

I'd just started to rethink this approach when the upheavals of the COVID era shook everything up, including the concept of deadlines. For the first time that I could remember, I missed a couple professional deadlines myself—and, lo and behold, it wasn't the end of the world. I successfully finished what I needed to finish, just a little later than planned. I know, right? Who knew? During the pandemic pivot, as part of my increasing understanding of how complex students' life circumstances could be, I also gained a new awareness of the fact that every student at some point will encounter an obstacle that interferes with their ability to meet a deadline. We can increase trust when we've planned and created policies that allow some flexibility in accommodating late assignments. Emphasis on "*some* flexibility." "Turn it in whenever you want" is not good planning, does not cultivate clarity, and doesn't increase trust—not really. On the surface, it sounds like "I trust you to turn it in when you can," but the strongest takeaway for most students will be that the professor doesn't care when they turn it in or, even more problematically, that the professor doesn't care, period.

One technique for framing assignment deadlines in a trust-building way that helps students maintain progress by completing assignments—and lets faculty maintain a reasonable schedule of assessing assignments and providing formative feedback—is the "'oops' token" or what I call a "flex pass." It allows students to submit one or two assignments late for full credit, no questions asked.[13] Other faculty use a "Best by" schedule for assignments that gives some, but not unlimited, flexibility for students without creating unsustainable labor for themselves.[14] I can check for student understanding before the first due date with an ungraded but required "quiz" with one question: *"What is the 'flex pass' in this class?"* or *"What are your options in this class if you miss an important deadline?"*—and, to ensure students understand it must be completed, I lock access to whatever comes next in the LMS until that "quiz" is submitted.

Another assessment strategy that offers some flexibility around deadlines is a set of regular assignments in which a certain number of lowest assignment grades, including a zero for incompletion, will be dropped before the final grade is calculated. Again, we can check for student understanding around this aspect of assessment and grading by asking them directly to recall and explain what the policy is and how the grade will be calculated. For instance, I sometimes do an in-class chorus reading of a specific late and/or dropped assignment policy: everyone reads it out loud together. Then I can do a quick check for understanding via an anonymous poll or class exit ticket: *"How confident are you that you understand how I will grade all your [fill in the blank] assignments?"*

These are effective ways to add some flexibility to deadlines, but, in addition, we can cultivate clarity by emphasizing that meeting deadlines is a valuable academic skill that requires a lot of practice. For example, at the beginning of the semester, I often have students identify what they expect will be the greatest obstacles to their own individual successful completion of the class. Virtually everyone will at least mention "time management" or "procrastination." Bingo. Now I've got a way to link meeting deadlines with their own individual success for the whole rest of the term. So every time something is coming due, when I send reminders or mention it in class, I can say, *"I know procrastination and time management is challenging and this will be an opportunity for you to increase your skills.*" I've also sometimes had students, especially early in their college careers, do low-stakes but required assignments reviewing and self-assessing their progress in overcoming procrastination and meeting course due dates and deadlines, helping them engage in metacognition and recognizing their own improvements or need for improvement in this area.

Helping students develop this skill and engendering their trust in us as their guide to help them develop that skill may require us to provide many reminders about upcoming deadlines. However many reminders you currently give students, I'm going to go out on a limb and say: They need more reminders. Reminders do not bother the (infinitesimal number of) students who are so on top of their planning that they don't really need reminders. And reminders can be a make-or-break situation for some students. Students will never complain that you reminded them "too often" about upcoming due dates and deadlines.

The high-impact course policies around meeting deadlines, late assignments, assessment, and grading—and all our communications regarding these policies—are some of the most obvious ways we can increase cultivate clarify. But clarity is a useful trust-building practice in all aspects of teaching. Nothing in our work with students should be a secret or a bad surprise to them. Whatever we're undertaking to help students learn and to succeed will benefit from being as clear as we possibly can, anticipating where lack of clarity will trip up a student and questions they will have. Questions such as: "What is a 'learning center' and how would I use it to get assistance?" "What do you mean that highlighting and reading aren't a good way to study for a test? That's what I've always done before, so why should I try a different way?" and "Where do I go in the LMS to see my grade? Formative feedback means I did it wrong, doesn't it?"

And then there's a question almost guaranteed to stir up distrust: "Why should I attend class?" Attendance is a hot-button issue for college educators who are teaching on-site, in-person, and synchronous classes at any time, but it's blazingly, molten-lava-level hot after the upheavals of 2020–21 emergency remote instruction. And with questions of accessibility and equity on the line, class attendance is increasingly a point of contention between students and faculty, exacerbated by the conflation in far too many instructors' minds between "sitting inertly in a room while I talk at you" with "attendance" and by pandemic-era educational experiences that seemed to prove to many students that their physical presence was not a necessary part of learning and academic success.[15]

Such tension around attendance increases its potential as a source of distrust: students don't trust that attending class is a good use of their time, and faculty don't trust that students will make every effort to attend class. In this volatile context, crafting an attendance policy that increases trust should be a priority for anyone teaching a face-to-face class. But cultivating clarity isn't enough. To truly increase trust around attendance, we need to enlist students as partners.

Enlisting Students as Partners

Sherri Spelic is an author and leadership coach who teaches physical education at the elementary level. In one of her many thoughtful and thought-provoking online posts, she described a note she'd received from one of her students that said simply, "Thank you for sharing all the power with me." This comment speaks to how Spelic effectively implements pedagogical practices that encourage students to see themselves as active participants, not passive recipients, in their learning. It illustrates how effective it can be when we, as educators in the classroom, seek to share the power by partnering with students rather than relying on traditional hierarchies.

"Sharing all the power" and creating partnerships with students as part of effective teaching and authentic learning is the subject of a growing body of scholarly research on the benefits of creating classroom environments that systemically dismantle educational hierarchies and empower students to actively partner with faculty in building their skills and knowledge.[16] The students as partners (SaP) framework can extend into educational development and other campus programs as well.[17] In this section, I focus on two very specific causes of distrust snafus in on-campus classes that can be proactively reduced by enlisting students as our partners: attendance and phone/device distractions.

I first began to deliberately enlist students as partners when I started noticing a growing gulf of bafflement between professors on my campus who couldn't imagine why they needed to explain to students that attendance is important and students who couldn't imagine why going to class every single time would be worth exerting their limited time, energy, and willpower.

> **Professor (bewildered, bordering on angry):** You need to attend class.
> **Student (bewildered, bordering on angry):** I can't attend every class. I don't need to attend every class.
> **Professor (insulted, discouraged, frustrated):** You can't succeed if you miss class. Why don't you believe me?
> **Student (insulted, discouraged, frustrated):** I can succeed if I don't attend every class. Why don't you believe me?

This distrust speaks to more than a lack of transparency. There's a lack of clear, meaningful student motivation for attending class. "Because I will get points docked from my final grade" is certainly one kind of extrinsic, cop-adjacent motivation for attending class, but in the long run, and when things go wrong or things get hard, it won't empower student self-efficacy, let alone productive participation in class. It imposes a top-down, instructor-centered rationale for why a student should attend class, which is often a precursor to distrust.

Moreover, you've got as many reasons for attending class as you have students, because every student's unique life circumstances create unique reasons for them being in class. The best attendance policy will tap into those reasons. You may have what sounds to you like a compelling list of reasons why a student should attend your class, but unless they're connected in some way to what matters most to the student, it's not compelling for them. In addition, rigid attendance policies can contribute to inequities and ableism in higher education by directly penalizing students who are capable of successfully completing the learning objectives and demonstrating their learning but may also, because of their life circumstances, not be able to attend the minimum number of classes required in the attendance policy. That's a distrust snafu just waiting to happen.

I know what you're thinking: If it's about trust, then, hey, we don't need any policy at all; we can just tell students we trust them to come to class, and if they're not in class, we trust them to uncomplainingly face the consequences of missing class. That'll work! No. It won't. Whatever our intentions, having no attendance policy whatsoever conveys to many students the message that the professor doesn't care if they attend class, nor does their attendance matter to other students. If we want to increase trust, just saying "Trust me, you need to come to class" isn't enough, and it's not enough to think only in terms of "required attendance," "permitted absences," or even "makeup for absences."

Focusing on the positives of attendance instead of the negative consequences of not attending, we can incentivize attendance with external motivators that encourage student choice and offer supportive flexibility. For example, math professor and scholar of teaching and learning Robert Talbert offers his students numerous and varied opportunities to earn "engagement credits"—points for things such completing an optional assignment, reflecting on an activity, and, yes, attending class.[18] He enlists students as partners in this practice by inviting them to suggest ways they can earn engagement credits while providing an extremely clear and specific motivator for attending class (which might be especially useful for some students who, for cognitive, developmental, or experiential reasons, strongly benefit from some structured, external motivators in academic settings).[19] Other educators have found that using non-punitive strategies such as nudging and gamification improves attendance.[20]

However, there's no miraculous course design to fix it so that every student will be able to attend every class you teach forevermore and you'll never have to talk or think about attendance and the issues of equity and learning it raises ever again, hallelujah and huzzah. But redefining class attendance as working together with students as partners can give students and faculty a better starting point. In recent years I've moved from a class attendance policy to class attendance contracts, agreements, or goals. Instead of a punitive attendance policy, I enlist students as my partners. I have students set their own individual attendance goals, including identifying exactly how attending class will increase not only their own individual opportunities to advance toward their own unique personal, academic, and professional goals but also how it will increase the learning and success of everyone else (including me, as the facilitator) in the class.[21]

When we shift away from top-down punishment to co-created expectations and goals, conversations about attendance can go more like this:

Professor (recognizing student as an individual and demonstrating care for learning): *What are your goals? How will attending our class regularly help you achieve those goals? How could missing class become an obstacle in meeting those goals?*

Student (appreciative that professor shows an interest in student as an individual): Here are my goals and why I should attend class regularly."

Professor (framing class as a learning community, valuing diversity as an educational asset): *How will your regular attendance benefit the other students in our class?*

Student (thinking about the class as a group of people working together): My presence matters for these reasons.

This approach to attendance can increase trust because it conveys to students that you view their presence in class as vital to their success—their own, specific, individual success—and that you view your role regarding attendance not as the class policeperson ticking names off a list like a warden doing a cell check but as encourager in chief, helping students build the self-regulation and time management skills needed in order to attend class. It conveys quite explicitly to students that I want to help them figure out how to make the best decisions for class attendance for them but they need to do their part as well and take time to reflect on those decisions. I've increased trust with students, sometimes even directly as part of the wording in the attendance agreement with students, saying: *"I value your time and I know you're trusting me to facilitate effectively, but it takes everyone's efforts to make class meeting time valuable. I trust you to invest your tuition wisely by prioritizing attending this class."*

Admittedly, attendance plans and contracts require extra work on my part at the beginning of the semester because I have to review them and make revisions with the student to plans that aren't realistic ("I won't miss any classes") or will not enable student success ("I'll come to half of the classes"). Sometimes I combine attendance plan completion with visiting me (on-site or via Zoom) during office hours, so it's a twofer: increase student usage and understanding of office hours while talking about and planning for class attendance. It also requires that I take attendance throughout the semester, checking it against the attendance plans and following up with students who miss more classes than they said they committed to attending. None of this is especially difficult but it takes time, and while it could be modified for classes of larger than fifty students, it's easier to implement with smaller classes.

The payoff for me is not only increased trust but also a reduction of certain kinds of teaching labor. Specifically, I no longer regularly get emails or have interactions with students where they feel compelled to detail the reasons why they couldn't attend class. When attendance isn't linked directly to grade penalties, much of the potential conflict and resulting emotional labor around absences is removed. I still regularly discuss attendance with students, but it's far less taxing to express concern that a student has not met their own attendance goals—and that this could have a negative impact on their work—than to get mired in conflict about what constitutes "excused" or feel the emotional onslaught of a desperate student doing desperate things to avoid being penalized via grades for missing a class.

Partnering with students didn't come naturally to me at first. It felt at times like I was ceding some hard-won pedagogical and academic authority, neither of which was automatically granted to me as a woman teaching about pop culture, and would be even less granted to faculty without my social privileges. Also, my teaching persona relies primarily on the think-y part of being professor: I connect with students by being enthusiastic and fascinated by their ideas and their academic work. I'm not as skilled at projecting warmth and friendliness, and "student partnerships" has a touchy-feeling subtext that made me feel uneasy at first. I've gotten a lot more comfortable with it for the simple reason that what I was doing before wasn't working for me or for students. The standard penalty-based attendance policy was making my teaching life increasingly difficult: the back-and-forth about absences, my fear of unfairly granting "excuses" to some students and not others, and my increasing sense of arbitrary and inequitable parameters, like why three absences was fine but four absences was unacceptable. It wasn't working to incentivize attendance and it actively contributed to obstacles facing students with physical disabilities or chronic illnesses. The attendance agreement or contract system won't translate perfectly into every teaching context, and I'm not pretending that it fixed all attendance issues forever. I'll be forever tinkering and adjusting attendance policies (just like every other aspect of my teaching). But when we are looking to increase trust, it's worth our time and effort to consider where we can partner with students to shape our big-impact class policies.

One such policy issue is at the nexus of a complex, common distrust snafu: distracting, non-class-related phone, device, and laptop computer usage during class. In mainstream press and educational commentary, the discussion often centers on a ballyhooed research project that promises to make a truly thorny problem simple, such as studies trying to definitively prove whether people take better notes on a laptop than by hand.[22] The topic of device distraction in the college classroom is an example of how reluctant we can be to accept that the answer to our pressing question about teaching is: "It's complicated." There will never be one easy-to-implement, works-always-and-forever way to guarantee absolute attention on everyone's part, with nobody ever being tempted or distracted by their devices. There is, however, a compelling case to be made that this situation necessitates enlisting students as partners.

For the foreseeable future, every college instructor who wants to increase trust in the classroom and limit device distractions will have to engage in ongoing and ever-evolving classroom strategies—sometimes even changing from class to class—to figure out ways to help students cultivate focus and resist being distracted by phones during class. Smartphones are quite possibly the most effective human attention-getter that's ever existed, by deliberate design. So, like attendance policies, putting trust at the center of phone and device classroom policies cannot be a matter of just saying, "I trust you not to be distracted by your phones. If you are, oh well, whatevs, that's on you." Such an approach is not really trusting one another to make the classroom environment as productive as possible for the most people possible. It's also not going to give structure to those students—which is most students—who need some assistance in figuring out how to best engage in class and to build the attention skills needed to turn off the phone when they don't need it. But on the other hand, going to the other extreme, a punitive no-phones-ever policy, will automatically generate distrust.

Implementing a total ban makes you the phone police charged with "catching" banned usage and does not take into account the situations, including academic accessibility, when people truly need to view their phone. Like class attendance, we can change the whole tenor of phone and device usage by enlisting students as our partners in tackling this major teaching and learning challenge for in-person classes. This builds on the approach taken by critical pedagogy scholar Kevin Gannon, who writes: "I didn't go to graduate school to be a cell phone cop."[23] In response to the real problem of phone and device distractions, Gannon decided to revise his approach and policies to emphasize "choice, collaboration, and agency," explaining that "I could continue to try and police devices and behavior. . . . [O]r I could collaborate with my students to find solutions that worked for all of us."[24]

In practical terms, for me this means discussing the issue with students at some length in the first week of class, framing reducing phone distractions as a challenge for everyone in class and outside of class, and asking for their ideas and strategies for creating class meetings that help them build their attention skills and ability to resist mindlessly, habitually picking up their phones and/or social media-ing. (We need a new verb.) I emphasize that I am going to do my part by making class meetings a valuable use of their time and tuition dollars and that I want everyone to trust that we may occasionally have personal health or family issues that make checking our phones necessary. The goal is to co-create, as a classroom community, a statement of values, classroom norms, or mission statement that includes how we will, together, deal with phone and device distractions.[25] Like attendance agreements, a class values statement takes time to set up and then to maintain. It's also not a one-and-done deal. It must include what we think, as a class, should happen if someone breaks the agreement or violates the values we've stated.

What I find especially useful with the contract or agreement approach to phone distractions and enlisting students as partners in the process is that it becomes automatically folded into more meaningful goals for the class. For instance, one of the first shared values that students will usually arrive at independently is something like: *As a class, we value everyone's time, so we'll work to avoid wasting time during our class meetings.* I can then chime in with concerns about how unnecessary texting or scrolling can waste a student's time in class or be a distraction to other students, thus not allowing them to make good use of the class time. We can hash out then what to do when—not if—this happens. What kind of one-word reminder from Professor Neuhaus would you find helpful, for example? Maybe we do regular anonymous class check-ins, and if students report that they're finding themselves being tempted by phones and distracted, we revisit our values statement. Perhaps we schedule a few minutes in every class to look at our phones. I sometimes assign a low-stakes but required "class values" reflection, asking students to recall our shared values and identify ways they've met them or fallen short and ways they can keep improving.

Students with a bad case of academic entitlement, invested in their own passivity, may not be able to easily engage in this type of class contract co-creation as partners with the professor. The class values statement may need a lot of tinkering and it may require more time and discussion than you want or feel able to give it. And, of course, a class values statement is not the be-all and end-all solution to the phone and devices conundrum. But it does redefine the phone and devices conundrum as a problem we as a class must contend with together as partners in teaching and learning, transparently and very clearly defining attention as an important skill to master, and device distraction as a problem we all have to battle at some point. It won't prevent students from sometimes being unable to stop scrolling or doing non-course-related stuff on their computers. But it builds trust between students and faculty by moving away from us (faculty = phone police) versus them (students = phone felons) and instead it's us, *all* the people in class, versus the attention vampires living in our phones, pinging and chiming and latching directly onto our brainpans and making our valuable time disappear. It redefines us less as phone cops and more as attention coaches, guiding and encouraging students to build valuable personal, professional, and academic skills.

Similarly, a class values statement enlists students as partners to address other major trust-busting issues such as cheating and microaggressions. A class values statement can go beyond the punitive "This is what will happen when you cheat" syllabus statement required by most colleges and universities. It can include why it's important for students to develop their own ideas and the instructor's responsibility to ensure the class assignments and activities help students do exactly that. It can state the importance of respecting other people's experiences even if we disagree about something. It can make more explicit and transparent, using students' own words, the ways we need to be able to trust one another in the classroom.

Enlisting students as partners helps everyone think about a class not as "the" class or the instructor's class but rather "our class." This practice encourages students' responsibility for their own learning and for contributing to the positive classroom environment and is also one of the most viable ways to effectively respond to the dramatic increase of readily available generative

AI. Colleges, universities, and instructors in every higher education setting are scrambling to revise everything from the biggest policies to the smallest assignment details to account for ChatGPT and other language and visual analytical and predictive generative tools. The results vary wildly. On one end of the extreme, some instructors are forcing students to handwrite everything and some schools want to unleash the harshest of academic penalties if a student even *whispers* to themselves, "Hey, maybe ChatGPT could write this boring essay for me?" On the other end, some commentators are insisting that unless every single student becomes a generative AI expert immediately, their degree will be for naught, and anyone who's not using ChatGPT right this very minute is a Luddite chump.[26] It's one of the biggest academic hullabaloos of our time, with heated debate and tussles, resulting in draconian policing of students, head-in-the-sand, fingers-in-ears "La-la-la, I can't *hear* you!" refusal to deal, and everything in between. But if we look at generative AI as an issue of trust first and foremost, it's easy to see advantages of enlisting students as partners.

Turnitin is not going to save us.[27] Generative AI is not, technically, "plagiarism" and all those technology systems for nabbing student plagiarism will not work. (Also, don't forget that language-generating technology grew in part at least from the millions of student papers that faculty cheerfully uploaded for decades into the ed tech database maw; the phrase "hoisted by our own petard" comes to mind.) They will result in false positives and therefore unfounded accusations of student academic misconduct. Even more troublingly, the false positives around generative AI writing seem to be more likely when the writer is not a native English speaker.[28] Short of harassment and violations of physical safety, I can't think of a more trust-destroying and professionally problematic action than accusing a student of cheating when they didn't cheat.

We can help our students and make our own work life less onerous when we enlist students as partners to figure out how we will use, cite, and/or not use generative AI in our classes. For instance, this can be included in the co-created class values or norms statement written by faculty and students together at the beginning of class, deciding as a learning community what kinds of problems AI causes for learning, where it may be of benefit, how we should cite it if we do use it, and so on. Since 2022, I've included this statement on my syllabus to set the stage for enlisting students as partners:

> *One of my favorite parts of teaching is helping you improve your writing skills. While AI tools can generate written statements and even whole assignments, I am here as an expert writer to help you develop your ability to express your own unique and individual ideas in written form. That's what your tuition is paying for! As part of our co-created class values statement, I hope we will decide together when and how we'll limit the use of ChatGPT so everyone in our learning community will have the maximum opportunity to develop their writing voice.*

Like attendance, and like resisting the lure of device distractions in class, enlisting students as partners to figure out how to contend with generative AI is going to be more effective than a top-down, authoritarian model. Not perfect but more effective.

There is, as always, an important stipulation: sharing responsibility and partnering with students can be more difficult when, because of a professor's embodied and social identities, and student biases and expectations, an instructor is not automatically granted respect for their academic authority and subject expertise.[29] But co-creating with students in this way can help students overcome their biases and stereotypes about instructors, as some of research on SaP shows.[30] Also, enlisting students as partners in these ways does not mean we as the instructor relinquish all authority. In fact, providing leadership and effectively facilitating class meetings is vital to student-faculty trust. We can all strive to be "team leaders," as social psychology scholar Erik Simmons argues in "Black Man in a Strange Land: Using Principles of Psychology and Behavior Science in the Classroom," noting that faculty "must create a sense of 'we-ness' in our classrooms to encourage social cohesion, to promote vulnerability and communication, and to remain resilient amid a constantly shifting landscaping of higher education delivery."[31]

We take a risk when we decenter ourselves in the classroom, and it is risker in some teaching contexts than others. But it gives us a good approach for contending with some of the most complicated and challenging classroom issues of our time. Ultimately, enlisting students as partners increases students' trust in themselves and in you as the team leader and facilitator of their learning. It also increases trust in ourselves as faculty members—trust that we know how to help students learn and succeed; trust in our own pedagogical abilities and teaching self-efficacy.

Nurture Your Teaching Self-Efficacy

I was happily watching a new crime drama procedural, when suddenly there he was: the Super Teacher, entertaining hundreds of students in a lecture hall with his mesmerizing Oscar-worthy soliloquy—oops, I mean "lecture." I shouldn't have been surprised because the formulaic premise of this formulaic show is that a supersmart but emotionally damaged psychology professor (okay, that part is believable; I mean, a lot of college professors are super smart but emotionally damaged) is regularly tapped to provide his keen insights into human behavior when police and detectives are baffled. This is almost always the only time a college professor character gets airtime in fictional entertainment. Mostly, when they're on-screen, college professors aren't teaching. They're studying grisly crime scenes or eruditely discussing psychopathy over a body in a morgue or, occasionally, engaging in sexy workplace drama in opulent offices furnished with antique fainting couches and bookshelves filled with leather-bound tomes. But whenever there is a fleeting glimpse of a professor doing some actual teaching on TV shows and in films, they're almost invariably lecturing to a large class and, moreover, lecturing in such a compelling way about such utterly fascinating things that every student is completely transfixed and, presumably, having knowledge effortlessly transmitted into their brains by Super Teacher.

I'm happy to report that this version of the Super Teacher isn't a white guy, which is progress on the pop culture front for representations of college faculty. Unfortunately, in every other way, Professor Alec Mercer (played by Jesse L. Martin) on NBC's *The Irrational* conforms to some of the biggest, most damaging stereotypes and misconceptions about teaching and learning reiterated throughout the show. For example, in one episode, Professor Mercer's graduate student assistant Rizwan (played by Arash DeMaxi) subs for Professor Mercer, who is, once again, solving crimes instead of putting in his contracted contact hours in the classroom. "Sub" means lecturing, naturally, and Rizwan makes a hash of it because he's nervous and doesn't deliver a monologue worthy of a lauded Shakespearean thespian, so the students are—OMG—*bored*. Unthinkable! What a disaster! Students walk out of the lecture hall in protest!

In the next scene, Rizwan and another grad student are "reading the reviews" online, and of course they're terrible. (Memo to scriptwriters: Yes, once upon a time there was a website called Rate My Professors that was essentially a compilation of "reviews," but I promise you that students do not routinely rush out of every class meeting to submit online reviews like disgruntled diners complaining about poor customer service at Olive Garden.) Happily, Rizwan's next lecture combines humor, insight, prizes, and—I kid you not—confetti cannons. Students cannot help but be dazzled. Their "reviews" for this lecture are much better.

I ask you: *Confetti cannons?*

This depiction epitomizes the things I hate most about how college teaching is represented in the popular imagination. Things like how knowledge and expertise are only expressed via uninterrupted lecturing; that learning means sitting and listening to an expert; and how "good" teaching is only ever equated with entertaining lectures about inherently interesting subjects. Such oversimplified portrayals do students and professors alike a real disservice by idealizing the standard lecture format as the best way to learn and suggesting that mesmerizing performance/lecturing is the most important characteristic of an effective educator. It sets all of us up for failure, because this isn't how learning works, it isn't how teaching works, it isn't how any of this *waves hands toward all aspects of education* works.

I found this episode of *The Irrational* particularly galling because of an additional scene in which Rizwan is discussing his poorly reviewed lecture with his mentor. Professor Mercer reassures Rizwan that Mercer's own first lecture was terrible too, explaining that it takes practice to give a good lecture in a hall full of students, many of whom would rather be doing other stuff than sitting in class. The intimation is that, with time and practice, Rizwan too will become adept at performance lecturing and therefore, presumably, a good teacher. This exchange comes infuriatingly close to naming a central truth about effective teaching: it takes practice. A *lot* of practice, coupled with informed, reflective pedagogical learning and growth. Not #@$! confetti cannons.

Educator self-efficacy—knowing that we know how to help students learn and, when things go wrong, we can get back on track—takes a lot of time and a lot of ongoing effort to develop. This chapter focuses on increasing trust between students and faculty but we also need to consciously and regularly pay attention to increasing trust in ourselves. Building trust with students requires us to first trust in our own unique abilities to help students learn how to do things in and with our subjects.[32] Two of the most useful and immediately actionable ways anyone in almost any teaching context can nurture their self-efficacy and build trust in themselves is by (1) finding and getting support for ongoing pedagogical reflection and learning, and (2) paying attention to teaching wins.

As discussed in chapter six, talking about teaching with other people who care about teaching helps us create and maintain connections. It also nurtures our self-efficacy. Mentors, both informal and via formal programs, can provide that support. So too can campus teaching centers, faculty learning communities, and attending teaching conferences support our work to increase our knowledge about effective teaching. Ideally, scholarship of teaching and learning—books like the one you're reading or listening to this very minute—can nurture teaching self-efficacy. All these things take time and may not be immediately accessible in every teaching context. But when teaching is our main job, being able to engage in study and work with other educators helps us keep improving at our work, and doing so is a necessary part of maintaining our self-efficacy. It's the heart of what we most need to do to be effective and to know we are effective: engage in pedagogical learning about effective teaching.

For people who care deeply about student learning and are fully aware that teaching effectively is something we must always keep learning how to do, cultivating trust in ourselves and our teaching ability can sometimes be a bigger obstacle than cultivating trust in students. This is especially true when we are working in precarious employment conditions, fighting extensive systemic discrimination, or trying to survive a truly toxic workplace environment. On top of that, we have to fight the Super Teacher myth. If I start comparing myself too much to that guy, I'm going to feel less and less able to trust myself, no matter how many books on teaching I've read or faculty learning communities I join.

One vital way to counteract this tendency is to pay close, regular attention to what we call #ProfessorWins on social media—noticing and ideally recording even minuscule gains and positive interactions. Did you greet some students by name? Make a note, because that's a win. Did a student who's been falling behind ask for assistance? That's a win too. Did a quiet student ask a great question in class, to which other students responded thoughtfully, and you remembered to compliment her after class for her contribution? Win, win, win. Paying close attention to our wins in the classroom and during interactions with students is predicated on knowing and understanding ourselves and our teaching personas. The above examples are from my own teaching experiences because these are notable wins for me. I often feel self-conscious about greeting students, must make an effort to cultivate approachability so students will ask me for assistance, and highly value productive classroom discussions. So, for me, these count as wins that I know will help me build meaningful connections both to students as well as to the work of teaching itself.

We need to keep track of what's going well, not just notice or mention it in class. We should make sure that we've noted, summarized, or recorded in some concrete way our teaching successes. As I've written elsewhere, for some educators this can take the form of a gratitude practice—not as a way of ignoring negative situations or putting a veneer of facile positive thinking over problems, but as a way of improving our understanding of the entirety of our experiences as educators.[33] Recording in some detail our successes is a concrete way of rendering more visible the emotional and cognitive labor effective teachers do every day. A monthly teaching activity log that includes estimated hours spent on specific tasks can show us and anyone who's assessing our work how much time we spent preparing materials, assisting students, assessing learning, and so on. I don't want to overstate the case: the best-kept activity log in the world won't by itself undo systemic inequities or fully protect us from toxic departments or colleagues. Nonetheless, there is power in keeping close track of our teaching labor. Keeping better track of what, when, and how we're working to increase teaching and learning success will build our teaching self-efficacy.[34]

Conclusion: We've All Got Trust Issues

Building trust isn't easy and it doesn't look the same in every teaching context. Sometimes it feels like students have given us little reason to trust them or even to try to trust them. We get burned. The snafus sink us. Conversely, the same goes for students who can feel like they have little reason to trust us or even try to trust us. Often, trust boils down to being able to see each other more clearly as individual people rather than as stereotypes, or vague outlines through a fog of assumptions and miasma left over from previous negative interactions with other students and other instructors. Think of everything you do to build trust with students as money in the bank, saved up against the possibility of more stressful interactions or potential conflicts. Down the road, if a problem arises with a student, there's some positive past experiences to draw on.

For example, one time after I showed a documentary film in class about the history of Indigenous residential schools, a student suggested to me that in the future I might want to include a content warning before showing the film because it contained descriptions of child abuse and violence. I know she felt comfortable giving me this constructive feedback because of the foundation of trust I had been building in the class. I frequently emphasized that I cared about student success and learning: I regularly asked students for their constructive feedback and input and made a few minor adjustments; I chatted pleasantly about not much of anything with students before class; and I checked their understanding. I cultivated clarity and enlisted students as partners. This student had come to office hours before, where I tried my best to listen more than I talked. We trusted each other: she trusted that I would appreciate constructive feedback because I care about teaching, and I trusted her to offer feedback constructively. I trusted my own teaching efficacy as well. She wasn't hostile and I wasn't defensive. That trust didn't happen by accident and didn't happen overnight. We built it slowly and through deliberate choices I made to increase trust between myself and students.

Making a pointed effort to build trust with students took me a ton of time, study, and ongoing, persistent effort (all of which was very much enabled by employment security), but my efforts have paid off. Most students most of the time trust that I want to teach effectively and help them succeed. Sometimes it's hard to quantify, but a comment that I will always treasure indicated progress in regularly building trust with students. I was helping a student practice for her senior research project presentation, and she said that she appreciated my support, stating that "it really helps to know that you *like* us." As someone who works very hard to build rapport with students and to clearly convey my care for their learning, this was one of the best compliments I could get about my teaching practices. She wasn't saying that I had transformed my nerdy self into a socially skilled butterfly, gregariously and easily connecting with students, or had become a Super Teacher wowing students with amazing lecture-y entertainment. She meant that I had successfully communicated that I saw them as individual people, that I wanted them to succeed, and that I was glad to be working with them. She knew she could trust me.

We all have trust issues. We need to build trust with students not solely because meeting deadlines, attending class, and minimizing phone distractions is a big part of their success as learners but because these things are also a part of our success as teachers. If we have conveyed to students that meeting deadlines is super-important but not easy to do and that it requires practice and support, students may be able to return that attitude if we miss a deadline ourselves. If we've crafted and maintained attendance policies that convey our trust in students, with some flexibility built in for personal or health emergencies, we've increased the possibility that students will not quickly condemn or resent us for missing a class due a personal or health emergency.

Before we risk our necks making that leap from motorcycle to car, we need to ensure our vehicles are in sync. We have to trust the other driver and they have to trust us. Then the gap between our separate speeding conveyances will shrink, and we'll both be able to get where we want to go.

Gear for Your Go-Bag

- In course materials, classes, and individual interactions, we can consciously and deliberately welcome students in ways that are authentic to our teaching persona.
- We should strive to make every aspect of our classes clear and transparent to students and check frequently to ensure students understand our grading practices.
- Enlisting students as partners—especially for co-creating and maintaining high-stakes class policies around attendance, deadlines, and phone distractions in class—is both a practical as well as a pedagogically innovative way to increase trust.
- Build trust in your own individual teaching efficacy by regularly noticing and keeping track of all the things you are doing well as an educator.

PART IV

FAILURE

If you are completely buried, chances are you will be
too injured to help yourself.

—"How to Survive an Avalanche,"
The Worst-Case Scenario Survival Handbook

Chapter 10

FAILURE FOULS UP LEARNING AND TEACHING

I love eating homemade meals but I don't enjoy preparing homemade meals. For one thing, the gendered ideals of domesticity, including home cooking, have irritated me my whole adult life, and I've devoted a lot of my brainpower to studying and deconstructing them.[1] But the thing I dislike most about cooking is how easily it can fail—how sometimes, after hours of planning, shopping, and working, the soup scorches, the cake doesn't rise, the crust won't brown, or the fancy heirloom grains transform into tasteless sludge. Even worse, the people sitting down at your table are going to find out that you failed.

I've always remembered my friend Stephanie telling me about the time she tried a new recipe for a big dinner party she was hosting. The main dish looked fine, but after the guests had gathered and everyone ate a few bites, Stephanie discovered something had gone wrong and her main dish tasted awful. So she announced: "This is terrible. I'm going to order a pizza." I remain in awe of the self-assurance and poise that enabled Stephanie to take the necessary steps to repair her dinner party situation. Instead of becoming immobilized by shame (as I would have been), Stephanie was able to STIR this situation.

Stop: Put down the fork.
Think: Do a mental inventory of what's in the fridge right now.

Identify: This is inedible.
Repair: Everyone likes pizza!

An unappetizing main dish is an abnormal occurrence in Stephanie's kitchen, because she is an excellent cook. That's one of the reasons that she was able to handle her cooking disaster with aplomb.

When we are skilled at something, we know when we stumble, take a misstep, or just fall flat on our face in front of everyone, we will be able to address it and move forward. In fact, becoming skilled at something always includes some failures. It's one of the most proven facts about "how humans learn," to use scholar of teaching and learning Joshua Eyler's memorable phrasing.[2] Failures make teaching and learning hard for everyone at some point, and it's a driving cause of many higher education snafus. But unlike the snafus discussed in the previous chapters, failure has a valuable role to play in effective teaching and learning. In contrast to inequity, disconnection, and distrust—aspects of education that are unremittingly harmful to students and to faculty—failure plays an important and necessary part of our work.

As the authors of *Make It Stick*, a trailblazing book on the science of learning, succinctly put it: "Making mistakes and correcting them builds the bridges to advanced learning." Moreover, they continue, understanding this key fact about learning means being able to "view failure as a sign of effort and as a *turn* in the road rather than as a measure of inability and the *end* of the road [original emphasis]."[3] Scholars of teaching and learning routinely emphasize that inclusive course design, equity-minded classroom practices, and effective pedagogy fully take into account the essential role of failing as part of mastering skills and abilities.[4]

Failure is not only integral to how humans learn but also integral to how humans human. We fail sometimes when we do anything at all. Expecting successful educators and students to never fail at anything whatsoever is absurd, yet there is little leeway granted for this aspect of being a human in higher ed. Eyler asks, when some failures are inevitable, desirable, and necessary to learning, "Why is it, then, that our educational systems stigmatize failure so profoundly for students themselves?"[5] And, I would add, for teachers as well. At so many points throughout our educational system a single small failure can be like accidentally kicking a pebble that then starts rolling down the hillside, gathering momentum and accumulating more dirt, then more pebbles, then rocks, then trees, than the whole mountain itself comes crashing down and buries you alive.

We need to plan for and create ways to allow the passage of necessary pebbles—the mistakes and setbacks that we must withstand in order to learn and to build our skills as learners and as educators—down the hillside. We need to keep them from becoming big boulders of failure that will crush us and render us unable to go any further or to ask somebody else for help or to help ourselves. It's a difficult balancing act, creating conditions that focus on facilitating teaching and learning successes while at the same time assuming there will be failures aplenty. By its very definition, failure is the definitive example of things going wrong in the college classroom, so we have to recognize the ways it can foul up learning and teaching, plan for what to do when a failure avalanche threatens to completely bury us, and strategize ways to increase success.

Failure Fouls Up Learning

One of the most valuable things I help students understand about any aspect of their academic work is the predictability of a "shitty first draft," as memoirist and author Anne Lamott calls it.[6] Good writing requires rewriting, sometimes a lot of rewriting. Often, students erroneously believe that writing is a single-step process. Experienced writers know that sometimes the shitty first draft is a whole freaking book that you tearfully must chuck into the garbage before you can write the book you really wanted to write all along (not that I speak from personal experience or anything). Helping students unlearn how they think about writing—and making sure they have the structure and support they need to write a not-great first draft without suffering grade-based penalties or becoming overly discouraged (or feeling compelled to outsource to ChatGPT)—is an ideal example of how we can keep a smattering of pebbles from becoming a full-blown avalanche.

Unfortunately, far too often, academic failures bring enormous, even education-ending consequences for students. The most obvious failure for any college student is attrition: matriculating, paying tuition and fees, but then permanently withdrawing without successfully completing enough credits to earn an advanced degree. According to a 2023 study by the National Student Clearinghouse Research Center, that type of failure currently accounts for close to 40 percent of all students across all institutions, a rate that has not changed since 2015.[7] This disheartening statistic is the most observable way we define "failure" in the college context, but it represents only the culminating event in a much more wide-ranging and complicated series of failure experiences. Because what failure feels like, means, and does to students cannot be easily or simply summarized, varying as it does in highly individual and idiosyncratic ways. At the same time, systemic failures—not individual choices or actions—can also significantly foul up learning for students.

In some senses, failure is a deeply personal experience for students, affecting them socially, emotionally, and cognitively at an individual level.[8] Each student possesses their own unique qualities, life circumstances, embodied and social identities, and concepts of their selves that significantly shape how they define and experience any type of academic failure. To take a common example, people with perfectionist tendencies are more likely to view one small academic setback as a failure and will struggle to regulate their emotions and behavior in its wake.[9] The scholarship of teaching and learning is chockablock with research on how a student's individual mindset, self-concept, locus of control, expectations, goal orientation, sense of belonging, and other attributes impact their ability to withstand failure and exercise resilience.[10]

One important aspect of this work is the clear evidence of how much the *fear* of failure alone can foul up student learning.[11] For instance, fear of failure might fuel problematic coping mechanisms and behaviors, such as procrastination, which in turn directly interfere with student learning and success.[12] In her work on students' fears, higher ed scholar Rebecca Cox shows how fear, rather than actual mistakes in learning, creates failure because of the avoidance behavior and shame it generates. She explains that fear of failure "afflicts students' possibility of success" because "the same strategies that relieve their fear also prove counterproductive to their completing college coursework. While avoiding assessment, they also avoid the opportunity to prove their academic merit. The fear of failure—rather than actual failure, or substantial evidence of unsuitability"—inhibits their learning and success.[13] As Sarah Rose Cavanagh notes: "When you avoid situations that involve something you fear, you also deprive yourself of the possibility of ever extinguishing that fear . . ."[14]

Fear of failure (an individual student trait), and limited exposure to and understanding of how learning works (a systemic problem for students), create conditions for failure to foul up student learning. Many students have not had experiences in school that would enable them to value and embrace what the science of learning and SoTL terms "productive struggle," "desirable difficulties," and "productive failure." The research on how we learn clearly demonstrates that a highly effective way to learn how to do a thing is to try without having a good idea—yet—of how to do it well. There are nuances to how educators can best implement these theories about learning, such as identifying the tipping point when productive struggle just becomes overwhelming, and taking into account variables in different disciplines, but research convincingly demonstrates that educators can and should create learning conditions that support and encourage students to attempt things that are just a bit beyond their ability.[15] To be clear, "it's not the failure that's desirable" but rather "the discovery of what works and what doesn't that sometimes only failure can reveal. It's trusting that trying to solve a puzzle serves us better than being spoon-fed the solution, even if we fall short in our first attempts at an answer."[16]

However, "falling short" in attempting to learn and succeed academically can wreak havoc on students' self-efficacy. Increasingly, scholars of higher education are attentive to the high emotional cost incurred by individual students when they experience failure.

It's not an overstatement, asserts one group of researchers, to describe academic failure experiences as akin to a type of trauma:

> Academic failure is one of the commonly reported "most stressful or traumatic life events" among college students. Although academic failure is not typically considered a "trauma," it can become a life crisis and lead individuals to experience severe negative psychological outcomes such as depression. Failure can also contribute to increased negative affect and shame, and in the case of academic failure, individuals may experience a loss of self-esteem and self-concept, especially those who have experienced repeated failure.[17]

A "life crisis" or "severe negative psychological outcomes" in the wake of academic failure will obviously snafu learning.

As another group of researchers argue, academic failure is so uniquely awful that educators and educational institutions must stop "intellectualizing and distancing ourselves from it" and develop better awareness of failure's emotional impact on students: "Analyses which do not engage with the present tense, lived experience of failure—which is deeply affectual and often deeply vulnerable—are in danger of misunderstanding what "failure" really means. . . . [F]ailure is *felt* differently, and is not always identifiable within its normative framings" (original emphasis).[18] It's easy to see the inadequacy of "normative framings" for failure, considering all the contributing and complex factors that make failure so "deeply affectual."

These complex factors include both individual and systemic reasons for why and how students define and experience failure. For instance, stereotype threat will interact with a student's own individual psychology and life circumstances, shaping how they contextualize making even a small error in the college classroom.[19] A student's fear of failure is never solely an isolated psychological trait but is shaped by what failure means to that student in the context of their family, economic, health, and institutional circumstances. Students' academic failures are not caused either by individual or universal conditions but a combination of both. As a study on the causes of college attrition concluded: "Individual, situational, and institutional factors interplay in experiences of failure and persistence; that is, there is interdependence of individual *and* system factors" (original emphasis)."[20]

Failure is more than a personal and emotional challenge. It arises from a combination of dispositional, situational, and institutional factors.[21] Even a small failure can escalate to avalanche proportions in higher education. For example, consider how many classes a student must take to earn a degree, and let's say out of all *those many classes* they do poorly in one of them. Percentagewise, a single class is only a small portion of their college education. Beyond the emotional, cognitive, and social costs to a student, though, that lone F on their transcript can impact financial aid and student loans, increasing the literal cost of their education, and limiting their eligibility for other educational and professional opportunities. Moreover, how a student experiences that F depends on factors such as: Was this course an elective they took early in their college career? Is the course required for completing their degree? Were they planning on graduating, and does failing this course mean they won't graduate when they expected to? If failing this class helped them realize they really don't want to major in this subject, is that a 10-point earthquake on their internal Richter scale or just a little tremor? When the stakes are high—graduation is on the line, for instance—failing has life-altering consequences.

Failure creates obstacles to learning because the consequences can dramatically increase the costs, literal and figurative, of making mistakes. Even if somehow, some way, every student in our class was personally, constitutionally, and academically prepared to engage in productive struggle and resiliently spring back from mistakes and errors (actually, this would be a pretty creepy group of students, like *Children of the Corn Go to College*), the grinding gears of higher education would soon catch some of these unicorn-y students in a failure snafu. Arcane curricular requirements and steep financial costs, for example. In addition, we who care deeply about student success may forget that there is a small group of instructors who *don't* care, and because of employment status or campus culture they face few or no negative professional consequences for their ineffective teaching practices. It's a minority of faculty, but their poorly designed and badly executed classes create prime conditions for a failure avalanche.

We must be able to make mistakes. But so many aspects of higher education seem to function utterly oblivious to this very basic aspect of learning. One of the most widespread ways that individual college classes fall short when it comes to facilitating productive failure is course design that limits assessment of a student's learning to a tiny number of extremely high-stakes assignments or exams, such as when the instructor calculates a student's final course grade based on a single midterm exam and a single final exam. Doing poorly on the midterm—no matter how much the student learns during the whole second half of the semester—will doom the student to a poor class grade. In low-structure courses like these, doing badly on a single assessment becomes a crushing failure avalanche.[22] Yet failure does not need to become an avalanche, especially given that some productive struggle and making mistakes is so central to learning. I've been dancing around it for a while but now it's time to take a hard look at the most salient, most powerful, most relentless way that failure fouls up learning: grades.

In *Geeky Pedagogy*, I wrote about how important it is to cultivate complete transparency with students around grades. I advocated for low-stakes assignments; giving timely, actionable feedback as part of grading; spacing out assessments; and creating assignments that faculty might actually *enjoy* assessing and grading. I further argued that because, "eventually, we have to assign grades," I urged educators to be closely attuned to the fact that, for students, "grades are a source of a great deal of emotional baggage, and the only lens through which most students see their academic progress, or lack thereof. In short, they're a big honking deal."[23] I haven't changed my mind that planning and transparency are vital, and I unequivocally stand by my statement that grades are a big honking deal. But I've become much less resigned to the unavoidability of traditional grading systems.

A growing body of SoTL critiques traditional grading structures and suggests alternatives. Some advocates and researchers argue that the entire system of ranking student learning via grades needs to be eliminated—that a letter or point-based rank-ing of students is not only morally wrong but also directly under-mines learning.[24] They point out that A-to-F grading systems are not some kind of metaphysical reality set in stone for all eternity but are like any other human invention: a social construct main-tained by discourse, economic systems, and political interests.[25] These scholars make a strong case for alternative grading prac-tices and what's become known as "ungrading," an umbrella term for a variety of nontraditional assessment practices that remove the point-based or ranking component of assessing student learn-ing.[26] Ungrading does not mean eschewing expert feedback and assessment in higher education, but it does mean acknowledging the harm traditional grading does to students and student learn-ing; questioning the utility, accuracy, and equity of traditional grading systems; and challenging the idea that grading is an ines-capable requirement for education.[27]

I'll discuss specific assessment strategies, including nontra-ditional grading, in chapter twelve. What I want to underscore here is how grading, as it has become synonymous with failure, fouls up learning. It is almost impossible to untangle letter and point grades from how students perceive themselves as learners because it's almost impossible to untangle letter and point grades from how teachers, college instructors, and all aspects of all edu-cational institutions perceive them. Grades can wholly define a student's status and identity as a student. With that kind of power, grades can easily overshadow and render irrelevant actual learn-ing, because actual learning requires trying to do something you've never done before or doing something better than you've done before, which in turn requires struggle and, in the short term, non-success. When schooling appears to reward most richly the external motivator of success defined as one's ranking via a letter grade, why on earth should students bother to slowly, pains-takingly build the internal motivation and self-efficacy to tackle the non-successes that authentic learning demands?

Why would students embrace the mistakes and failures neces-sary for authentic learning when grades are the barometer of aca-demic success, and a failing grade is tantamount to failure as a student? As Kevin Gannon writes, for students, a failing grade is "the quintessential representation of everything they have been conditioned to avoid. An F grade carries a stigma; there is no credit that accrues from it, as if the course in which it was 'earned' never happened. An 'F' is a dead weight on one's GPA, one that needs four or five times its mass in As to overcome."[28] Grades interfere with students' ability to productively engage in trying new things, make mistakes, get and understand feedback, and try again. They inhibit and impede the very things that people (reminder: students are human people) need to do in order to learn.[29] Grades cannot very accurately encapsulate or summarize the widely varying and often incremental progress that students make in their learning over the course of any class. Grades are a crude, blunt instrument better suited for metaphorically smashing in skulls than for measuring or even reporting on something as complex and wildly diverse as how well human beings are increasing their thinking skills and abilities.

Research supports this statement but so too does wisdom of experience.[30] Because any teacher, if they are being totally honest, can tell you about those times when a grade did not accurately reflect a student's learning. The limits and limitations of letter- and point-based grading can create situations where the instructor enters a final course grade for a student and gets a sinking feeling that something just doesn't seem right. Even the most conscientious, equity-minded educator, with the most carefully planned and executed learning assessments, can find themselves assigning a point or letter grade that's a bad, or at least incomplete, indicator of a student's progress and learning. This hit home for me when I was working with a student whom I'll call Dan.

Dan was one of my favorite students, and I know he enjoyed my classes and appreciated my teaching practice. (I know because he told me, and he recommended my classes to other students.) He possessed the rare gift in a seminar class of being able to unfailingly improve discussion with one thoughtful, insightful comment. Never once dominating discussion or making an extraneous remark, he was one of the best students I've ever worked with in terms of his understanding of the material, ability to listen and respond to his colleagues during discussion, and willingness to engage with new ideas. But in two of our classes, although I'd scaffolded assignments and sent numerous reminders, he never completed the major project. So I ultimately entered a final failing class grade for Dan. I could point to the necessity of students completing tasks and documenting their increased understanding and show that Dan did not adequately do this. Still, entering a failing grade for Dan just did not seem right to me because of its rigid definition of failure. One letter grade couldn't sufficiently encompass Dan's learning in my class.

It was surprising when Dan continued to enroll in my classes, because, in my experience, the power of a failing grade—the way it's conflated with personal failure and its concrete power to negatively change a student's educational experience, including incurring additional financial costs—ensures that assigning students a failing final grade means the end of my opportunity to work with that student productively, let alone elicit praise for my pedagogical approach. At a minimum, I probably won't ever see them in a class again, but with a failing grade there's also always the chance for negative interactions and hostile responses. In every case, the grade—not what the student truly learned how to do or learned how to do better—takes center stage, hogging all intellectual and emotional attention.

Unintentionally but unmistakably, Dan showed me how grades were interfering with my own perceptions of teaching and learning. Dan's final grade—instead of all the achievements he'd made in class discussion and the engaging, thought-provoking conversations we'd had one-on-one about the course content and other topics he was researching—became the frame for how I remembered and perceived Dan. Looking back, and knowing what I know now about how irrevocably and thoroughly failure as filtered through systemic grading practices fouls up learning, I'm still not sure if I could have done something at any point to change the outcome of my work with Dan. Within the semester structure, I couldn't provide him the entirely different timetable he seemed to need for completing the required academic tasks.[31] But I do know that the letter grade obscured my understanding of Dan's real skills and his potential and made it impossible for me to facilitate a way for him to learn from his mistakes without incurring major tangible and intangible costs as a student.

Being caught in the confines of traditional grading systems is only one example of how failure can foul up teaching. Institutions and their populations—colleagues, departments, and student populations—can up the ante for a pedagogical failure in ways that truly foul up teaching. And failures can lay waste to our teaching self-efficacy and consume our pedagogical energy, leaving instructors disengaged and burned out.

Failure Fouls Up Teaching

In my most popular tweet @GeekyPedagogy, I imagined a supernatural manifestation of certain anxieties and worries I have when I'm teaching:

> **Me, a professor:** Class is going great! 24 out of 25 students are learning and engaged.
> **A demon** That one student tho. Probably you're a bad teacher.
> **Me:** But—
> **Demon:** Settle in. I've got slides.

Based on the number of likes and retweets this got, many other educators could relate to the feeling of a Failure Demon plaguing their thoughts about their own teaching. When we want to be effective teachers and we care about student learning, a single student doing poorly in a class (which, as some on #AcademicTwitter pointed out, was perhaps an unrealistically high percentage of students doing well in any class) can consume us with a sense of a failure.

Again, "us" refers to college educators who want to be effective teachers, regularly reflect on their practices, and engage in pedagogical learning, i.e., the people reading this book. The small number of instructors who choose to ignore their own shortcomings yet face few professional consequences for ineffective teaching do not tussle with these demons—demons that scholar of teaching and learning Stephen Brookfield might label "conversional obsession." Conversional obsession is "when you become obsessed with converting a small and easily identifiable minority of hard-core resistant students into becoming enthusiastic advocates for learning." Brookfield explains that this is a no-win teaching situation:

> You pour all your energy into provoking a response from this group, visualizing them leaving your course at the end of the year wreathed in beatific smiles of self-actualized gratitude for the wonderful transformations you have wrought in them. . . . The transformation you envisage will almost never happen, leaving you feeling that you've failed. . . . [and] you start to call your competence as a teacher into question.[32]

Moreover, he continues, when we're trapped in conversional obsession, "The legitimate learning needs of the majority of students take second place to your efforts to prove to yourself that you're a *real* teacher" (original emphasis).[33] Conversional obsession fouls up teaching at two levels: our own self-efficacy and our pedagogical efficacy with the rest of our students.

There's an element of negativity bias at work here, when our brains catch on the one or two things going wrong instead of the many things going right in the classroom, and then they balloon into a failure.[34] It is one element of the "downward spiral" described by Harriet Schwartz in her book *Connected Teaching: Relationship, Power, and Mattering in Higher Education.* In a chapter titled "Disappointment and Failure" she writes: "We think we are doing our best and yet students resist both us and learning; students perceive the course as unfair and, concurrently, we think they are unduly resisting the work; and though we try and try again to fix the course and reconnect with students, the problems feel insurmountable. . . . [O]ur attempts at repair fall short . . . [T]he chasm only widens and a downward spiral ensues." The downward spiral, Schwartz continues, often ends in a sense of failure: "Teaching experiences that go so wrong can rock us to the core, bruising our sense of efficacy, identity, and purpose."[35] For people who care deeply about student learning and success, teaching failures are more than just an ordinary workplace difficulty: they "rock us to the core."

A downward spiral when things go wrong is understandable because teaching failures are emotionally and psychologically taxing. Negativity bias about our own teaching efficacy is understandable because advances and accomplishments in teaching and learning are often incremental. Major breakthroughs and light bulb moments occur occasionally, but more often we advance slowly and laboriously. It takes regular, effortful practice to notice that something is working well and to identify when we've improved our skills. If we're struggling in a particularly inequitable and burnout-inducing teaching context, it's even more difficult. But in addition to the basic human tendency to have our attention seized most powerfully by things that stir up negatively charged emotions, and perhaps also because of a disproportionally high number of perfectionists in higher education, I think the image of a demon clicking through a PowerPoint slideshow about my teaching struggles resonated with other educators because of the discourse, policies, and institutional structures that portray teaching and learning as a perfectible endeavor, and anything less than 100 percent success at all times as a pedagogical failure.

"Perfection is an illusion," states Brookfield, dryly noting that "the image of the fully formed, omniscient teacher trained to respond immediately and appropriately to any and all eventualities is indeed part of the veil of illusion that comprises the physical world of pedagogic practices."[36] One notable part of this "veil of illusion" is the myth of the Super Teacher (don't even get me started again on those confetti cannons!), an important factor in how failure undermines teaching at an individual level. When the imaginary perfect professor skulks in our subconscious, it's hard to see our mistakes or missteps as anything less than total failure.

For college instructors highly trained in their academic subjects but with fewer hours of study and research on effective teaching under their belts, confidence can be even more easily shattered when things go wrong in the classroom. Far from being able to calmly recognize when something's not working and order a pizza instead, an ungodly demon may take up residence in our minds and start showing us an endless slideshow of how badly we've failed as a teacher. We'll never live up to the impossible professor ideal, which means that the routine, normal, totally-to-be-expected times when we make a mistake or don't do something as well as we'd like as part of our pedagogical work can easily transform into the feeling that we're a complete failure.

The damaging Super Teacher myth even lurks beneath many scholarly discussions about college teaching, contributing to educators' self-perceptions and internal measurements of teaching efficacy. Scholarship of teaching and learning, published advice about college teaching, and language around teaching awards does not emphasize enough the recurring and predictable occurrence of failures in teaching and learning. It's one of the reasons that even a minor non-success can foul up teaching. People who want to be effective college teachers are precisely the people who will seek out research on teaching and learning. If they don't read or hear experts normalizing failure, then they won't be able to see failure as anything except their own personal pedagogical shortcomings. Or, just as problematically, they'll view it exclusively as an indicator of their students' shortcomings. In both cases, that instructor is hurtling toward a world of hurt, depleted teaching self-efficacy, and, ultimately, burnout.

We'll make mistakes when we're teaching, and things will happen that could objectively be seen as failures (and are not just our demons talking). That should be a normal and expected part of teaching and learning. But when institutions implement inadequate, ill-informed assessments of teaching efficacy, faculty—especially VITAL faculty—mistakes are too often perceived as a summative judgment rather than an opportunity to keep improving. When something isn't working in our course design, learning assessments, or any aspect of our teaching practice, being able to critically reflect, make informed revisions, and try again is the primary way we improve our teaching skills. But contingent employment and standard review practices can prevent instructors from engaging in this essential reflection and learning.

Standards and measurements for teaching efficacy as part of the tenure review process can also be hazy or even completely unstated. This vagueness makes them susceptible to triggering Super Teacher stereotypes and unsubstantiated assumptions about what "good" teaching looks like. It can give vastly unbalanced weight to one failure, such as one class with a high DFW rate (the percentage of students in the class with a final grade of D or F, or who withdrew). This is particularly likely if review committees are assessing teaching efficacy solely via anonymous standardized end-of-the-term student evaluation of teaching forms. Unfortunately, you'll find inadequate or even actively damaging teaching evaluation practices everywhere from small regional community colleges to prestigious R1 universities.[37] And if a faculty member doesn't fit the racialized, gendered, and embodied stereotypes of what a professor "looks like" and/or what "good" teaching looks like, students can and do pounce on an instructor's minor misstep as a pretext for questioning the faculty member's entire subject area expertise and knowledge.

Faculty themselves tend to view teaching failures primarily as their own individual faults and flaws, which prevents us from being able to fully recognize factors like inequity, disconnection, and distrust that may be contributing to things going wrong. That view of teaching failure obscures all the ways that our failures may be "collateral damage" of contemporary academic workplaces "characterized by intensifying competitiveness, individualism, rationalization, ramped-up expectations, strategic aspirationalism, marketized hype [and] performance management."[38] Like failures during learning, teaching failures occur in a context that is highly personal yet simultaneously situational and institutional. When things go wrong, we first need to be able to identify intersecting complexities at various levels in different contexts before we can utilize a repair strategy.

Gear for Your Go-Bag

- Although some element of failure—struggle, setback, and mistakes—is a vital part of how our brains work when building new skills (including pedagogical skill), academic institutional systems, higher education employment inequities, and traditional grading create obstacles to learning and success.

- In addition to systemic and institutional ways that failure fouls up learning and teaching, individual and personal factors—such as perfectionism or fear of failure—contribute to how both students as well as faculty navigate learning and teaching failures.

Chapter 11

REPAIR STRATEGIES FOR FAILURE SNAFUS

When I began teaching, I quite wrongly assumed that students would just naturally understand that one poor grade on one small assignment was a minor setback. I didn't grasp how the ramifications for any type of failure can vary widely from student to student, based on their previous academic and life experiences and whatever current issues they may be having as a learner and, you know, a human person living in the world. Today, I know that a student's "interpretations of the experiences of failure" are shaped by a complicated "confluence of factors that contribute to academic failures—complex lives and contested identities," and that for students there is a "compounded effect of failure" on any other stressors in their lives.[1] For many students, writes scholar of higher education Moira Peelo, "failure is not an event but . . . a combination of moments of failure."[2]

In this chapter, I discuss how to identify those moments when a failure may become an avalanche and enact a repair strategy. I then show how four of the strategies described in part one and part two are especially valuable tools when we spot failure snafus—use a script, apologize, convey care, make revisions—and detail one final repair strategy that I call "lean into learning."

Identifying Failure Snafus

Failures in teaching can range from subtle and hard to spot to glaringly obvious. One persistent #ProfessorFail that hasn't grown easier over my decades of teaching is when my joke falls flat. I'm no stand-up comedian and don't aspire to be, but to make someone crack a smile (and vice versa) with one of my wry comments, mild snark, or witty wordplay is pretty much my favorite social interaction with anyone. So, when my joke lands with students in the on-site classroom—a live audience—man, what a rush! I'm not trying for guffaws but smiles and a chortle or two; that's a major win. Conversely, for me, it's a big fail when my joke flops. Crickets chirp as the tumbleweed rolls by, the sad symbol of my dead, dusty, unfunny joke. The absolute worst is when the joke worked in my 10:00 a.m. class but stunk up my 11:00 a.m. class with the reek of failure, even when I used the exact same words with the exact same intonation.

I'm describing this moment when things go wrong in Professor Neuhaus's classroom to illustrate an important point about identifying failure snafus. While we may be able to readily identify, by some objective measures, a failure in learning (i.e., a student cannot do the thing they need to be able to do) or teaching (i.e., joke ≠ funny = failure), we may very well not be able to immediately fully understand the experience of that failure. For some ultra-confident and outgoing professors, rattling off a jokey comment that misses its mark wouldn't be worth a second thought. For me, well, I'm stricken with remorse, asking myself why, oh, why did I ever open my big mouth? This is why STIR is useful when things go wrong because of failures. Stopping, thinking, and identifying are vital when navigating something as complex and as emotionally, socially, and cognitively fraught as failure.

Some failure snafus are foreseeable, while others can spring up seemingly out of nowhere. Some are within our power—our power to both cause them as well as to repair them. Some are not. In all cases, we can strive to identify the failure fissures and rumblings before they cause an avalanche.

Stop: Whether ours or a student's or multiple students', failure is never fun and the temptation to rush past it, to ignore it, and/or to pretend it's not happening is enormous. We need to resist that urge and instead halt and pay attention to what exactly is happening and be alert to the many different iterations and experiences of failure that might be occurring.

Think: Remembering the complexities of failure can help up identify what's going wrong, particularly the ways that academic failures are simultaneously highly individualized but at the same time deeply enmeshed with systemic failures. While not overintellectualizing the emotional and social impact of failure, we can productively apply our knowledge and understanding to what is happening.

Identify: We want to be able to name and begin to understand exactly how this mistake, misstep, or nonsuccess is manifesting as a failure.

Repair: Complete restorative repair may not be possible, but often we can at least lessen the negative consequences of teaching and learning failures.

Identifying failures is going to require concerted effort at stopping and thinking because, again, failure won't look the same for everyone all the time.

It won't be experienced the same way because frequently "failure may be *attributed* on the basis of poor performance but it is likely to be *felt* as a result of the constructs and personal interpretations the individual makes of the world" (original emphasis).[3] We have to discern different components of failure and be alert to different individual interpretations (including our own), in our classroom practices or student work or interactions between students or ourselves and students. Those failure pebbles are going to be rolling down the hill, but if we can build our ability to notice them while they're still pebbles, we may be able to make repairs before they accumulate into an avalanche. Eyler summarizes that "we should envision student failure as a spectrum that begins with small errors like inaccurate calculations and extends to significant conceptualizations that impede a student's ability to build knowledge."[4] Similarly, for faculty, small setbacks like a lecture that tanked, a poor choice of words during a class, or getting behind on providing feedback can accumulate into a big feeling of failure.

On the other hand, sometimes the failures are obvious but we need to prepare for what to do when we identify them. We know that sometimes a student will fumble, stumble, or fall and not be able to get back up. This is probably the most universal way that something can go wrong: a student enrolled in your class cannot successfully complete it. They can't do the necessary learning for any number of reasons, ranging from intensely personal to purely academic, or sometimes they've engaged in egregious academic dishonesty that leaves you no other option, or sometimes they simply disappear. Sometimes students really and truly fail, period. We can't casually accept it or lightly disregard it, and we really can't stop continually trying to reduce and mitigate its impact on students. But there will be times when there's no repairing a student failure.

Some educational philosophers and reformers might argue that when higher education is so flawed and inequitable, disconnection, and distrust undermine learning and success at every turn, we cannot let any student ever fail in our classes. It's certainly incumbent upon us to exert maximum efforts as instructors to do everything we can to ensure small student failures don't escalate, especially by planning assessment structures that do not reinforce the harms of traditional grading. But it would go against the very premise of this book to suggest to readers that we can, through our own individual pedagogical efforts, prevent students from ever failing our course completely. For people like us—educators who deeply care about student learning and success—one of the hardest, most painful parts of our job is when a student fails. Not in a small, non-success-as-part-of-growth, mistakes-leading-to-mastery kind of way but a no-class-credit or even withdrawal-from-college kind of way.

This can and should be as rare as it can possibly be, but there are times when things go so wrong that a student simply cannot succeed. Unless everything about every cultural, social, and educational structure in the entire world changes before this book is published (#UtopianVision), sometimes a student will fail your class. Occasionally you can even see it coming a mile away, so you pour in a ton of extra effort and time, throwing them every lifeline you can, hoping they'll get back on track, and then . . . they don't. At times it's almost made me physically ill, draining my supply of pedagogical and personal energy until my tanks run dry. The pandemic times magnified this dynamic, since so many external factors made student failures even more frustrating, fruitless, and stomach-churningly terrible. And for instructors also contending with employment precarity and/or student biases and stereotypes, personal frustrations about student failures can't be disentangled from broader teaching inequities.

Some hard-bitten professors accept students' major failures with no qualms whatsoever. They may even see failing students as an indicator of their own almighty academic "rigor."[5] *Snafu Edu* isn't for them, since they've entirely absolved themselves from any responsibility for student failures, are unbothered by student failures or have convinced themselves that they are, and certainly have zero interest in identifying their own teaching failures. Lucky them, I guess. It must be nice to live on Irreproachable Island where you never have to worry your big academic head about your teaching efficacy.

This is for the rest of us: when something goes so wrong for a student that they fail the class, there is still some benefit for employing STIR. Stopping and thinking—not torturing ourselves over what we maybe did wrong or endlessly rehashing the moment or moments that a student just really screwed up—can offer us some clarity. Stopping and thinking can be especially helpful for us when student failure is combined in some way with student incivility or outright hostility or has led to baseless accusations made toward you. Thinking through all the possible larger factors at play, including how inequity, disconnection, and distrust shape students' experiences, can provide some needed breathing room in situations crowded with all the extreme emotions and real concrete consequences of student failure. Similarly, STIR is a valuable tool for when *we've* made an error, our teaching has fallen short, and we've got a pedagogical failure on our hands.

Repair Strategy Redux: Responding to Failure

Utilized as part of STIR, there are four previously described repair strategies that can be especially useful when we, instructors and students both, feel like we have failed: (1) Use a script, (2) apologize, (3) convey care, and (4) make revisions.

Respond to Failure by Using a Script

Scripts enable us to do some advance thinking and preparation for how to respond when failures arise. The exact wording matters less than the approach of planning, and to some extent rehearsing, things we can say when our verbal response is an appropriate STIR strategy. In her article "Dealing with the Aftermath of Student Failure: Strategies for Nurse Educators," Nancy J. Franks includes some excellent examples of scripted statements that instructors could readily adapt for one-on-one meetings with a failing student:

> ➢ *"I have something to tell you that will be difficult to hear."*
> ➢ *"It sounds like you are angry."*
> ➢ *"I understand that you are disappointed."*
> ➢ *"The student handbook provides instructions for appealing this grade on page xx."*
> ➢ *"You may repeat this course next semester."*
> ➢ *"Sometimes when students struggle, there are other factors involved, such as excessive work hours or family concerns."*
> ➢ *"You demonstrated strong clinical skills, and I believe with additional time to study, you will succeed when you retake this course."*[6]

Importantly, in addition to the script recommendations, Frank spells out the need for faculty to take safety precautions in the emotionally volatile context of failure:

Some students become aggressive during these conversations, and potential for violent behavior exists. Positioning oneself near the door allows a quick exit if necessary. Carrying a phone with preprogrammed emergency numbers provides options for securing assistance quickly. Furthermore, asking campus security or other faculty to walk by during the conversation creates the opportunity for someone to intervene if necessary.[7]

This kind of advance preparation for student failure, folded into our scripted responses, is especially important given the increased likelihood of inappropriate, demeaning, or threatening student behavior during interactions with professors from historically minoritized groups. It's also a vital part of how instructors need to be prepared for the big emotions students experience around big failures, including stunned disbelief. As Frank notes, "Students often experience shock when hearing news of course failure. Despite verbal and written warnings and prescribed remediations, many students remain unaware of [inevitable imminent failure]."[8]

Respond to Failure by Apologizing

Coping with teaching failures can absorb a huge amount of cognitive and emotional energy. However, I've found that the second strategy that I discussed in chapter two—apologize—has been the most personally pedagogically empowering kind of scripted response in my go-bag. Identifying and repairing my teaching failures has become more automatic, far less draining, and easier all around since I got comfortable with apologizing when I've caused something to go wrong. I can stop obsessing over the mistake or, even better, not even start.

Crucial caveat: It's no accident that it got a lot easier for me to apologize to students after I got tenure. Also, I am white and able-bodied and I benefit from other social privileges. Context always matters. But when it's possible, and our failure is clear to us, we can own it. Owning it, and apologizing for it, can be extremely effective at helping everyone—you and your students—move forward, which is what we all want to do when we've made a mistake.

Respond to Failure by Conveying Care

We can't apologize when the failure is not ours to own, but we can—and should—convey care when students are mired in a failure experience. Because the experience of failure can have such an impact on students, conveying care at a pivotal moment can be extremely effective. Similarly, prioritizing care and compassion for ourselves when we flub something is essential to navigating failure snafus. Fully "fixing" failures in teaching and learning is frequently not possible, but conveying care can reduce their negative impact.

Respond to Failure by Making Revisions

Sometimes, with this previously discussed strategy—make revisions—we can minimize the fallout of a failure, and making revisions can also lead to fewer failures in the future. Again, context matters. When something goes wrong, when something fails, being able to scrap, rethink, and revise whole huge swathes of my classes and my pedagogy is possible in part because I have tenure, in part because I have certain embodied and social privileges, in part because I have been reading and writing and learning SoTL for years now, and in part because, as a writer at heart, I have a lot of learned skill at and even fondness for revising. It may take a lot of time and effort, but there's no agonizing over jettisoning what isn't working to try something new. Failure can be a catalyst. However, all that smugly said, revision isn't a cure-all; sometimes failures can't be fixed, and revising for future classes or interactions or assignments doesn't repair the failure at hand.

In *Connected Teaching*, Harriet Schwartz describes a process akin to STIR that includes a step for making revisions. This three-step model, gleaned from research on the psychology of workplace failures, is called "Stop. Regroup. Learn." Schwartz writes that "stopping to recognize the failure is an important first step. When we recognize failure in the midst of the experience, we might be able to make productive adjustments." We might also be able to "see the failure as concluded," notes Schwartz, which "allows us to begin to reflect, process and consult with others so as to gain clarity." Next, we regroup, seeking to "restore emotional balance and well-being [and] identifying one's emotions, which may include embarrassment, shame, guilt, dejection, frustration, and anger": "naming our emotions" may "help reduce the intensity of the feelings."[9]

Schwartz rightly reminds us that, just like students, educators are swimming in a messy soup of cognitive, emotional, and social experiences of failure, and being more cognizant of how to identify and name what's happening can keep one failure from crushing us. In the final step, continues Schwartz, "we seek to learn from the experience" because "people who operate from a learning orientation are more likely to successfully navigate failure." For educators, this learning step includes "recalibrating a sense of what is our responsibility and what is our students'," a vitally important part of pedagogical learning when we're grappling with perfectionism (I see you lurking over there, PowerPoint-wielding demon) and tend to overstate our own role in any one student's failures.[10]

I want to turn now to a final repair strategy that we can use not only when failures are snafuing teaching and learning but also pretty much anytime things are going wrong: lean into learning.

Lean into Learning

Listen, college professors are hella smart. They're highly trained, top-notch scientists, linguists, scholars, artists, researchers, and thinkers. They're the bona fide, certified authorities in their fields. To say that faculty are expert learners is a huge understatement. Pursuing new knowledge in their scholarly fields is more than a job: learning is their passion and their vocation. So, in what possible scenario could these people—academics with vast neural networks of sophisticated thinking skills in their skulls—flat out refuse to learn? I'll give you three little hints: L. M. S.

In 2023, when the SUNY Plattsburgh faculty had to learn how to use a new learning management system (from Moodle to D2L Brightspace, if you really want to know, you geek), I saw up close and in excruciating detail exactly how difficult learning how to do something new can be when one is (a) supersmart and completely capable of learning how to do a thing but (b) doesn't feel meaningfully invested in learning how to do the thing and resents being told they have to learn how to do the thing. It was a powerful reminder of just how difficult it is to learn how to do something new, period. When learning something outside their area of expertise—a whole new set of skills—most faculty were like any other human person learning something new: they found it to be frustrating, confusing, and wearisome. Surprise! Professors are human people! And for people, learning is often more than merely "challenging" or even "hard to achieve." Lots of times, learning is a real bummer.

I need to emphasize this harsh reality before describing my final strategy for when things go wrong, and especially when failure—ours or our students' or both—fouls up teaching and learning. Because when I advocate that we "lean into learning," I want to make it absolutely clear that this is not a facile admonition to make sweet, lip-smacking learning lemonade out of the bitter lemons of failure. I'm not suggesting everything always works out or that every failure can, should, and will lead to personal and professional learning and growth, so we should just sit back and enjoy the journey to Flunksville and tell our students to do the same. But I am arguing that when failures threaten to bury us as educators, we can name those failures and try to understand them as part of the long, slow, laborious work we must do to accrue pedagogical knowledge and skills over the course of our teaching careers. When our students struggle with failures, we may be able to help them reframe what's happening as one part of some (difficult, draining, expensive, exhausting, often overwhelming) necessary learning in college and preparation for the future. Leaning into learning when we fail can also help us see more clearly how systemic and situational factors contributed to the failure.

Needless to say, "we can learn from failure" isn't an original idea. But what I want to strenuously acknowledge here is that failure can make us, educators and students both, feel horrible. Learning from failures is rarely if ever a PG-rated tale about a plucky protagonist who faces hardships but triumphs over adversity with a song in his heart and the friends he made along the way by his side. Learning from failures is more frequently a hard-R-rated, gritty, unpleasant slog punctuated by profanity and characterized by isolation, pain, and unsatisfying endings with little resolution. We can lean into the learning that failure generates but not before we discard some of the biggest clichés and oversimplifications that we may have picked up about failure from our culture in general and academia specifically. In an essay on failure in higher education, John Horton reminds us that

> we should guard against the impulse to speak about failures in ways which become instrumentally self-aggrandizing, which perpetuate a sense that failure should lead to individualized success or personal development, or which exert a kind of pressure to triumph-over-adversity. Instead, a more critical and careful apprehension of failures in the academy should permit other kinds of less acknowledged experiences: of failures with no happy endings; of failures which just go nowhere; of situations where there is just no good news or redemptive story . . . of disappointment, distress, devastation, hopelessness.[11]

I would add that our teaching failures and our students' academic failures may frequently feel exactly like the last types of failures described by Horton. They have a horrible tendency to tick all those boxes: "no happy endings," "situations where there is no good news," and "disappointment, distress, and devastation."

As Harriet Schwartz notes, teaching failures can feel like a "grievous injury."[12] So when I say that failure leads to learning, and as educators we can lean into learning when failure strikes, I'm agreeing with the SoTL authors who encourage us to view and to help our students view failure as an "agent of change" and that "to learn from failure we need to engage in systemic, deliberate

reflection through exploration and analysis of failure in our practice."[13] But I'm also emphasizing that such change, reflection, and
learning, whether it's the skills and content learning our students
do or the pedagogical learning we do, is emotionally and cognitively grueling. Still, at those times, I believe we can lean in.

"Lean in" means "persevere in spite of risk and difficulty," a
concept problematically promulgated by Sheryl Sandberg in her
2013 book by the same name.[14] Sandberg was roundly criticized
for seeming to suggest to women that our workplaces are inequitable and rife with sexism—but suck it up, buttercup, and get
to climbing that corporate ladder, because it's all about your individual determination.[15]

I want to reclaim and redeploy this phrase "lean in" in the context
of teaching and learning. For educators and for students, "lean into
learning" is never easy and might not fully repair a situation. Learning won't always lead seamlessly to an improved situation or a personal victory. However, it can keep our heads above the rocks and
debris of the avalanche by allowing us to deploy one of the best skill
sets that educators possess: we know how to build our knowledge
about something. We know how to assess, reflect, study, examine,
test, and stretch our brains to absorb new ideas and increase our
understanding of a topic. It can help us understand and gain what
we can from failure. We will need to identify what's working well
and address what's going wrong when we are becoming effective
teachers. That's going to entail using the ol' noodle and puzzling it
out. As Yoda might say, learn must you, and I'm confident that you
are really, really, really good at learning. Really.

"Lean into learning" can also be a good way of understanding
the more systemic and institutional aspects of failure. By positioning failure as a site of laborious, sometimes gut-wrenching
learning, we are going to be able to better see all the outside and
contributing factors in failure and not letting ourselves default to
thinking we're just "bad teachers" or even that a student is simply
ill-prepared for college. Instead, we can try to identify what kinds
of inequities, disconnections, and distrust snafus are being exacerbated right now by our educational systems, political pressures,
national and global events, and having a direct impact on this

particular non-success. For most scholars and researchers like us, "Strap on your thinking cap and get to pondering big issues and problems, some of which are beyond your control" is a welcome invitation. It's an empowering and uplifting modus operandi for cerebral people, and it can armor us against the slings and arrows of failure. I would argue that this is not overintellectualizing or distancing ourselves from the big emotional taxations of failure but rather making good use of the exact same abilities that got us through our advanced degree getting: our big nerdy noggins and our high-octane brain juice.

Happily, leaning into learning is not only a repair strategy for failures; it can also help us cultivate awareness of everything we and our students do that is successful. If you're paying attention because you are intent upon extracting every ounce of learning you can, you will increase your ability to spot successes alongside the failures. Because learning is hard, because the "downward spiral" is powerful, and because perfectionism is endemic, it's all too easy to miss the wins. Getting in the habit of documenting and recording and noticing everything you've done to facilitate student success is professionally, personally, and pedagogically energizing, especially because, when we're teaching, the wins can feel so small and the failures can feel so boulder sized. Systemic problems like bad teaching evaluation practices and inequitable teaching conditions heap boulders on top of boulders. So we've got to lean in and look closely for the successes.

That's what "lean into learning" will mean for our students too. You do not ever want to be in the position of unctuously reminding a distressed/discouraged/economically exhausted/irate student that their failure is just a stepping stone on the road to success and knowledge. When students are stuck in a failure experience, that's not the time or place to bring out the "lean into learning" speech. The best implementation of "lean into learning" for our students is to work toward creating assignments and classes that give students opportunities to engage in productive failure no matter how their individual, situational, and institutional context is shaping their experiences of failure. By doing so, we can increase the odds of their success—and ours.

Gear for Your Go-Bag

- There's no getting around it: failure feels bad and it can have significant negative consequences for learners and educators.
- Four repair strategies that can be especially helpful for responding to students' failures as well as our own failures are: Use a script, apologize, convey care, and make revisions.
- Without suggesting that all failures result in positive learning experiences or oversimplifying how hard it is to learn, as trained scholars and expert thinkers faculty have a valuable tool for understanding failure: our ability to study, reflect on, and embrace the opportunity for increasing knowledge that often accompanies failures.

Chapter 12

INCREASING SUCCESS

When we're trying to dodge the failure boulders that constantly threaten us, we can feel like Wile E. Coyote opening a laughably tiny parasol to protect himself from a Road Runner–engineered avalanche or Acme brand falling anvil. It's not humanly possible to eliminate failure altogether but we can reduce the negative impact of some failures and create more chances for success. Strategies discussed in the previous chapters for increasing equity, connection, and trust all go a long way toward increasing success for students and for instructors. Additionally, we can scaffold assignments, make time for lots of practice, and create grading and assessment structures that increase success. Perhaps most importantly, we can normalize setbacks and mistakes, establish psychological safety for learning, and create some big, strong, boulder-proof shelter against all those falling rocks.[1]

Scaffold and Practice

Being aware of the important role that productive failure plays for human beings who are increasing their knowledge and skills, we can design our classes, and especially our assessment and class grading systems, to create pathways for the failure pebbles to roll harmlessly to the bottom of the mountain instead of starting a deadly avalanche. Namely, we can increase opportunities for students to demonstrate their learning. Offering multiple ways throughout the class for students to show what they've learned is not only a key part of inclusive teaching practices as discussed in part one but also an essential part of increasing success.

But hold up a minute: students may not readily perceive it this way! Even as you're conscientiously planning more opportunities for students to demonstrate their learning, students themselves may be arriving to your class most familiar with the do-or-die assessment structure of a couple of high-stakes exams or assignments. On the face of it, without a good understanding of how learning works, students may only be able to view more opportunities to demonstrate their learning as unnecessary additional work or, even worse, pointless "busywork"—or, the real kicker, just more ways that they could fail.[2] Right about now I can see readers throwing up their hands in despair. "Let me get this straight," you're saying. "Students *need* more opportunities to demonstrate their learning, but many students might *resent or be hostile toward* instructors who design their classes this way?"

I hear you. Because they're usually so intertwined with grades and so shaped by outside academic systems and students' previous experiences, assessment structures can be an abundant fount of teaching and learning distrust, disconnection, inequity, and failure. So we return to the need for cultivating clarity and transparency with students. As part of cultivating clarity when scaffolding, we need to concertedly frame and make sure students understand that such additional learning opportunities are not a matter of meaningless quantity but rather scaffolded to increase success. "Scaffolding" means providing support for complex learning tasks by structuring assignments explicitly built on previous knowledge, such as dividing large projects into smaller assignments that give students time to make changes and improvements.[3] Ideally, we can also help students to reflect on and identify their own progress toward the major learning goal as part of a scaffolded assignment.

Take, for example, the research paper. When I began teaching as a graduate student whose main talent in life was writing research papers, I assigned research papers to my own students much like I did them myself in graduate school: "Do a research paper. Use lots of sources. It's 50 percent of your grade." This didn't work, for many reasons—not the least of which was that I was practically handing students an engraved invitation to hire someone else to write the damn thing for them. My students needed a lot of practice and feedback for each step of the research paper process. They needed instruction and support for finding, reading, and summarizing sources. Students needed more chances to not do very well on something, get my feedback, apply my feedback, and then do it better.

Today, when I give a research paper assignment, students first submit a required and assessed but ungraded research proposal, then a low-stakes preliminary bibliography, followed by a revised bibliography where they apply my previous feedback. Subsequent assignments incorporate a range of grading techniques, including a self-assessment component. Fortuitously, my revisions to the research paper also correspond nicely with proven ways to increase student learning with scaffolded assignments. This revised assignment structure has some major advantages over the high-stakes, do-or-die, one-shot-is-all-you-get, previous iteration of my assignment. Most relevant to this chapter, my revised assignment structure fully accounts for the reality of failures.

For example, it accounts for the difficulties I know many of my students will have locating, accessing, and correctly citing sources by requiring a preliminary bibliography—required and assessed but not graded. When they flub it the first time around, and many of them *will* flub it, they'll get my feedback and then have the chance to apply my feedback and locate, access, and correctly cite sources. This time it will be for a grade, which includes assessing how well they applied my previous feedback. This not only reduces the negative impact of failure but also encourages the exact type of productive failure that increases skills and learning. That necessary step is built in—required, assessed, and graded—but the next step of revising and improving creates opportunities for what I heard Sara Rose Cavanagh term "early wins" in the long process of writing a research paper, starting from a place of strength with a small stake but successfully completed step forward.[4] Yay! Woohoo!

Built on early wins, my scaffolded research paper assignment gives students meaningful opportunities to receive and apply my feedback. Effective feedback is a vast topic, a book unto itself.[5] What I want to highlight here is that assignment and class design that includes scaffolding to allow productive struggle and failure without unduly harsh consequences creates a framework for instructors to give timely, applicable feedback. In my research paper assignments, for example, after the first assignment, each subsequent assignment requires students to briefly summarize my previous feedback and explain how they've applied it to their current work— to identify where they've gotten my expert assistance, correction, and encouragement, and how they've applied it to increasing their skills and abilities. Feedback in this context is more readily meaningful for students, who benefit from seeing the clear (mandatory) line between "what Professor Neuhaus told me about my writing" and "making sure I understand what Professor Neuhaus told me about my writing because I have to apply it to the next assignment."

Giving students truly formative feedback that they are required, not just suggested, to think about, engage with, and apply is at the center of scaffolding. It also encourages students to build their metacognition skills when we incorporate self-reflection assignments, incentivizing learning from mistakes. For instance, when students can earn partial credit for a corrected exam question, including explaining why they got it wrong the first time and how your feedback helped them understand it better, that is a real, tangible way that your feedback is useful and frames errors as learning opportunities. I often assign general self-reflection assignments to students, asking them questions like *"What mistakes have you made so far this semester?" "How do you plan on correcting this mistake going forward?"* and *"What can you do better now that you've made this mistake and figured out what went wrong?"* Scaffolding in this sense is reframing "failure" as a to-be-expected part of learning.

More broadly than a single project, scaffolding for increasing student success often begins before undertaking specific tasks related to the content. It can start with relearning what they thought they knew about how to succeed academically—namely, how to study effectively. One of our first scaffolded steps may therefore be providing study guides, tips, and information about how, for example, rereading and highlighting are much less effective than spaced retrieval practice.[6] Depending on your student population, discussing time management skills may be part of this preliminary scaffolding. And in all my classes, we spend time—like, a lot of time—going through the LMS setup, including having each student locate exactly where they will find my feedback, grades, and so on, on whatever device they're most likely to be using in the future.

We are, together, right off the bat, using our valuable, expensive, on-campus class meeting time for hands-on doing. We're practicing. In combination with scaffolding, such tasks as course design, class activities, and assignments that prioritize practice will increase student success. It's an inclusive teaching practice, because allocating time for practice means we are also planning for student variability in student reading, study, and research skills, and different life circumstances that create additional obstacles to completing reading and research for some students. Setting aside class time for hands-on work instead of delivering new information or content won't set back any students because *all* students need practice—repeated practice—to learn. Allotting more in-class time for review, workshopping projects, or practicing problems helps everyone learn.

Moreover, most students also need practice asking for clarifications and assistance from their professors. In-class work time normalizes students needing time to practice and, when they've hit a bump, discussing the issue with you and, ideally, other students. In-class work time emphasizes that this incredibly valuable educational real estate is for students to actually do stuff and not for professorial windbaggery. It can ensure that you are giving time and attention to students learning how to do exactly what it is you are going to grade and assess, rather than limiting assessment to final products shaped in part by their individual and variable life circumstances, such as employment and family responsibilities. It can increase equity, connection, trust, and student success, one class meeting at a time. Practice is nothing short of central to what science says about learning and what the evidence points to as equity-minded teaching practices that assess the skills they're building rather than their life circumstances.[7]

As James M. Lang emphasizes: "Students should have frequent opportunities to practice *in-class* whatever cognitive skills that you want them to master, and that you will be assessing for a grade [original emphasis]."[8] So instead of plowing ahead to the next chapter, concept, or reading, use the class meeting solely for review activities. Instead of presuming that every student is going to complete the entire project outside of class, schedule workshop days when students work on assignments in class and you're on hand to provide feedback and assistance on the spot. Instead of shrugging off the fact that the majority of students got problem X wrong on the exam, use class time to practice problem X and allow students to resubmit corrected answers for partial credit.

One final note on scaffolding and practice: scaffolded assessment structures like the one I've developed for my research paper assignment is not just a tried-and-true, pedagogically effective approach to learning but also the way of the future. It minimizes the odds of student plagiarism and cheating because AI generators, paper writers for hire, Chegg, etc., are not good at applying individualized feedback, explaining how that feedback has been applied on the next assignment, or engaging in self-assessment and reflection based on one's own specific, unique learning and progress.

Thwarting ChatGPT while providing numerous, ongoing opportunities for practice draws on a whole bunch of proven evidence-based teaching and learning strategies, such as "flipping" the classroom, active learning, and interleaving.[9] However, it's not easy to cede valuable in-class real estate in order to give students supervised practice time. It means reducing content "coverage" for more time dedicated to practicing, correcting, and revising. We may face outside pressures—from departments and accreditation institutions—to cram in as much subject area info as we can. We may also be stuck in "should-ing" mode, as in students *should* be able to do these things on their own outside of class. Should-ing might make you feel self-righteous for a minute, but it won't help you figure out how to increase students' success. Not the students you *should* have because you are so very smart and learned. Not the students you *should* have if K–12 education wasn't going to hell in a handbasket. The students you *do* have, period. The ones sitting with you in the classroom or logging onto your LMS. When we want to be effective teachers, we must pay attention to and set aside class time for doing things that will help the students we do have to succeed, sometimes in ways that can feel unrelated to the subject area learning outcomes.

Forcing yourself to cut down on subject area content when possible and making time for lots of practice is going to help your students learn and succeed. What may be even harder for us to do, being the expert academics we are, is to accept that practice is also required for our own pedagogical learning. In other words, there's no shortcut to increasing our teaching skills. It takes a lot of skillful, informed, reflective practice, emerging out of what we learn from SoTL, from talking with other teachers, and from our own lived experiences, including all our #ProfessorFails. Yet, I would be remiss if I didn't also remind you that pedagogical learning and reflection as part of our teaching practice must be sustainable, especially if we're working in a particularly inequitable, precarious environment and/or in the face of majorly disruptive outside factors. As human beings with limits to our cognitive, psychological, and physical resources, our pedagogical learning, reflection, changes, and improvements need to be feasible and realistic.

This is a good place to note that all the time, energy, and emotion given over to teaching labor must be sustainable because next I'm going to delve into the single biggest time and energy suck in college teaching: grading.

Reduce the Harm of Grades

As an undergraduate student at a small liberal arts college in the late 1980s, I had a good but not outstanding GPA. I earned high grades in the classes I took as part of my major, but my effort was sporadic in other courses. I coasted through many classes on my strong writing skills, so I expected to ace a required English class.

To my surprise, I earned a low grade on a big paper, and while I don't remember the professor's specific feedback or exactly what we talked about during my subsequent visit to his office, I do remember feeling stuck in a power struggle with the guy and fuming resentfully about it while I laboriously made every one of his suggested revisions. When I got the paper back, there was a big red A+ on the top. I honestly don't know if it was the professor's intention or not, but I was convinced that this A+ had little to do with the quality of my work and everything to do with my compliance and acquiescence to his ego-driven need to feel superior.[10] It just really seemed to me that this was a *sarcastic* A+, like he was telling me that by making every single change and revision he suggested, I'd transformed my previously unacceptable writing into a shining example of sheer A+ perfection.

I doubt that you will ever need to deal with a student complaining about a "sarcastically" high grade they earned in your class. But the underlying cause of my experience is very typical, and every college instructor *will* have to deal with it on a regular basis, i.e., the ways that grades snafu learning. I did not view this A+ grade as constructive feedback that would help me improve my writing skill—a skill that I genuinely cared about and wanted to build. The final grade did not measure or reflect my authentic learning but rather signified my willingness to do precisely what the man in charge was telling me to do with my intellectual labor. I had to figure out exactly how to "do what the teacher wanted," no more and no less, or suffer the grade-related consequences.

Ungrading advocate and scholar of education Susan D. Blum would call this an example of "the game of school," in which compliance is students' main task.[11] In this "game," a student's experience of grades and experience of failure are often indistinguishable. Blum and other critics of traditional educational systems assert that standard grading practices are an integral part of the ways schooling can systemically interfere with rather than facilitate student learning. They argue that the problems with standard grading make the adoption of nontraditional grading and assessment practices at all levels a pedagogical imperative in the twenty-first century.

As much as I dislike traditional grading structures for how they inhibit intellectual and academic growth and development and how they do not adequately account for necessary, productive failure, I am not a hard-core ungrading evangelical. I don't believe in all-or-nothing when it comes to using nontraditional grading. For one thing, inequities and disconnection facing educators makes ungrading a significantly heavier lift for some faculty than for others. When a faculty member is already navigating student biases, the additional teaching work, including intellectual and emotional labor, required to transparently explain ungrading practices and build student trust around it increases. Scholar and professor of higher education Laila McCloud points out that "the discourse around ungrading as a liberatory pedagogical practice has ignored the ways that white supremacy and whiteness impact its implementation" and offers this cautionary note: "I do believe in the transformative potential of ungrading. I also believe that this practice warrants additional consideration of the labor associated with it, particularly for Black women faculty. Black faculty are often celebrated for our innovative pedagogical skills; however, the implementation of these skills come with a cost that cannot be overlooked or misunderstood."[12]

Because of this "cost that cannot be overlooked or misunderstood," I too am cautious about overemphasizing the "transformative potential of ungrading" and nontraditional grading. Additional "costs" of ungrading arise when we also consider employment precarity, teaching load, class size, and support (or lack of it) for productive pedagogical reflection.

It's also important to acknowledge that ungrading assessment practices increase the need for clarity, transparency, scaffolding, and practice. Equity-minded instructors interested in ungrading, or any nontraditional grading, need to be aware that neurodivergent, first-generation, and historically minoritized students may have previously thrived with, and continue to appreciate, external motivators and traditional grading systems in academic settings. Additionally, the advisor, tutors, counselors, and coaches who work directly with students rely on letter grades as a basic communication of and shared language about how the student is doing academically. If final class grades are an institutional requirement—as they are at most colleges and universities—but the instructor has not provided students with clear, ongoing, and grade-informed feedback, implicit biases are as likely to impact the final course grade in an "ungraded" class as it would the final grade in a traditionally graded class.[13]

One of the main reasons that I use a mix of traditional and non-traditional grading—and advocate for this approach in my work as an educational developer—is because of how grades intersect with deeply entrenched student fears of failure, exacerbated by elements of inequity, disconnection, and distrust. Decreasing those fears and increasing success depends on utter transparency, which is a lot more difficult to achieve if you are implementing a grading schema totally unlike any the student has previously encountered. It's like when you throw open the cage door for a creature raised entirely in captivity. Yes, freedom awaits, but they're extremely cautious about stepping out into the wild, and rightly so. There are unknown deprivations and deadly predators out there! The cage is confining, but at least every inch of it is familiar ground. So I plan, with my assessment mechanisms, a way to ease students out of that grading cage bit by bit with what I think of as a grading combo platter that mixes traditional grading with nontraditional grading and assessment. In this way, I'm doing what many faculty member do: adapt and use various *combinations* of different systems and schemes.[14]

You'll recall the original research paper assignment I used to give to students was assessed identically to how professors assessed my own graduate level work. A visual representation of the assignment would look like figure 2. The only assessment was a final, summative assessment, culminating in a standard letter grade. In my revised research paper assignment, the one I use now, a visual representation of the different types of assessment and the proportional breakdown of those assessments looks like figure 3.

Students must complete each component before submitting the subsequent assignment. For instance, students must submit a preliminary list of sources for which I won't be giving them a letter

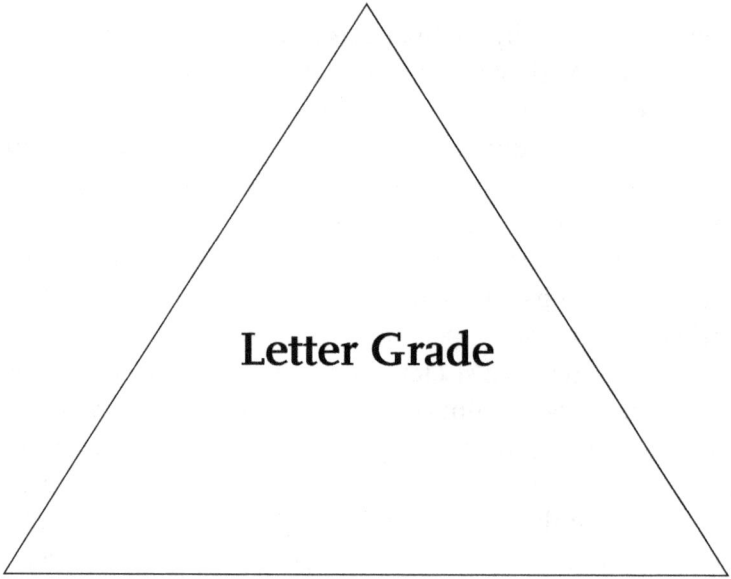

Figure 2

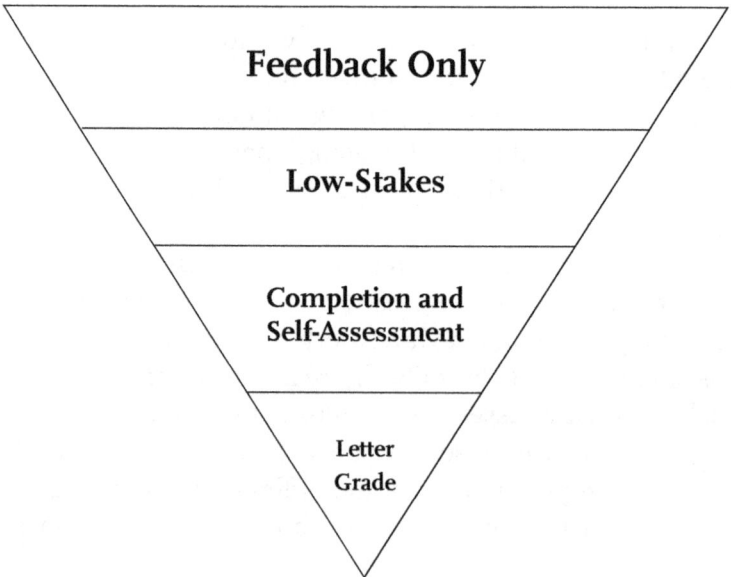

Figure 3

or point grade, only feedback. But they can't submit the graded list of sources assignment without a summary of how they applied my previous feedback. In this pyramid structure, I've made plenty of room for errors by scaffolding and creating a lot of opportunities for formative feedback and corrections without penalty.

In their landmark SoTL work on nontraditional and alternative grading, including their 2023 book *Grading for Growth*, mathematics professors David Clark and Robert Talbert define many of the techniques we can draw on when designing these types of assignments, showing how faculty can implement nontraditional grading in a variety of teaching contexts. They argue that all varieties of effective alternative grading are based on four "pillars":

1. Student work is evaluated using clearly defined and context-appropriate content standards for what constitutes acceptable evidence of learning.
2. Students are given helpful, actionable feedback that the student can and should use to improve their learning.
3. Student work doesn't have to receive a mark, but if it does, the mark is a progress indicator toward meeting a standard and not an arbitrary number.
4. Students can reassess work without penalty, using the feedback they receive, until the standards are met or exceeded.

Clark and Talbert go on to emphasize that, rather than "devise a new grading system with a cool name, we think it's more beneficial to set up a big tent with a lot of room underneath for anybody who wants to implement these elements in their grading process, no matter what they call it."[15]

Again, our teaching context matters. The classes where I assign research papers are relatively small, and I am a white, tenured full professor, factors that directly contribute to my ability to include nontraditional graded components without fear of unduly incurring a professional cost or creating an unsustainable workload for myself. And frankly, no matter what your teaching context, moving away from low-structure class design where a final grade is based on a few high-stakes, traditionally graded assignments and instead using any amount of nontraditional grading. . . well, that is a lot of work for instructors. Let me repeat that: it's a lot of additional work.

Here I could say, something about how the extra work is so worth it, my friends! That's true, but I think it's more convincing and equally true to say that although using some or a lot of nontraditional grading does not reduce teaching labor per se, it makes the labor of assessing student learning less onerous. It won't reduce the number of minutes you spend reviewing and assessing student work; it might even increase them. However, while nontraditional grading—especially adding nongraded assignments and self-assessments to a scaffolded project—may technically take more time to review and grade than one big high-stakes exam, in many ways it is not as difficult and can be far more rewarding. The labor to reduce the harm of traditional grading systems and grades to *students* can also reduce the harm of grading to *faculty*.

For example, if you're an equity-minded instructor, you're probably concerned about the ways traditional grading practices are shaped by unconscious biases.[16] Institutional and situational aspects of a student's academic experiences weigh heavily on us when we're assigning traditional grades that, within our current systems, are the biggest factor in determining if a student is successful or not. Nontraditional grading practices may relieve some of that stress. Or take again the issues of plagiarism and cheating: using nontraditional grading as part of scaffolding and practice can reduce the temptation to cheat or plagiarize. Dealing with such ethical breaches is one of the most unpleasant, demoralizing aspects of our grading work.

Just in terms of our work time and what daily teaching encompasses, which would you rather do for hours on end?

> **Option A.** Delineate in tedious detail the difference between a C– and a C and go over the numbers repeatedly to make sure you didn't make an error in your calculations because one of these grades will enable a student to continue in their major and one won't. So, the stakes are huge for everyone, including yourself, because you happen to know that

this student is going to go ballistic if it's a C– and complain to the chair, the dean, and the president and make your life a living hell for months to come.

Option B. Craft some formative feedback, based on your subject area expertise, that the student will use to improve their work in a revision of the assignment or the next assignment.

Yup, it's a real brainteaser all right. Which would you rather?!?

This is my ace in the hole, the real selling point: alternative grading practices can significantly decrease the number of frustrating, irritating, emotionally shattering interactions you have with students who are frantic, angry, baffled, indignant, or devastated by their grade. Most of us don't find arguing about a B+ versus an A– with a hostile, disrespectful student—or listening to a tearful student beg for a better grade as they relate horror show–like details of a personal trauma—gratifying and fulfilling aspects of teaching work. To reduce that type of labor, we should seriously consider anything we can do to lessen the eviscerating harm—for students and for ourselves—that grades can do.

Normalize Mistakes and Setbacks

I was once part of a campus "Student Success Consortium" that met to discuss the wide variety of issues that contribute to or impede student success. As a thought experiment, we all had to answer this question: "If you could choose one thing to change on campus that would help students succeed, what would it be?" It was supposed to be realistic, so "Throw out the whole concept of 'general education' and instead help every student craft their own unique learning program" probably wasn't going to fly. And "Surgically implant the desire to be an effective teacher, and the willingness to engage pedagogical reflection, directly into the brain stems of the few tenured professors on campus who are objectively awful in the classroom but will never face any professional consequences for their terrible teaching" wasn't on the table. This is what I said instead: "More instructors should plan for and communicate to students that when students hit an obstacle or fall behind in class, there are numerous ways to get back on track."

We have the power, as individual instructors, to increase success for all students by providing and helping students access "on-ramps" to get back on track when they've had a setback. This doesn't necessarily require extensive course revision, but it does require that we build in ways for students who miss some work or do poorly on a few things to recover and to continue forward in the class successfully. We can create conditions for students to safely stumble in a class, learn from their mistakes, and get back on track, because "the key to dealing with failure in higher education is to accept it as a normal and desirable part of the learning experience."[17] We can normalize mistakes and setbacks.

Personally, it's not too difficult for me to convey to students that I want them to succeed. In addition to course design that implicitly gives students this message, I've gotten in the habit of saying clearly and frequently "I want you to succeed." Simple and to the point, "I want you to succeed" can be readily tailored for specific occasions as well:

> ➤ *"I know that some of you are nervous about your presentation and I want everyone to do well. That's why we're spending the next two class periods practicing."*
> ➤ *"I want everyone to successfully complete this assignment, so we're going to workshop it today in class, and I'm offering a help session later this week."*

What's more difficult to convey to students is that I also want them to fail—not in any way that undermines their academic progress but in all the ways people we need to trip up, struggle, and push through to build our knowledge and skills.

Perhaps the most direct and essential way individual instructors have the power to do this is in how we assess and grade students' work. Kelly Hogan and Viji Sathy point out that in order to normalize making mistakes, grading structures must provide students the opportunity to do exactly that, without knocking them totally off course. They point out that grading systems are "how we show students it is OK to make mistakes" and offer some specific examples of how our grading structures can do this: "Allow a score on a cumulative final exam to replace a previous exam, enabling a student to demonstrate growth. Weight assessments early in the semester less heavily than assessments later in the semester to help students learn from mistakes. Drop the lowest grade or quiz, designating some quizzes available for retaking, and giving points back after a student makes corrections to an exam to encourage students to reflect on their responses and motivate them to aim for proficiency of the material." Grading schemes like these, argue Hogan and Sathy, help convey to students that "one bad day or one misstep need not derail a student's plans" or be interpreted by the student as a sign they don't belong in the discipline or in college.[18]

Similarly, Kevin Gannon asserts that we need to carefully consider how we can prepare students "to encounter failure with the tools to render it merely an interruption in, not the end of, their story in higher education." He suggests faculty "consider strategies you might adopt to allow students the opportunity to learn from initial experiences of failure: perhaps revisions or rewrites accompanied by a brief self-reflection, or allowing them to submit corrected (researched and cited) answers for an examination for partial grade credit."[19] Reducing the harms of grades in the ways suggested by Hogan, Sathy, and Gannon goes hand in hand with normalizing mistakes and setbacks. It's a clear example of how we can plan for and help students engage in productive, necessary struggle while avoiding what educational developer and scholar Larry D. Spence terms "harmful mistakes," and instead "promote learning from mistakes and failures."[20]

To illustrate his point, Spence describes his childhood experience of learning to ride a two-wheel bike: After a day of "screwing up, recovering, and getting back on," his bike was "scratched and banged" and his legs were bruised, "pedal-dented and scratched." He could "barely walk," but after hours of physically harmful mistakes, he learned how to ride a bike. Training wheels would have reduced injury but would not have helped him learn because "to balance a bike, you have to shift your weight away from the direction the bike tilts" and "if the bike doesn't tilt you can't learn."

Spence then describes a better way to learn: "Start with a small bicycle that allows the rider to put their feet flat on the ground while sitting, take off the pedals, and have the rider use their feet to scooter and coast the bike around an empty parking lot. As soon as the rider can keep the bike balanced, add the pedals. . . . [The] bike can wobble but it won't fall. The rider's errors are learning opportunities. The mistakes aren't suppressed and they don't hurt." As Spence concludes, this method of learning how to ride a bike does not "eliminate errors" nor does it "reduce the challenge of learning, but it limits the consequences of errors to allow for quick recovery."[21] It's a highly apt metaphor for course design and grading schemata that normalize mistakes and failures.

A class that accounts for making errors but also provides support for "quick recovery" from those errors has what the SoTL describes as a positive error climate or constructive error climate.[22] Joshua Eyler argues that we need to facilitate "an error-positive" classroom climate, in which "faculty believe that errors and mistakes provide valuable opportunities for growth and learning, and they design courses and assignments that reflect this belief."[23] While the concept of positive error climate and productive struggle has been especially well explored in STEM-specific SoTL, dance professor Donna Mejia draws on these approaches to normalize mistakes and errors in her college classes, especially those that challenge students to engage in critical reflection and small class discussion about such complicated and "hot" topics such as race, ethnicity, and embodied identity.[24]

In Mejia's classes, everyone agrees ahead of time that they will support each other's efforts to "fumble forward":

> To keep a space of inquiry open in a charged subject matter, students will preface their public commentary by saying "I'm about to fumble with my words." The community responds as a chorus with "Fumble Forward!" It is our social contract to let confusion be a part of our discourse. Perhaps the student is unsure of the terminologies needed to join the conversation. Perhaps they are unsure if their questions will be

offensive. Perhaps they don't have fully formulated ideas and opinions yet. But for the next few minutes, we've all agreed to suspend judgement, lean in, and help each other clarify [our ideas].[25]

Struggle, errors, and less-then-perfect articulation are not road-blocks but milestones as the student stumbles forward in their progress. It's an excellent example of encouraging students to "fail forward."[26]

Mejia's approach powerfully normalizes making mistakes. "Fumble" is a gentler word than "fail" and far less entangled with standard grading structures in which "fail" means "completely and utterly fail forever, goodbye and good luck, you'll need it." Yet "fumbling" contains elements of productive failure that can move us forward toward better understanding and increased skill, even as we're dropping the ball. The underlying concept is one that can be adapted to different types of classes and content, with the emphasis on how, in the classroom, we will be accountable to each other when we mess up, but part of being accountable includes helping each other regain our footing when we stumble.

As Mejia emphasized in an interview on the *Tea for Teaching* podcast, "Fumble Forward" is "not intended to be an escape route" or a way to jettison responsibility for harmful mistakes:

I think communication is always about trying, about leaving the door open and ajar to a possibility. But I've also done quite a bit of study around harmful individuals that quite honestly may have pathological levels of communication dysfunction, or may thrive [on] or enjoy inflicting pain, and being tormenting in the kind of words they slang around. So I think we've all encountered those high-conflict individuals. And so fumble forward again, is about giving them the possibility to choose differently. But if at times they're not willing to make that choice then a boundary is needed. And safety is more important than everything.[27]

It's an important caution: providing students with the opportunities for errors and missteps necessary for learning does not mean allowing unchecked harm or endangerment to us or to other students. Fumbling forward requires psychological safety.

First identified in organizational research as a feature of successful workplaces, psychological safety is considered by scholars of teaching and learning to be necessary for successful classroom environments as well.[28] The term "psychological safety" describes an atmosphere in which the members of an organization feel able to "move away from default ways of doing and thinking and learn, innovate and grow (i.e., unfreeze)" and the "degree to which people perceive their work environment as conducive to taking interpersonal risks."[29] Facilitating psychological safety doesn't mean removing challenge, fear, or stress: "the goal of psychological safety is not to remove all external pressures or learning anxiety, rather, it is to mitigate that anxiety so it is productive."[30] While psychological safety doesn't eliminate risks per se in learning, it "helps students to take risks with low concern about embarrassment, rejection or punishment from teachers. It allows students to focus on their learning rather than being distracted by worries of being ridiculed" and has been shown to positively affect "motivation, engagement, long-term memory, and academic achievement."[31] Because "risk averse behavior is often reinforced in educational practice" and "students are taught to view failure as a deficiency, and are conditioned to associate error free work with teacher approval and learning," the cultivation of psychological safety takes a concerted effort: we're swimming against the current.[32]

Psychological safety is crucial to normalizing mistakes and setbacks. As one group of organizational behavior researchers wrote, when members of an organization feel confident that "others will give you the benefit of the doubt when you make an error," they feel able to take the "interpersonal risks" necessary for learning:

> Psychological safety is key to enabling effective learning processes that involve reflective thought by which judgment is suspended, a healthy skepticism enabling the rejection of traditional presumptions is maintained and an open mind is exercised. Because learning is a process in which members

are engaged in 'asking questions, seeking feedback, experimenting, reflecting on results, and discussing errors or unexpected outcomes of actions a shared belief that members are psychologically safe becomes vital.[33]

Members of a classroom learning environment need this sense of safety to engage in asking questions, receiving feedback, and reflecting on the errors that learning requires. In classroom settings, psychological safety "has been shown to (1) free learners from being constantly self-conscious about image and competence, (2) enable them to be present in the learning moment and concentrate on the task at hand, and (3) reduce fear of asking questions."[34] Psychological safety allows students to make errors in ways that benefit their learning, helping to create a "fault-tolerant" environment in which it is "safe to take risks" and engage in "learning-oriented behavior" such as "the ability to ask questions, share ideas and ask for help without fear."[35]

Providing numerous "on-ramps" for students to overcome small setbacks—and indeed any place in our course design where there is a bit of flexibility—can benefit us as instructors as well. Not only does it help reduce the most fraught and miserable grade-related interactions with students, but it also provides us with some leeway for our own missteps. For example, if your entire syllabus is building toward a huge high-stakes exam, what will happen when you discover that many students do not understand the concepts they need to understand and have flunked the first exam? If we've planned our classes and our assessments with just a bit more wiggle room, a little bit of flexibility, we can make some adjustments and changes if we discover something's not working without having to try to rebuild the entire course halfway through or, even worse, proceeding along like everything's peachy keen when we know full well things are going wrong.

We can decrease the damage that failure can do if we anticipate stumbling blocks during the semester. We need to anticipate those times in class when everyone—instructors and students—will experience emotional and mental pinch points. When will students be most likely to lose it? When will you be at your lowest levels of patience and stamina? The last couple of weeks in any class can feel especially tortuous and exhausting. As high-stakes projects and deadlines loom, everyone's cognitive and emotional resources will be waning while the odds of completely flipping out will be waxing. Sometimes those times can also arise unexpectedly so it benefits everyone and increases everyone's odds of success if we can schedule in some kind of rebuilding-our-resiliency time. We can anticipate at least some of the moments when energy will be low and frustrations high. Those are the times we schedule an extra support session, a message of encouragement, or reminders of ways some failure is expected and accounted for, like *Hey, did you remember that you can drop the two lowest quiz grades/revise and resubmit a reading response/complete an extra credit assignment if you're concerned about your final grade?*

The research on class error climate, psychological safety, and productive struggle usually focuses on student errors but it's just as useful for educators. Fostering a class climate that encourages and supports everyone trying new things and encountering setbacks along the way should be extended to teaching practices, empowering ourselves to make those moments when we mess up just that—mere moments only. Recognizing that something didn't go well, that we made a mistake, does not need to spiral into fears of being a bad teacher. In fact, recognizing when something didn't go well but that it's something we can adjust or change in the next class meeting or at some point in the future is an essential part of effective teaching. To be sure, it's a lot easier to tell yourself, *Wow, that really tanked. I'd better try something else next time,* when you have employment security and are not also navigating numerous intersectional student biases. But to whatever extent possible in our unique teaching context, cultivating the ability to identify, reflect on, and learn from teaching mistakes as a normal, expected part of teaching goes a long way toward keeping the failure boulders from burying us.

At every opportunity when I'm with students, I try to directly acknowledge productive struggle and the reality of everyone making mistakes as part of learning, saying things such as:

> ➤ "A lot of people had trouble finding and restating the main argument of this article. Let's look together at it again, and if you would like to revise your reading journal after our discussion today, I've reopened the drop box."
> ➤ "Just a reminder that everyone has some revising to do on their first drafts and that my feedback is going to help you make the necessary changes and corrections."
> ➤ "Whoops, I'm talking too much right now. Let me zip my lip and we can hear from people who haven't had a chance to contribute yet."
> ➤ "This was a hard chapter to understand, so we're all going to reread the summary points again right now, in class."
> ➤ "Thank you for that question. You're on the right track but let me clarify something that I bet a lot of others are also unclear on."
> ➤ "I could have asked that question better. Let me try that again."
> ➤ "Because a lot of people need to do some major revisions, we're going to go over the rubric again in class."
> ➤ "Thank you for making that point. I hadn't thought of it that way before."[36]

I'm constantly framing mistakes as a normal part of everyone's work in class. My employment security and a certain amount of identity privilege increase my ability to do this. Also, I'm not interested in constantly affirming my academic ego by wielding my professorial power to make students kowtow to me and my Big Brain. These factors enable me to acknowledge when something isn't working in class. It's not always easy. Sometimes I make a fairly big change to an assignment or other aspect of my class plans when I see unnecessary failures looming ahead for too many students, and that makes me nervous. It's not what I planned, and I like doing what I planned. Plus, a small part of me fears that if I admit I've changed my mind, I'll appear weak or—hey there, demon with the slide deck—like I'm a bad teacher.

But changing your mind isn't an educational crime. In fact, when the point is to increase student success, and you've been as transparent as possible with students that this is why you're changing your mind, and the whole class understands the need for "fumbling forward," it's an indicator of pedagogical strength. Kevin Gannon reminds us that as educators we can "model failure:" "When we model constructive ways to engage with adversity and failure, we are also giving our students (and ourselves) that vital permission to be not-perfect, not-expert, not-polished . . . and not yet." It's in this "liminal space," Gannon concludes, "that deep and meaningful learning occurs."[37]

Open communication and discussion about our mistakes, errors, and setbacks is central to normalizing them and helping both faculty and students withstand their complicated emotional, professional, and cognitive costs. For instance, a 2022 study of first-year biology students found that the most agreed-upon potential strategy for normalizing failure was acknowledging it openly as a fact of life: "In student suggestions on how to reduce the stigma of failure within and beyond the university context, the most common theme identified across both contexts was for increased discussion and open communication about experiences of failure."[38] Or, as another group of researchers concluded, "creating a safe-space in which the socially-shared nature of failures could be explored was, in itself, a powerful intervention."[39]

The "socially-shared nature of failure" is just as important for academics and educators. Talking about our mistakes is a critical feature of "talk about teaching," the strategy discussed in chapter six. Faculty do not get sufficient opportunities and support for reflecting on failure in the classroom with our colleagues. By and large, we do not ever see other faculty members working in the classroom. We may share our syllabi at times but we don't meet over our syllabi to discuss all the things that went wrong with our course designs and what happened when things went sideways. In a survey of accomplished college faculty, one group of scholars identified this isolation as a major factor in how we experience teaching failures. Sadly but not surprisingly, in this survey none of the faculty they interviewed mention any kind of collaboration between instructors and academic or educational developers. This reflects our experiences that, even at universities where extensive support for educational development is available, there are issues around faculty accessing it, or making the choice to access it, for reasons ranging from not knowing it is available to not valuing it at an individual, department, or institutional level.[40]

Classroom and teaching failures compound when experienced entirely as individual mistakes or missteps, yet it is common for faculty to experience failure this way. In contrast, imagine a campus-wide "Whoops Day," when every instructor shares their biggest mistake of the term and then everyone brainstorms together about what they might do differently in the future. Imagine framing teaching failures in this way, as something expected, to be shared with colleagues for ideas about making any necessary corrections and adjustments. Failure would begin to look less like a demon's PowerPoint slideshow and lot more like pedagogical learning.

Just like we can take care to normalize mistakes and struggle in class, we should also consciously point to and celebrate successes. When there's been a breakthrough in understanding, a particularly perceptive comment, a high percentage of completed work, or progress in any way, take the time to acknowledge it for the whole class. I especially like to note and have students pay attention to how they have helped each other learn more, meet a deadline, make it to class, or just do better. Take a few minutes that you were going to spend lecturing and instead do some class shout-outs. It's not a frivolous or extraneous activity but an effective, low-prep, no-extra-teaching-labor-needed way to reduce the negative impact of minor setbacks and failures. Along with more closely paying attention to our successes, the constructive and positive error climate normalizing mistakes and building psychological safety that we've cultivated in class can help everyone in our learning community—including ourselves—to find a way forward when things go wrong.

Conclusion: "The Only Thing That Never Fails"

In many ways, we as individual instructors and students as individual learners possess the power to normalize mistakes and recover from failure while learning. But this can't fully, effectively be achieved solely through individual effort. Reducing failure and increasing success must be supported at the departmental, campus, and institutional levels. For example, students won't be able to absorb and implement new, more effective ways of studying just by hearing one faculty member talk about it in one class. They need repeated exposure to those strategies and opportunities for practice in programs such a first-year experiences, structured study sessions, and peer-to-peer mentoring.

Faculty cannot effectively engage in pedagogical learning, let alone the scholarship of teaching and learning, if their department tacitly or even overtly discourages instructors from doing so or if employment precarity or other teaching inequities make the costs of failure personally and professionally devastating. It is one of the greatest ironies in higher education that our mission is supposed to be learning, and yet failure—which is at the very core of all learning—is often so harshly, ruthlessly penalized. Our institutions fail us and fail our students even as we might strive to learn from our own individual mistakes and failures.

One of the most memorable things I ever experienced as an educator made me wonder: What would it look like if there were more, well, *forgiveness* for our mistakes as teachers and learners? Here's what happened:

On a June morning several weeks after classes had finished for the year, I found a small gift in my office mailbox with a note attached. The note was from a novelty stationery pad printed to look like those old-fashioned "While You Were Out" message pads. (Gather round, whippersnappers, and let me tell you about how, in the times of yore, you could leave your place of work and be, like, *not* in your place of work. People had to "leave a message" with another person who answered your work phone, which was in one fixed place and not in your pocket.) Instead of "While You Were Out," the sheet was titled "Apology." In the "From" box, the student had just written "A HIS 102 student," meaning a student from my introductory history class.

For the space labeled "Infraction," the student had filled in "Writing a mean course assessment last semester." Being professionally and personally damaged by needlessly cruel and demeaning comments on anonymous student evaluation forms is a near-universal experience for college faculty, and I'm no exception. But until that moment, it had never occurred to me that a student might later regret making such a comment. (Reminder to self: Students are human beings.) It's not an overstatement to say this note forever enlarged my understanding of teaching and learning by showing me how easy it can be during the arduous work of teaching *and* learning to make missteps that we will later regret. Missteps that we can't undo but only apologize for and maybe, eventually, find a way to lean into the learning.

The apology memo sheet also had a wide selection of boxes to check under "Reason for My Behavior." Things like "I was in a foul mood." "I was feeling insecure." "I was tired." "I forgot." The student had checked: "I was being selfish." "I wasn't thinking." "I had no idea it would hurt you." "I'm a schmuck." They'd also checked a box at the bottom that read: "This note represents my awareness that my words or actions in some way upset, hurt, or otherwise alienated you. In light of this understanding, I will not do it again." Without knowing who the student was or being able to connect them to their comment, I have no idea what they said on their anonymous evaluation or why in retrospect they realized the comment would hurt me. All I know for sure is that this was evidence of a student's continued learning and growth after they left my class, that they now regretted their behavior during an interaction with me as their teacher, and that they planned on doing things differently in the future.

I think of that note often. We just never know how long learning might take or what forms it might take. A big failure that we can't undo is probably inevitable sometimes, and that stinks, because nobody wants to fail. Nobody wants to check the box "I'm a schmuck." In academia, with its toxic, misogynistic, ableist, and sometimes racist strains of perfectionism linked to completely outdated and unrealistic measures of what constitutes professorial and scholarly success, failing can be perceived as unacceptable, and genuine apologies are scarce. Part of our work in accepting the predictability, reducing the occurrence, and mitigating the impact of higher ed snafus is accepting the predictability, reducing the occurrence, and mitigating the impact of failure.

Sometimes an apology is our only recourse when we fail, but then again, sometimes an apology can be a sign of authentic learning, which is, after all, the reason we're all here in higher ed.

Arguably, authentic learning is the reason we're all here on this earth. It's the work of being human. Learning is the only constant, consistent good in a frequently terrible, hurtful world, as the wizard Merlin in T. H. White's *The Once and Future King* explains:

> "The best thing for being sad ... is to learn something. That's the only thing that never fails. You may grow old and trembling in your anatomies, you may lie awake at night listening to the disorder of your veins, you may miss your only love, you may see the world about you devastated by evil lunatics, or know your honour trampled in the sewers of baser minds. There is only one thing for it then—to learn. Learn why the world wags and what wags it. That is the only thing which the mind can never exhaust, never alienate, never be tortured by, never fear or distrust, and never dream of regretting. Learning is the only thing for you. Look what a lot of things there are to learn ... ."[41]

We can lean into learning—figuring out "why the world wags and what wags it"—with the confidence that we will never be "tortured by" it or "dream of regretting" it. It is the best thing. It is "the only thing that never fails."

The small victories and advances in our pedagogical skill can easily become lost under the rubble of own individual mistakes and setbacks, not to mention the situational, institutional, and systemic boulders coming at us. We in higher education who care about creating more equitable learning opportunities for all students and who value diversity as an educational asset are most assuredly seeing our honor "trampled in the sewers of baser minds." We are watching our world "devastated by evil lunatics"— the politicians imposing dreadful legislative mandates on our public institutions, and the commentators and campaigners waging a culture war on "woke" and decimating our ability to teach and learn effectively. Learning in this situation can be acutely discouraging. But learning is what will keep our heads above the avalanche when failures threaten to bury us.

Lean into learning, because there's no certainty ahead, except that mistakes, errors, problems, and failures await us. But learning itself? Never. Fails.

Gear for Your Go-Bag

- Scaffolding content and assignments, especially large projects, and providing students with extensive low-stakes opportunities for practicing new skills significantly increases student learning and success.
- Any steps we can take to reduce the harm that grades can do—transparency, low-stakes assignments, alternative grading practices—will increase student success and improve our teaching life.
- We can design our courses with numerous "on-ramps" for when students get off track to increase student success.
- With every aspect of our classes and our words, we can strive to normalize setbacks and mistakes for everyone in our learning community—including ourselves.

PART V

FEAR

Floating on quicksand is the best way to avoid its clutches.

You are more buoyant in quicksand than you are in water.

—"How to Escape from Quicksand,"
The Worst-Case Scenario Survival Handbook

Chapter 13

FEAR FOULS UP LEARNING AND TEACHING

As an avid TV and movie consumer, I've always enjoyed sci-fi scares (aliens!) and supernatural thrills (vampires!) but never horror movies or TV shows. Until, that is, the spring of 2020. As emergency remote instruction and the subsequent blender semesters (teaching and learning course modalities puréed together, with new elements like synchronous Zoom added to the mix) dragged on, horror shows and films began creeping regularly into my Netflix queue and podcast downloads. Why this shift in my media habits? Why did I suddenly start enjoying narratives of violence and mayhem?

Horror on the screen is about scaring us but scaring us about things that are not actually happening to us and are thus—and here's the reason I started down this disemboweled-corpse-strewn path—completely controllable. Unlike, say, a highly contagious, airborne, potentially deadly virus. Watching a horror movie stirs up a bunch of adrenalizing fears and then the credits roll and, yay, we survived, we made it, everything is A-OK now. Also, we know danger's coming. The soundtrack alerts us! Ominous strings in a minor key as the camera pans slowly toward the gloomy house or the gloomy woods or the gloomy face. Menacing piano chords build as the hapless victim drives down the dark road or opens the creaky door. I'm going to jump at the jump scares, yes, but I knew that would be part of the deal when I hit "play." It's fear but a completely predictable fear, with a start and stop time that I command with a touch of a button. I'm entirely in control. *Ahh, that's the stuff!*

People have different levels of tolerance for uncertainty, so not everyone shares my personal struggle to accept the basic change-ability of existence or gets mental relief from their real-life fears by watching scary movies.[1] But everyone experiences fear sometimes, and fear is the thrumming undercurrent running beneath many of the things that can go wrong in teaching and learning. Fear is the quicksand that can engulf everyone's ability to think, engage, and interact in the college classroom. It's a sucking bog hidden on our path, deceptively disguised as just another sandy part of the road. We're strolling along, learning and teaching, teaching and learning, and then, suddenly, we're stuck. The ground beneath us isn't traversable after all. The quicksand of fear can catch us any-where and can foul up learning and teaching all on its own, but it's also entirely twisted up with those snafus I've already discussed. In this chapter, I show how inequity, disconnection, distrust, and failure feed student and faculty fears. I revisit the strategies I've outlined for responding and repairing when a snafu rears its ugly head, synopsize the proactive measures previously detailed for reducing the odds and impact of major snafus, and frame them as a means for increasing student and faculty agency.

When the ground beneath our feet dissolves into sludge, and we get sucked into a teaching and learning quagmire, trying to pretend we're not being ensnared, or flailing around in a panic, trying to extricate ourselves, will just speed up our sinking. We can, however, float instead of struggling. We can float just enough to keep our heads above the surface, and we can build up the buoyancy we'll need for when the quicksand catches us.

Fear Fouls Up Learning

"Fear" is too small and narrow a word for the panoply of emo-tional, mental, and physical conditions identifiable as being in a state of fear. My irrational yet overwhelming need to run away screaming when I see a totally harmless garter snake slither across the hiking trail is not the same kind of fear I feel when someone I love is seriously ill, which is not the same kind of fear I feel when I sense something going wrong in the classroom, and so on. The cause, scale, and scope are all different, but one thing they have in common is that fear is going to do a number on my ability to cope with, let alone learn from, the event as it's happening. In a 2021 presentation about pandemic-era teaching and learning at SUNY Plattsburgh, professor of counseling education Portia Allie-Turco vividly explained how fear negatively impacts the brain's ability to learn. If you are being stalked by a tiger, she said, your brain is going to be entirely focused on escaping from the tiger. You're looking for a tree to climb or a place to hide or a weapon to use to defend yourself. There's not going to be much left over in your cognitive energy repository for grappling with new ideas and creating new knowledge.

Fear—in small doses, occurring in an overall psychologically safe learning environment—can spur learning when it's signaling the magnitude of issues and ideas with which we're grappling as part of learning, for both teachers and as students.[2] But overwhelming fear is primal and powerful, doing what it can to help us survive when we're under attack and threatened by things with sharp teeth and claws. In the article "Recognizing Student Fear: The Elephant in the Classroom," T. Scott Bledsoe and Janice J. Baskin offer this overview of how fear effects learning: "It impacts our cognitive processes—how we perceive our environment, how we remember things, whether we can focus and pay attention, how well we plan and then execute that plan, and how well we problem-solve." In short, "its effects on learning and academic performance can be profound."[3]

Similarly, Sarah Rose Cavanagh writes that "fear and anxiety are psychological states that have at their base an ancient neural circuit wired for defense, the activation of which triggers behaviors that will help the organism survive a perceived threat to safety." One of these survival moves, she continues, is "behavioral inhibition"—that is, "the shutting down (inhibiting) of those behaviors required for exploration, play, and social connection—all components of effective learning." Fear severely interferes with learning, she points out, because "fear arrests all other processes."[4] During traumatic events, when someone feels under threat, "all aspects of individual functioning change—feeling, thinking and behaving," and as the threat grows, "the less capable he or she will be of learning or retrieving cognitive content; in essence, fear destroys the capacity to learn."[5]

This fact about how our brains work is the starting point for trauma-aware pedagogical practices.[6] Awareness of how trauma and traumatic stress interferes with effective teaching and learning is on the rise, including scholarship about its intersectional impact on students.[7] The pandemic era dramatically increased both the need for, and faculty engagement with, trauma-aware teaching.[8] Yet, even as campuses as a whole are becoming more attuned to trauma, fear still abounds in the classroom. Student fears are almost as numerous and unique as students themselves, but the SoTL identifies some consistent types of fear, such as fear of failure, fear of missing out, fear of shame, fear of crime, fear of disappointing family members, fear of public speaking, fear of negative evaluation, and fear of making a mistake that will create judgments from other students and the instructor about their intelligence, academic abilities, and belongness in higher education.[9] The sociocultural contexts of our present historical moment, such as school shootings, the dissolution of reproductive rights, and climate change, create additional fears. Fear of being negatively compared to one's peers appears to be increasing, meaning that students' "attention is divided between attempting to understand course-based information and worrying that their skills will not match up to the abilities of others, which may cause them to feel anxious, confused, or overwhelmed."[10]

In fact, the classroom is uniquely positioned in our society to exacerbate those fears. The classroom is "an emotional minefield," write T. Scott Bledsoe and Janice J. Baskin, noting: "Each student holds a mental template of classroom environments made up of incidents both positive and negative from earlier occurrences in school . . . and brings into the classroom the resultant fears. Individuals with disabilities, past traumas, or unique historical backgrounds (e.g., being poor but attending an affluent school) may experience fears that are deep-seated and fraught with painful memories."[11] While they are varied and diverse, some "deep-seated" fears accompany every student into the college classroom. Simultaneously both highly specific as well as collective, fear creates obstacles to learning. For instance, while a person's individual educational and life experiences will impact their feelings about taking tests in school, test anxiety generally is one of the most common fears shared by many different students.[12] Emotions can be socially "contagious" too, so any one student's anxiety about an upcoming test can ratchet up if other students are freaking out. One student's panic can infect others in a very unfortunate feedback loop.[13]

Influential pedagogue Parker Palmer asserts that we learn and teach in a "culture of fear"—that, "from grade school on, education is a fearful enterprise." In the college classroom, Palmer writes, students are "afraid of failing, of not understanding, of being drawn into issues they would rather avoid, of having their ignorance exposed or their prejudices challenged, of looking foolish in front of their peers."[14] He argues that many college students also fear "a live encounter with alien 'otherness,'" which is "actually a sequence of fears that begins in the fear of diversity," which in turn creates "fear of the conflict we know will ensue when divergent truths meet" and "fear of losing our identity" and "our sense of self."[15] So many aspects of school can be scary, and fears will routinely create obstacles to student learning.

Fear Fouls Up Teaching

Like student fears, faculty fears are both highly individualized as well as commonly shared. Factors that shape an instructor's unique teaching context can give rise to fears—legitimate and valid fears, such as fears for basic security and safety generated by contingent employment, or ongoing discrimination based on one's embodied and social identities. But in addition, some fears that foul up teaching apply widely to college faculty in every teaching context. Unless we've totally ostriched our heads in the sand, pretty much everyone teaching college classes should be at least a little bit afraid of today's major political, social, cultural, and economic stressors on institutions of higher education.

Fears engendered by perfectionism also pop up in many academics' headspace. Fear about making mistakes or looking foolish is rampant among people who pride themselves on their intellectual prowess. Relatedly, many of us fear that when anything goes wrong, it is an indictment of our teaching abilities. We fear that we are not good teachers. Yet, like student fear-based avoidance behavior, the fear of being a bad teacher can lead to self-sabotaging actions. It can result in faculty actively avoiding reflecting on teaching, engaging in pedagogical learning, or taking steps to improve their teaching.[16] The fear of the thing sabotages our ability to reduce the likelihood of the thing happening. The "culture of fear" described by Palmer extends to faculty's experiences of teaching. A brain in fear is a brain that has trouble gaining knowledge: it's hard to learn how to teach effectively when we are afraid.

SoTL and general teaching advice on trauma-aware pedagogy has only begun to address how educators must contend with their own traumatic stress and how clinical anxiety and all types of fear interfere with effective teaching. Educational developers are beginning to call directly for trauma-aware supports and programming for faculty, and scholars who address intersectional teaching inequities have drawn attention to the physical, emotional, and cognitive stress and toll extracted on faculty of color, for example.[17] But as much as we know about fear's impact on human learning, fear itself is idiosyncratic. Some people are terrified of snakes (hi, it's me) and some people love snakes. (How? Why? How???) We experience fear in our own individual brains and bodies, but fear can also be more generalized, commonly arising at the convergence of certain circumstances in certain contexts. Fear arising on both a highly individual level as well as social and systemic levels contributes to all the things that foul up learning and teaching.

Snafu Redux: Feeding Fear

Inequity, disconnection, distrust, and failure directly feed fear. These things dump a dangerous slurry of grit and muddy water into our paths, causing quicksand to grow and spread, ready to sink everyone in teaching and learning snafus.

Inequity Feeds Fear

Inequitable learning and teaching conditions contribute to a fundamental fear that you—the individual instructor or the individual student—will face additional, unnecessary obstacles to your academic success because of your positionality. You can't be certain that you will be able to fully access all available opportunities for effective teaching and authentic learning, unimpeded by other people's stereotypes and systemic biases. For faculty with visible and invisible disabilities, and faculty from historically minoritized social groups, labor disparities, ableism, and students' racialized, gendered, and other assumptions about scholarly expertise create major uncertainties about pedagogical efficacy. Trying to discern where students' biases are interfering with their own learning, as differentiated from those aspects of a class that you could change and improve in order to help students learn, is an emotionally and cognitively strenuous task that cannot ever be definitively concluded. For VITAL faculty, labor inequities and employment insecurity create uncertainty and fear about their teaching context—namely, fear about their ability to keep teaching at all, including the ability to learn from mistakes and subsequently make changes to pedagogical practices.

For students, inequity creates ongoing uncertainties and fears about their basic sense of belonging in college. It can continually cause fear about what will really matter and ultimately be evaluated in their college classes. Are they being evaluated on what they're supposed to be learning in that class, or are they being evaluated on how their past and present life circumstances shape their abilities to fulfill the requirements? What aspects of the hidden college curriculum are going to negatively impact their opportunities to demonstrate their learning and to make connections to other students, faculty, the course content, and the college itself?

Disconnection Feeds Fear

Educators who feel disconnected from students, institutions, and each other face uncertainties and fears about the point and purpose of their work in higher education. Systemic inequities underscore isolation and disconnection from the institution at large, from the act of teaching, and from individual students. Negative interactions with students, which are more likely when such inequities are at play, cause disconnection from students and from teaching and undercut teaching self-efficacy. Negative interactions with department colleagues, staff, and administrators can also further any educator's disconnection from teaching and learning. A toxic work environment in which we must disconnect to protect ourselves professionally and personally creates all kinds of potential for fouling up our teaching and exacerbating fear. When labor conditions combined with world events (pandemic-era Zoom school, I'm looking at you) create a near-perfect recipe for teaching burnout, a sense of profound disconnection can swiftly arise. Fear and uncertainty are inherent to this type of disconnection, generating doubts about whether the enormous and time-consuming work of planning, implementing, reflecting on, assessing, and continually revising our teaching practices is worth our effort.

For students, disconnection generates major fears and uncertainties about whether the financial, mental, and emotioime and effort. Without some meaningful connections to other students, succeeding academically can become significantly more difficult, intensifying fears and uncertainties about even being in college at all, especially among first-generation students and students from historically marginalized groups. Lack of connection to the course content will undermine anyone's ability to learn. These deep uncertainties, morphing into fear, intertwined with disconnection, sap students' self-efficacy, reducing their ability and willingness to persist and to work at overcoming obstacles. Fear about whether their academic efforts matter at all can truly foul up a student's learning.

Distrust Feeds Fear

In the college classroom, distrust feeds fear in especially noxious ways. Faculty distrusting students, students distrusting faculty, and everyone distrusting the institution—together these epitomize the destructive snafus caused by fear and uncertainty. For instructors, uncertainty about students' willingness to engage productively can quickly become the kind of distrust that generates punitive class-room and coursework policies. Such uncertainty can trap faculty into policing students instead of working with them—a teaching snafu if there ever was one. When this uncertainty is threaded through our view of students, things like attendance and device-based distractions in class become less a pedagogical puzzle to examine through the lens of teaching effectiveness and more of an enervating power struggle that will almost inevitably foul up teaching and learning. Distrust entangled with teaching dispari-ties and systemic inequities creates additional uncertainties that students will acknowledge and respect their own academic and intellectual expertise.

Similarly, students who are themselves navigating biases will face additional hurdles to building and sustaining the types of trust they need to learn and to succeed academically. And every student, no matter what their embodied and social identities, may distrust many aspects of the standard education system. Most stu-dents are not certain that their authentic learning—as opposed to their grades—matters. Many are not convinced that faculty truly want students to succeed, a fear exacerbated by their experiences with the small number of instructors who are objectively terrible teachers (and who, because of employment status or campus cul-ture, have no external incentive to improve, and face no negative consequences for their poor teaching). Opaque expectations or amorphous grading schemes contribute to students' fears about how their work will be assessed and graded, which in turn ups the odds of cheating, which in turn ups the odds of increasing the faculty member's distrust, thus entrapping everyone in a horrible cycle of snafus, driven by doubt and fear.

Failure Feeds Fear

While necessary for some aspects of learning, failure feeds fear. In higher education systems, failure too often has dire conse-quences, overriding its potential to help us learn from mistakes and setbacks. For instructors, failure feeds our fears about employment security and teaching self-efficacy. At many institutions, not only the stated procedures for but also the unstated assumptions around evaluating an individual's teaching practices—as linked to employment decisions—are structured and implemented in ways that do not sufficiently allow for learning from our teaching mistakes and making changes or corrections. Small mistakes that have the potential for productive pedagogical reflection and learning instead become financial and professional liabilities, possibly even job-ending failures. In such a context, aggravated by social and cultural stereotypes about teaching and the unobtainable ideals set by the Super Teacher myth, mistakes and missteps can set off doubts and fears about our own individual abilities to help our students learn. As faculty who want to teach effectively, many of us tend to personalize every failure, even failures with multiple, complex causes, including things totally beyond our own individual control.

For students, the most universal fear related to failure can be boiled down to a single word, "grades," because, in most educational systems, grades matter more in terms of recognized markers of academic success than anything else, with all the financial, emotional, and intellectual risks and rewards therein. When grades are at stake, any failure at all can explode into a snafu that shuts down learning while it ramps up the chances of potentially hostile and negative interactions with a faculty member—not to mention the allure and internal moral and ethical justifiability of cheating to avoid a failing grade. For some legitimate reasons, most students are deeply, profoundly uncertain that anything at all in their educational endeavors matters as much as their class grade, and failure of any type usually feels like a threat to their class grade.

Identifying Fear Snafus

Failure, distrust, disconnection, and inequity feed fear, and fear causes things to go wrong in the classroom. Yet it can be difficult to identify fear-related snafus, especially because fear can be linked to certain student behaviors that consistently drive most faculty right up the wall. If students' previous experiences include negative or even traumatic experiences related to education, they can lead to students being in a "state of alarm" and being "less capable of concentrating, more anxious, and more attuned to non-verbal cues such as tone of voice, body posture, and facial expressions," which in turn may led to them "misinterpret[ing] such cues because of anxiety-induced hypervigilance."[18]

Such "hypervigilance" can manifest in what looks like, at first glance, inattention, disengagement, or even disrespect:

> We may think someone is . . . capable of taking our directives when [they are] actually in a state of fear. A compound command such as "Take out your book, open to page 52, and write out the key concepts related to the lesson for today" is often processed inaccurately. The learner gets confused and therefore more anxious; this anxiety can then escalate, making the learner even less capable of following directions. If the learner makes a mistake or asks a neighbor to repeat the teacher's clear directives, the teacher can become frustrated and impatient.[19]

What a snafu! Fear is fouling up this seemingly simple interaction between the student and the faculty member, with fear derailing the student's cognitive processes, and the faculty member perceiving the behavior as failure to listen and to implement straight-forward directions.

As Palmer explains, "seeing is never simple" for educators when it comes to student fears, because there's always a chance that what we experience as "the Student from Hell" is a person wracked with fear.[20] Palmer describes an experience working with one such student—a young man who sat slouched and silent, eyes averted, in every class, radiating what looked like boredom and hostility. A chance one-on-one conversation with this "Student from Hell" revealed that S.F.H. lived with an unemployed alcoholic father who continually mocked and derided the value of college, seriously undermining the student's self-efficacy and motivation. Parker writes that the conversation was a light bulb moment because it "helped me understand that the silent and seemingly sullen students in our classroom are not brain-dead:

they are full of fear. . . . Their silence is born not of stupidity or banality but of a desire to protect themselves and survive."[21]

Palmer's point is that fear often drives a physically, emotionally, and cognitively overriding command in students' bodies and minds to "protect themselves and survive," resulting in behaviors that quite directly interfere with students' ability to succeed and that can be extremely difficult for faculty to identify when it causes things to go wrong. As one SoTL researcher points out, "Whenever physically fighting or fleeing isn't possible, people use avoidant and psychological fleeing methods that are dissociative."[22] Fear may be driving student behaviors that are deeply distracting, discouraging, and frustrating for faculty—behaviors such as avoidance (procrastination, tardiness, repeated absences, not turning in assignments) and disengagement (nonparticipation, scrolling or sleeping in class, nonresponsive/glazed expressions). Perhaps most vexingly, fear can be an instigator of students' acting out behaviors, like disrupting class with side conversations, making sarcastic comments, and complaining.[23]

When it comes to student fears, then, educators are faced with a complex task: trying to remain attuned to the pernicious ways fear fouls up learning so we can identify those snafus while at the same time coping with the problems that fear-based student behavior creates. And we can't eliminate either individualized or systemically induced fears from teaching and learning. But as I discuss in the next chapter, we can take meaningful steps to increase and amplify our agency as educators and our students' agency as learners.

Gear for Your Go-Bag

- Fear is a complicated emotion, shaped by both our unique and individual life experiences as well as systemic and institutional factors that contribute to inequity, disconnection, distrust, and failure in educational settings.

- Fear creates physiological, cognitive, and emotional obstacles to learning and to effective teaching.
- Fear can be hard to identify in the classroom, especially when it presents as student behaviors that are frustrating for faculty.

Chapter 14

EXERCISING AND INCREASING AGENCY

What's the opposite of fear, in the context of learning and teaching? Courage, invoked most memorably by Parker Palmer in his popular book titled *The Courage to Teach*, seems like a foolproof answer, but to my ears "courage" is just a bit too loaded of a term for explaining teaching and learning qualities we can and should cultivate. The flip side of courage isn't fear but rather cowardice, and that's too harsh when we're talking about navigating the intersectional, systemic, and individual challenges of teaching and learning in higher education. Arguing that we need to be more courageous implies personal moral fortitude, when in fact many of our fears are very well-founded, given all the ways that higher education hamstrings us as learners and educators. Additionally, at times courage and even confidence, another good contender for the opposite of fear, can be misplaced. We all know someone who possesses a level of confidence all out of proportion to their skills and abilities. It's way too easy to cross the razor-thin border between confidence and self-delusion.

Instead of "courage" or "confidence," I believe "agency" is the most appropriate term to use as the opposite of "fear" in learning and teaching.

Exercising Agency in Learning and Teaching

Agency is a complicated sociocultural concept, long theorized, politicized, and analyzed in academic discourse and applied to educational settings in work by critical pedagogues such as Paulo Freire and Henry Giroux.[1] A simple definition of "agency" would be something like "the ability to act and the understanding that you have the ability to act." However, agency is not simply free will or individual effort. As individuals with individual histories, we all exist at a specific moment in time, connected to various groups and communities, situated in a given set of contextual power dynamics that create limitations on agency: "Agency is bounded; one acts within certain constraints imposed by previous experience as well as context."[2]

Scholars have examined what role agency in academia plays in work-life balance, use of educational technology, professional networks, negative graduate school experiences, navigating gender biases, and contingent employment status.[3] Workplace agency for educators could be defined "having a sense of power, will, and desire to create work contexts that meet the individual's goals over time," but researchers emphasize that "organizational contexts and environments shape faculty agency" and "overarching power structures—administration, tenured faculty, formal and informal policies—may contribute to experiences of constrained agency and invisibility for key members of the organization."[4] For educators, "both personal and contextual/social factors—including personal and collective discourses—shape, facilitate, or restrict teachers' agency in their various professional and organizational contexts."[5] However, within these constraints, researchers consistently identify some means for faculty's individual agency and, to a lesser but still important extent, collective agency.[6]

SoTL research on student agency look for ways that student-centered classroom structures can increase students' agency and learning and, recently, how remote emergency instruction during the pandemic affected student agency.[7] Student agency in this work is variously theorized and defined. "Ecological agency," for example, means that individual students "act by means of their environment or 'ecology,' rather than being able to act separately from the conditions that surround them . . . [A]gency can be located not in learners but in the enablers and constraints of the context"—meaning that "students [act] by means of their environment, rather than simply in an environment"—making it "possible to understand why an individual can achieve agency in one situation but not in another."[8] Kevin Gannon argues that student agency is the opposite of a deficit-based approach to education and that facilitating student agency means "seeing our students as active partners in teaching and learning, as cocreators of knowledge and coparticipants in the scholarly conversation."[9]

Other aspects of student agency further defined in the research include "(a) dispositional dimensions of individuals who act and transform environments; (b) motivational dimensions of individuals who regulate their actions, exist within contexts, and make choices and decisions; and (c) positionality of individuals in that individuals negotiate and interact within complex social contexts."[10] According to one study, students feel they have agency when they have choices "in their roles as learners" and are "positioned as knowledgeable decisionmakers and individuals capable of exerting influence in their learning contexts."[11] Some researchers emphasize the links between agency and identity for historically marginalized students navigating systemic educational inequities, drawing on work such as bell hooks's argument that "the work of 'theorizing'—the work of naming and understanding one's experiences as connected to broader systems of oppression—is central to survival and liberation," defining "theorizing-as-agency."[12] Others focus on the positional and situational aspects of student agency, examining how "agency is not developed solely by an individual but co-created with other individuals such as peers and teachers" and "is not an isolated action where students exist in a vacuum, rather, agency is co-constructed in communities of practice" in which students "develop perceptions of themselves in relation to schooling."[13]

Some of the most compelling work on student agency is through the lens of our varying academic disciplines. For example, STEM SoTL scholars have argued that in their disciplines "the central concept of agency in science is the notion of authorship"— and students engage in "epistemic processes paralleling those of professional scientists" in order to construct new-to-them knowledge.[14] To facilitate student authorship in science classes, faculty need to create "safe learning environments for promoting agency" in which students can "willingly share ideas without being held up for ridicule" and "feel non-threatened personally and in their ideas."[15] One of our overarching goals in every discipline is to help students exercise their agency: *doing* math, *giving* a public presentation, *creating* art, *writing* a research paper, and so on. More than building confidence or even courage in the face of daunting aspects of our subject, we strive to help them rethink their (learned, honed, previously rewarded) academic passivity and to view themselves as learners with agency to do the things we most want them to learn how to do in our subjects.

As individuals working and learning in higher education, then, agency simultaneously offers us potential for action and recognizes limitations for action. For instance, building our ability to exercise agency in the college classroom can't and won't eliminate the ultimate control that an institution's grading systems have on some aspects of a student's academic success. But increasing our agency as educators, and students' agency as learners, can help us reduce the damage grades can do to self-efficacy and trust in the classroom. To take another obvious example, building our ability to exercise agency in the college classroom can't eliminate intersectional biases and discrimination, but it can help us name and reduce the damage they can do during class meetings and interactions.

In a 2020 article, one group of researchers describes what they call "an agentic perspective toward teaching and learning:

> Bandura (2001) wrote, "To be an agent is to intentionally make things happen by one's actions (p. 2)." Agentive teachers iteratively use their knowledge, experience, and theories of learning to actively create, critique, and adapt curricula (Wilkinson, 2005). They intentionally adopt, reject, or initiate instructional practices to support student learning (Paris & Lung, 2008). Agentic approaches to teaching and learning assume that teachers are unique, that strengths

and experiences should be respected, and that knowledge is socially constructed (Vygotsky, 1978).

Likewise, students possess unique strengths and experiences; they are capable of engaging agentively in their learning (Ivey & Johnston, 2013).[16]

An "agentic perspective" on teaching assumes that, within some systemic constraints, faculty can reflect on effective teaching, activate their own self efficacy, and apply pedagogical learning to their teaching practices. An agentic perspective on learning assumes that students possess "the capacity to act in ways that exhibit their own choices in learning, informed by their beliefs and careful consideration, self-regulation, and self-reflection about their ability to control and take ownership of their own learning."[17]

Building educators' and students' agency won't eliminate fear. Some fear and uncertainty always accompany authentic learning—including pedagogical learning—which will include moments of confusion, unease, and uncertainty. Some systemic and institutional aspects of higher education outside our control will create fears. But agency empowers us to traverse those moments, with the knowledge that we have the power to act in ways that have a positive and productive—if contextually and variously limited—impact on teaching and learning.

STIR and Repair Strategy Redux: Exercising Agency

As I've argued throughout *Snafu Edu*, when we're talking about teaching and learning, we need to pay a lot more attention to the fact that things go wrong. All the time. When we are more cognizant of how frequently and routinely snafus arise in the college classroom, we are going to be better able to act when snafus arise in our own classrooms. This skill is more than "quick thinking" or even "good preparation" for when things go sideways. When we are aware of and able to implement specific strategies for making repairs, we are increasing our agency as educators because "teacher agency fosters teachers' resilience in the face of multiple challenges."[18] Having a go-bag, including repair strategies for when things go wrong, is an important way that "teachers become agents": agents who "act (creatively), negotiate, and integrate pedagogical and digital resources into meaningful teaching practice," even "under severe and limiting constraints."[19]

STIR (Stop, Think, Identify, Repair) is the starting point for those strategies and for increasing agency. In all kinds of moments of uncertainty and potential problems—from student hostility and microaggressions in the classroom to grading disputes to an assignment that tanked to spiraling doubts about our teaching self-efficacy—pausing for thought can help us. We academics, we know how to think, and critical reflexivity is a key component of agency.[20] So we need to take the time to stop and think, to figure out what's going on, and to address it—maybe in the moment, or maybe after everyone's had a chance to cool off. This step should always include identifying what's working well, in addition to what's gone wrong. We proactively counter negativity bias—and combat the Super Teacher myth—by paying attention to what's going right, even when we're figuring out how to repair what's gone wrong.

And then what? I've previously detailed seven strategies that we can draw from, adapt to our own unique teaching contexts, and put into action when we're hitting a patch of pedagogical quicksand. These repair strategies can also be framed as ways to activate, and to increase, our agency as educators and learning facilitators.

Using a Script Activates Agency

When we're ready with a script—particularly in especially fraught and emotional interactions with students, such as when a hostile student is inappropriately challenging our expertise—we are better positioned to respond in an agentic way; to respond in a way that enables us to utilize and apply our pedagogical knowledge, reflection, and professional expertise to our teaching practice.

Apologizing Activates Agency

It may sound counterintuitive, but being able to say "I'm sorry" when we've made an error is ultimately an empowering ability and teaching skill. Even taking into account teaching inequities, acknowledging a mistake that we've made demonstrates confidence in our pedagogical abilities. Skillful practitioners recognize when they've made a mistake and can say so. In the process, they also clearly demonstrate that their missteps can be corrected, and they have the know-how to do exactly that. That's educator agency.

Conveying Care Activates Agency

Keeping in mind that "care" can take many forms within the constraints of higher education, conveying care for student learning and success is an agentic teaching strategy in that it communicates to students our desire and ability to help them learn. It can strengthen the necessary social connections that enable students' academic engagement and builds our agentic ability to "act in reflective, autonomous, and intentional ways based on personal and professional convictions of what is right."[21]

Making Revisions Activates Agency

Identifying a problem or mistake in teaching and making a necessary revision is a clear example of a faculty member exercising agency—by "assuming strategic perspectives and/or taking strategic actions towards goals that matter to him/her."[22] Pedagogical revisions arising out of careful reflection, undertaken with the goal of improving teaching and learning, is an effective, strategic, agentic practice.

Defusing Distrust Activates Agency

When things go wrong, particularly in the on-campus classroom where there is a live audience of students to witness the snafu, using defusing strategies increases faculty agency. Again, agency in this sense doesn't mean our individual will and effort, outside of all contextual components, but it does mean a sense of self-efficacy. Knowing we have tools ready to defuse a tense, problematic, emotional, or even hostile situation enables us to better do precisely that.

Rebuilding Trust Activates Agency

Rebuilding trust when it has weakened, or even broken, in teaching and learning is an act of educator agency. Rebuilding requires action—informed, intentional actions based on our knowledge and understanding of what's gone wrong and what teaching practices we can utilize in this situation. It strengthens our agency, even within institutional constraints, as facilitators able to productively respond and regroup when snafus arise.

Leaning into Learning Activates Agency

Fully embracing the career-long process of learning how to be an effective teacher is a powerful strategy for increasing our agency. It gives us the chance to metamorphose our mistakes, struggles, and missteps into pedagogical knowledge. Leaning into learning can even potentially help build "transformative agency" by allowing us to address a "'fractured' practice that requires transformation through new solutions," including "resisting and criticizing the current activity . . . explicating new possibilities, envisioning new patterns or models, committing to specific actions, and taking the consequential actions needed to change the activity."[23]

More than just a checklist of how to respond when things go wrong, these strategies enable us to exercise our agency as educators. I've used all these strategies myself and increasingly I view my teaching more through an agentic lens and less through a veil of fear. For years, when something went wrong in the classroom, my first response was reactive and defensive. Looking back now, I see this response was in large part fear-based and resulted in reducing my own agency. Frantically worried about doing something wrong, I flipped out when I did something wrong, or even when I didn't necessarily do anything wrong but things still went sideways, because students are people and people mess up/miscommunicate/misunderstand things.

In an essay about a class that completely tanked, English professor Tom Romano describes this kind of vicious circle of teacherly fear and pedagogical failure:

> Instead of letting go and enlisting the students' aid in solving the problem of the deteriorating class, fear ruled me—fear of losing control, fear of recriminations for incompetence, fear of being revealed a fraud. . . . Instead of acknowledging my fears and failings and confronting them with courage, I became defensive. I closed communication and sought to turn the class around by exerting autocratic control . . . [But] the stringent measures didn't work. The ship sank, with me singing stridently on the bridge at the top of my lungs. . . . Because I capitulated to fear, I didn't have a chance of improving the class.[24]

Embracing the concept of revision and being able to apologize when necessary has increasingly enabled me as an educator to not let fear rule me in the way described by Romano. When I don't "capitulate to fear" I have a real chance to improve. I better understand and can more effectively respond when things go wrong because it flips a switch in my brain, from a fear-induced feeling that "oh noooooooo, something's gone wrong, it must be my bad teaching/students being irredeemably horrible/the pointless futility of it all," to a far less fear-inducing *Well, this wasn't what I wanted to have happen, so what can I revise for the next interaction/class meeting/time I teach this course?*

No matter how skilled we become at responding to snafus, we can still be afraid that we're not good enough and feel powerless (lack agency) to engage in effective teaching, especially if institutional constraints on our educator agency are particularly restrictive. Fear can follow all of us into the classroom, as Parker Palmer writes: "After thirty years of teaching, my own fear remains close at hand. It is there when I enter a classroom and feel the undertow into which I have jumped. It is there when I ask a question—and my students keep a silence as stony as if I had asked them to betray their friends. It is there whenever it feels as if I have lost control: a mind-boggling question is asked, an irrational conflict emerges, or students get lost in my lecture because I myself am lost."[25]

Parker mentions just a few of the fear-inducing and agency-reducing things that can happen when we're teaching. A go-bag of repair strategies can help us withstand those moments, which are routine, predictable, and to be expected. But so too can we proactively reduce fear by increasing students' and our own agency in higher education with course planning and teaching practices—all the planning and practices I've previously discussed for proactively increasing equity, connection, trust, and success.

Proactive Planning and Practices Redux: Amplifying Agency

I may have slightly misled readers with the title of this book. I've fulfilled my promise to put teaching and learning foul-ups at the center of my discussion and provide specific classroom and teaching practice strategies for coping when things go wrong. But I've spent more pages discussing how to proactively decrease the odds of things going wrong. Sorry not sorry. While I want to completely and forever normalize the fact that teaching and learning can never be perfectible activities, I also want to ensure that this book sparks ideas and generates energy for readers to take initiative planning and preparing to reduce in the first place the possibility of getting stuck in a snafu. I said "reduce," not "eliminate," because the best planning and the best go-bag in the world doesn't change the fact that human beings mess up sometimes and things go wrong.

We can't stop things from going sideways sometimes, but we can increase our agency—that is, our "capacity to make professional choices based on the knowledge and expertise of ways to produce learning and development in students," and cultivating a "willingness to engage in iterational, practical-evaluative, projective and transformative action despite the existence of practical, personal, and institutional constraints."[26] I want us all to be able to purposely exercise agency and increase student agency in order to reduce those things that we know cause teaching and learning snafus. Those snafu causal drivers—inequity, disconnection, distrust, failure, and fear—are always lurking and ready to undermine student learning and effective teaching. But by the same token, the strategies I've previously discussed for reducing the occurrences of those snafus enable both faculty and students to better exercise their agency.

Increasing Equity Amplifies Agency

Planning for learner variability, with attention to accessibility and providing some options for students, creates classroom conditions that reduce student fears about being able to demonstrate their learning, and enables more students to exercise more fully their academic agency. Planning for learner biases can enable us, on an individual level at least, to exercise more fully some aspects of our educator agency. A major way to effectively plan for learner biases and reduce the professional and personal damage they can do to our teaching self-efficacy and agency is to actively lessen the harms of standardized, anonymous end-of-term evaluations of teaching by soliciting student feedback and reflection frequently (including students' reflection on their own actions and responsibilities as members of a learning community); framing all student feedback as formative only; and putting student feedback into its appropriate proportion.

Increasing Connections Amplifies Agency

Reducing the negative toll of disconnection on students and faculty, and upping the connections between students, between students and content, between students and faculty, and between faculty and other educators, can foster classroom conditions for increasing agency. By actively prioritizing ways to help students recognize the relevance of their academic work, structuring student interactions, and getting good at small talk, we facilitate stronger connections that reduce fear and build students' individual abilities to engage as agents in their learning. Talking about teaching with other people who care about effective teaching, especially if we're working in a toxic and agency-restricting context, increases our own individual connections. Those connections help us ascertain where and how we can exercise agency.

Increasing Trust Amplifies Agency

The concept of agency takes into account that sometimes trust is delimited by the situational realities in which a subject is living and working. However, the concept of agency also allows for the possibility of working individually and collectively to increase trust in the classroom space. Being continuously welcoming, cultivating clarity, and enlisting students as partners are all well-documented, evidence-based teaching practices that build student trust. Increasing trust with our students benefits both faculty and learners in ways that decrease fear and allow us to exercise our educational agency. And last but not least, nurturing your teaching self-efficacy is, quite directly, a means of increasing trust in yourself and your ability to facilitate student learning. That's agency.

Increasing Success Amplifies Agency

Student fears perhaps most obviously coalesce around fear of failure, which in turn undermines student academic agency. So too does fear of failure create quicksand bogs that trap educators and leave them floundering and stuck without the ability to act. There are things we can do to reduce fear and mitigate the negative impact of necessary setbacks and failures in learning, including pedagogical learning. We can facilitate as much scaffolding and practice as possible instead of trying to shoehorn in more and more new content. Key to increasing student success and building agency is reducing the harms of standardized grading. And for both students as well as for educators, increasing agency means normalizing setbacks and mistakes. Creating classroom environments that provide psychological safety for students and, as much as we can, for ourselves allows us to better exercise agency as novice learners in the subject and as pedagogical leaners with subject area expertise. Exercising agency to the maximum of our ability is only possible when we're working with others and within structures that enable us to encounter obstacles, make mistakes, and at times struggle without being decimated by failure and fear.

There are no simple shortcuts to increasing equity, connection, trust, and success, and using these practices to increase agency. The process of engaging in these practices will never be a straight-forward march but rather a twisting, turning path with numerous detours and side trips, some of which may end with our students and ourselves sinking into a quicksand-y snafu. Agency isn't easy, as one group of scholars note: "Developing agency requires time and effort. It requires thought, reflection, learning through trial and error, creativity, continuing assessment and no doubt, per-sistence and courage."[27]

Yeah, yeah, I know I said I didn't want to use the word "courage." But building our agency muscles, and concertedly developing our ability to increase our own knowledge and skill as learners and as educators, means overcoming at least some of our own individual and unique-to-us fears. That takes "time and effort, trial and error, creativity, continuing assessment, persistence," and, okay, yes, res-olution, "persistence, and courage." Entering the classroom, as a student and as an educator, knowing that things will go wrong and still insisting upon claiming your own academic agency to learn and to teach—that takes guts.

Gear for Your Go-Bag

- We can't eliminate all fears from learning and teaching, but we can increase our own and our students' ability to exercise agency in meaningful ways within institutional and systemic constraints.

- STIR and the repair strategies discussed in this book—
  use a script; apologize; convey care; make revisions;
  defuse; rebuild; lean into learning—are ways we can
  exercise and help our students exercise agency when
  things go wrong.
- The proactive planning and practices discussed in this
  book for increasing equity, connection, trust, and success
  also amplify agency.

CONCLUSION

Keep from Sinking

In *Geeky Pedagogy*, I described my recurring teaching anxiety dream where I'm back in college, sitting in a class or waiting in line in at the registrar's office, even though I know for a fact that I already graduated, like, a really long time ago. So why I am still stuck here here?!? Well, because I am still in college, in the sense that my body is still spending most of its working hours on a college campus and/or college digital learning environment.[1] But "School's Back in Session—Forever" is not my only recurring dream related to teaching. I regularly have another, much more embarrassing dream about teaching.

In this dream I have to go to the bathroom. Urgently. I find an open stall in a public restroom and relieve myself, but when I flush, disaster strikes. The toilet overflows, flooding the bathroom and covering the floor, my shoes, and basically the entire world with, um, you know. You don't need an advanced degree in psychiatry to interpret this dream. It is my deepest, darkest fear in a potty-training guise: my bodily functions and I will cause a horrible mess. Everyone will see and smell it. I can't keep everything shiny, sparkly, perfectly clean. I won't always be able to stop the stink or flush it all away. I'll have to grab a plunger and a bottle of bleach and clean it up. Sometimes things go wrong. Shit happens.

Right up until the COVID-19 pandemic years of my career in higher education, I had this dream routinely when classes were about to begin. Then, in the fall of 2020, I stopped having the

"School's Back in Session and Shit's Gonna Get Real" dream. My subconscious could no longer conjure or conceive of anything happening to me as a teacher that could be weirder, messier, and harder to clean up than what was happening IRL. I picture the committee of tiny subconscious Jessamyns who are in charge of my dreams saying, "Take five everyone! The coronavirus just made 'fear of exploding toilet' totally trivial." The fundamentally unpredictable and uncertain state of our whole entire existence—let alone the predictable routines of teaching and learning—during a global pandemic and concurrent intersecting social, economic, and political upheavals stupefied into silence my teaching anxieties and fear of making mistakes.

Things Will Go Wrong, That's for Certain

Before March 2020, I allowed the predictable aspects of college teaching to lull me (at least at the conscious level) into a false sense of security and assurance that during each semester things would go as expected. I'd design my classes and create my syllabi. Then classes would start. Then I would work with students, most of whom would successfully complete the course requirements. Then classes would end. But I was fooling myself. Every semester, every class, every single interaction with students—they all contain unpredictable elements, including things that can go wrong. Mistakes, missteps, and problems can occur at any time. So can unexpected breakthroughs, achievements, and learning. The pandemic years expanded my tunnel vision to see much more clearly how students too had to grapple with their own mistakes, in the context of their own individual life circumstances shaped by numerous factors, including those totally outside their control.

For all of us, the best course planning, the best pedagogical skill set, even the biggest, best-stocked go-bag cannot change the fact that some kinds of fear and uncertainty are a built-in part of teaching and learning. So too will we have to navigate inequities, disconnections, and distrust, all of which feed our fears. It's a part of learning: we start with some uncertainty (not knowing), which often causes at least some fear and stress, and then, over time, with practice and effort, we achieve more certainty (knowing) but never total and complete certainty, forever and ever. Uncertainty is just a part of being alive in this bonkers world of ours, including experiencing events and factors very much outside of our own individual control or influence. As students and as faculty, sometimes we'll be confused and unsure of where to go or how to get there, and there's always a danger that, like quicksand catching the unwary traveler, we'll get sucked down into a morass.

For people like me who crave predictability and find all aspects of uncertainty unnerving, there will always be some fear strewn throughout teaching practices. For those of us professor birds who revel in the silent perfection of our syllabi/eggs before the noisy arrival of the actual living chicks/learners discombobulates us, uncertainty and some fear that is associated with it is simply a fact of our teaching life. Even if you're someone more able to go with the flow of life's inherent changeableness, the high stakes around teaching and learning can create uncertainty and fear. By "high stakes," I mean the way that college teaching and learning is closely linked to things with huge, real-life consequences such as grades, tuition, degrees, self-worth, employment, intellectual development, and economic security. Fear can take a big toll on our self-efficacy and very much interfere with our success when the consequences of our actions in the classroom can incur such real figurative and literal costs.

What's more, avidly grasping for certainty and attempting to eliminate all fear will *increase* the odds that we'll suffer those high costs. Pretending that things will go exactly as we plan makes it more likely we'll snafu something when things don't go as anticipated. Trying to convince ourselves that we won't make mistakes, won't encounter inequity, won't ever struggle to stay connected, won't feel distrustful, and won't fail at any point will only make it that much harder when we do make mistakes, encounter inequity, struggle to stay connected, feel distrustful, and fail. Such rigidity makes us more, not less, vulnerable to breaking when we're blown around in an uncertainty tornado or even a brisk breeze caused by a slight change of course.

When unexpected and unplanned-for things happen, as they always will, fear can easily take over if you've been pouring all your energy into futilely attempting to create a classroom where the unexpected and the unplanned for never occur. Anything from a head cold to a hurricane, not to mention world-altering events like a pandemic or the advance of AI, can completely derail teaching and learning if we've left no wiggle room or pockets of flexibility for fear and uncertainty. We need to find ways, before the quicksand bogs us down, to build our agentic educator buoyancy, and to float instead of sink when we find ourselves in a quagmire.

Building Buoyancy

Educational developer and scholar of teaching and learning Travis Thurston notes in the introduction to the 2021 collection *Resilient Pedagogy* that "teaching is hard at the best of times, but when we are forced to change instructional approaches, modalities, and locations amid a global pandemic and social unrest, it's, well, incredibly difficult." Resilient pedagogy, he continues, is not a panacea that makes teaching less difficult when we're coping with upheavals and uncertainties but rather a reframing of teaching as a "nuanced and ever-changing" process. He argues that we are always continually adjusting our practices while we learn how to help our students—who are themselves constantly changing—in constantly changing conditions.[2]

In Thurston's description of resilient pedagogy, he acknowledges the kinds of factors that I've been discussing throughout this book and that can cause things to go wrong:

> The work of resilient pedagogy makes us vulnerable to heartbreak and disappointment because we know we can create a better future for our students one interaction at a time and that we will fail along the way. It means that we recognize the inequities that exist in our current structures and that we not only work to adapt and transform those structures but continue to visualize how that architecture will need to take

shape and be molded moving forward. . . . In other words, the work of resilient pedagogy is messy, iterative, and continuously reflective by emphasizing process over product.[3]

As Thurston writes, failure is built into that requisite process. Inequities abound and uncertainty is ever present. But we continue teaching and learning by embracing the "messy, iterative, and continuously reflective" aspects of being in the college classroom.

Defining effective teaching and successful learning as an ongoing "messy, iterative," and "ever-changing" process of reflection and adaption, setbacks and progress (and frequently reminding ourselves of this definition) increases our ability to exercise agency when things go wrong. It is perhaps the only entire certainty we can count on when we are teaching and learning—the fact that there is no certainty, that we will make mistakes and that if we want to be effective teachers, we must accept that we're never going to stop learning about teaching and learning. We also must accept that inequity, disconnection, distrust, and failure will create fears and problems that directly cause snafus for students and for faculty. They will cause things to go wrong. But as I've shown, there are ways we can increase equity, connection, trust, and success, thereby at least reducing many uncertainties we face in the college classroom. We can plan for snafus and plan ways to reduce them. Honey, I shrunk the snafu!

As an effective teacher, you can—and you should—carefully plan. Plan your classes, assignments, and a variety of interactions and communications with students. Account and plan for emotional labor, systemic biases, and teaching disparities. Plan for seeking student feedback while protecting yourself from the harm that anonymous, end-of-term, standardized evaluations can do. Plan for helping students connect with one another. Plan for relentless transparency and communication with students about how their learning will be assessed. Plan to fight the Super Teacher myth and to get support and encouragement for your teaching from a pedagogical community of practice. Plan on identifying and documenting all the successes you achieve as a teacher and your students achieve as learners. Plan your professorial butt off.

But don't get exceedingly attached to your plans. Because at some point your plans will be interrupted or upended, and you and your students will make mistakes.

Over two decades now into my teaching career, I can still be easily flustered when things don't go like I planned, and I expect this will be true for the rest of my life in the college classroom. What has helped me the most has been talking to and learning from other people who care about teaching, reading the SoTL, and continually trying new things to mitigate and to prevent some snafus while at the same time planning and preparing for snafus. Planning won't change the fact that things won't always go as planned, but it can reduce the frequency and intensity of certain snafus. We can build a go-bag of teaching techniques, scripts, and strategies for when things do go wrong.

A Snafu Is Not a Fubar

In his book about helping students cultivate engaged attention in academic settings, James M. Lang argues for viewing the classroom as a space for creating an "attention retreat": "a retreat space from distraction, where we make deliberate efforts to do the hard work of using our attention in support of our learning" and facilitate for our students "safe and supported spaces where they can pause from their distractions and engage with us, with one another, and with the fascinating questions of our disciplines."[4] This really resonated with me, particularly in terms of teaching in the same physical space as students. Entering an on-site, in-person classroom has long been the only thing that enables me to discard all distractions and be completely present. (I'm still working on replicating this in asynchronous online spaces.) The classroom fully and completely absorbs every ounce of my attention; it becomes, without conscious thought or almost any effort on my part, my most vital "attention retreat."

I have a monkey mind full of emotional primates screeching and chattering about what I did in the past and what I might do in the future. Except when I'm working with students. Then I'm somehow able to shut down those mind monkeys for a little while and focus only on the people in front of me and on things we're doing to learn. It doesn't happen by magic, but I do experience it as a kind of faith. When I step into a classroom, I always bring faith that the labor of teaching and the hard work of learning is meaningful and that our academic agency always matters, no matter what limitations on our agency exist, or how daunting the obstacles to effective teaching and authentic learning may be, or how many things went wrong before or will go wrong in the future.

My faith in teaching and learning didn't just appear one day. I laid the groundwork by consciously deciding that teaching effectively really mattered to me—a lot—and that I was going to utilize all my scholarly skills to learn from researchers and experts about effective teaching practices. Today it exists on its own: my stubborn optimism and faith in transformative education, even in the face of major, fear-inducing, agency-reducing factors such as the recent politically motivated attacks on equity efforts in higher education. I continue to have faith in the transformative potential of learning and the transformative power of teaching.

Until the pandemic lockdown closed my on-campus classrooms in 2020, I didn't understand how much that faith and optimism influenced my day-to-day teaching practices. I didn't realize how much I depended on the attention retreat of the classroom as the time and place I could count on my brain's continually spinning gears to be quieted for a while. Until it was gone, I didn't realize how much I drew on the predictability of this cognitive, emotional, and physical experience and the general predictability of the standard college academic calendar. Fortunately, I discovered that we can be as buoyant in the quicksand of things going wrong as we are in the smooth, untroubled waters of things going according to plan. Because there's a big difference between situation normal, all fouled up (a snafu) and situations fouled up beyond all repair (a fubar). Inequity, disconnection, distrust, failure, and fear will routinely foul up teaching and learning. But those foul-ups do not need to become fubars when we exercise agency, help students exercise agency, and have a go-bag for when things go wrong.

We can't ever totally avoid the fearful, fear-inducing clutches of all the things that go wrong in the college classroom. But when the ground beneath us starts dissolving into quicksand, we can stop ourselves from sinking and STIR instead, identifying it as a normal and to-be-expected snafu, an everyday snafu that can be mitigated with our agentive teaching practices, not a fubar we never saw coming that's going to drown us in mud and sludge. Buoyancy doesn't stop things from going wrong. It can't eradicate all fear or create absolutely equitable, connected, trusting, successful learning and teaching environments. Buoyancy won't dry up the quicksand . . . but it can keep our heads, and our students' heads, above the muck. We can help one another escape its clutches. Buoyancy enables us to float on the surface of the quicksand until we can reach up for help and scramble back onto more solid ground.

NOTES

Introduction

1. Rosemary Mosco, "Bird and Moon: Instinct Is Weird," Rosemary Mosco, n.d., https://rosemarymosco.com/comics/bird-and-moon/instinct-is-weird.

2. Kevin Gannon, interview with John Kane and Rebecca Mushtare, "A Return to Rigor?," August 9, 2023, *Tea for Teaching*, podcast and transcript, https://teaforteaching.com/301-a-return-to-rigor/.

3. Paul Emerich France, "Collective Efficacy or Toxic Positivity?," *Educational Leadership* 79, no. 3 (2021): 32–37; and Kerry Howells, *Gratitude in Education: A Radical View* (Sense Publishers, 2010), 93–107.

4. I appreciate scholars who are willing to discuss teaching mistakes in print, but usually the takeaways from these articles are framed as "Now I know better so now I do better." That's not a bad takeaway in and of itself, but, collectively, such work suggests that when things go wrong in the classroom, it's an individual problem that is fixable. Notable exceptions include Michelle Jackson, "On Engaging Students: What I Learned from One of My Biggest Teaching Mistakes," *Transformative Dialogues* 10, no. 2 (2017): 1–5, https://doi.org/10.5325/trajincschped.29.1.0099; and Brenda Miller Power and Ruth Shagoury Hubbard, eds., *Oops: What We Learn When Our Teaching Fails* (Stenhouse Publishers, 1996).

5. On the term "effective teaching" (rather than "excellent" or even "good" teaching), see Jessamyn Neuhaus, *Geeky Pedagogy: A Guide for Intellectuals, Introverts, and Nerds Who Want to Be Effective Teachers* (West Virginia University Press, 2019), 16–17.

6. Roxanna Harlow, "'Race Doesn't Matter, but . . .': The Effect of Race on Professors' Experiences and Emotion Management in the Undergraduate College Classroom," *Social Psychology Quarterly* 66, no. 4 (December 2003): 362, https://doi.org/10.2307/1519834.

7. Jessamyn Neuhaus, ed., *Picture a Professor: Interrupting Biases about Faculty and Increasing Student Learning* (West Virginia University Press, 2022).

8. Cate Denial, Clarissa Sorensen-Unruh, and Elizabeth Lehfeldt, "After the Great Pivot Should Come the Great Pause," *Chronicle of Higher Education*, February 25, 2022, https://www.chronicle.com/article/after-the-great-pivot-should

-come-the-great-pause; Virginia Gewin, "Pandemic Burnout Is Rampant in Academia," *Nature* 591, no. 7850 (2021): 489–91, https://doi.org/10.1038/d41586-021 -00663-2; and Mary McNaughton-Cassill, Stella Lopez, and Aaron Cassill, "What if the Faculty Are Not Alright? Burnout and Compassion Fatigue in Higher Education," *Change: The Magazine of Higher Learning* 55, no. 5 (2023): 23–34, https:// doi.org/10.1080/00091383.2023.2235250.

9. Traumatic stress is the fear, anxiety, distress, and other emotional consequences of traumatic events, even when you do not experience the event directly. It can significantly shape students' experiences in the classroom. Victoria M. E. Bridgland et al., "Why the COVID-19 Pandemic Is a Traumatic Stressor," *PloS One* 16, no. 1 (2021): https://doi.org/10.1371/ journal.pone.0240146; Yusen Zhai and Xue Du, "Trends in Diagnosed Posttraumatic Stress Disorder and Acute Stress Disorder in College Students, 2017–2022," *JAMA Network Open* 7, no. 45 (2024): https://doi.org/10.1001/jamanetworkopen.2024.13874

10. I'm indebted to Liz Norrell for helping me articulate these points and for the phrase "not a problem to be solved."

11. Power and Hubbard, "Introduction," in Power and Hubbard, *Oops*, vii, viii.

12. Specific definitions of "snafu" as a noun vary somewhat. *The Cambridge Dictionary* defines "snafu" as "a situation in which nothing has happened as planned," while Merriam-Webster defines it as "a situation marked by errors and confusion" and Vocabulary.com defines it as "an obstacle or glitch that keeps you from accomplishing something."

13. Glenda Bissex, "Scenes from the Inner Life of a Teacher," in Power and Hubbard, *Oops*, 90.

14. Tema Okun is credited with linking perfectionism to white supremacy culture in the workplace. See also Nancy Ehrenreich, "When Professors Get in Their Own Way: Law Teaching and Academic Perfectionism," University of Denver Sturm College of Law, legal studies research paper (2019), https://ssrn.com /abstract=3431301; Daniel Madigan, "A Meta-Analysis of Perfectionism and Academic Achievement," *Educational Psychology Review* 31 (2019): 967–89, https:// doi.org/10.1007/s10648-019-09484-2; Rebecca Pope-Ruark, *Burnout: Pathways to Reckoning and Renewal* (Johns Hopkins University Press, 2022), 69–73; and Janelle Raymundo, "The Burden of Excellence: A Critical Race Theory Analysis of Perfectionism in Black Students," *The Vermont Connection* 42, no. 1 (2021), https://scholarworks.uvm.edu/tvc/vol42/iss1/12.

15. Though this group does not consist solely of tenured full professors, it's worth noting that tenured full professors often never face any long-term professional consequences for ineffective teaching practices and, frequently, receive few institutional rewards or incentives for improving their teaching practices.

16. Brian Rosenberg, *"Whatever It Is, I'm Against It": Resistance to Change in Higher Education* (Harvard University Press, 2023).

17. See chapter five for a brief discussion of trauma-informed pedagogy.

18. SOAR is sometimes defined as "Stop, Observe, Assess, React" or "Stop, Observe, Analyze, and Respond." "Getting Started with Managing Classroom Conflict," Cornell University Center for Teaching, https://teaching.cornell.edu /resource/getting-started-managing-classroom-conflict/. Another variation for classroom conflict management is SOAR-UP, as in Stop, Observe, Assess, React, Use (active listening techniques), and Prepare (for the next time), described by the University of North Carolina at Chapel Hill's Center for Faculty Excellence, *CFE Newsletter*, November 2004.

19. The term "classroom" includes both on-site spaces where students and faculty gather on campus at the same moment in time as well as asynchronous online learning environments. While I don't examine issues unique to online or HyFlex teaching and learning in this book, the snafus and strategies I discuss are relevant in many modalities.

20. Joshua Piven and David Borgenicht, *The Worst-Case Scenario Survival Handbook* (Chronicle Books, 1999). I refer to this tongue-in-cheek but factual guide throughout *Snafu Edu*. I'm drawing on its premise—specific action steps for surviving ludicrously terrible situations—as a smarty-pants rejoinder to sanctimonious teaching advice that downplays or elides the reality of things going wrong.

Chapter 1

1. Lauren Stentiford and Georg Koutsouris, "What Are Inclusive Pedagogies in Higher Education? A Systemic Scoping Review," *Studies in Higher Education* 46, no. 11 (2021): 2245–61. See also Gary A. Berg, "Equity and Diversity in the 21st Century University: A Literature Review," in *Accessibility and Diversity in the 21st Century University*, ed. Gary A. Berg and Linda Venis (IGI Global, 2020).

2. Emily Brier, "Pandemic Pedagogy: Practical and Empathetic Teaching Practices," *Spectra* (The Social Political and Cultural Theories Archives) 8, no. 2 (2021): 31–37; Carla D. Chugani and Amy Houtrow, "Effect of the COVID-19 Pandemic on College Students with Disabilities," *American Journal of Public Health* 110, no. 12 (December 2020): 1722–23, https://doi.org/10.2105/AJPH.2020.305983; and Alyssa M. Lederer et al., "More Than Inconvenienced: The Unique Needs of U.S. College Students During the COVID-19 Pandemic," *Health Education and Behavior* 48, no. 1 (2021): 14–19, https://doi.org/10.1177/1090198120969372.

3. Nichole Margarita Garcia, "You Don't Look Like a Professor," Diverse Education, June 29, 2018, https://diverseeducation.com/article/113239/.

4. Chavella Pittman and Thomas J. Tobin, "Academe Has a Lot to Learn about Inclusive Teaching," *Chronicle of Higher Education*, February 7, 2022: https://www.chronicle.com/article/academe-has-a-lot-to-learn-about-how -inclusive-teaching-affects-instructors.

5. Tracie Marcella Addy et al., *What Inclusive Instructors Do: Principles and Practices for Excellence in College Teaching* (Stylus, 2021), 152.

6. Isis Artze-Vega et al., *The Norton Guide to Equity-Minded Teaching* (W. W. Norton, 2023), xxi.

7. M. L. N. Birdwell and Keaton Bayley, "When the Syllabus Is Ableist: Understanding How Class Policies Fail Disabled Students," *Teaching English in the Two Year College* 49, no. 3 (2022): 220–37.

8. On the use of the term "opportunity gap," see Kelly A. Hogan and Viji Sathy, *Inclusive Teaching: Strategies for Promoting Equity in the College Classroom* (West Virginia University Press, 2022), xi. See also Genyne L. Royal et al., "From Theory to Practice: Leveraging Identity-Conscious Student Success Strategies to Close Opportunity Gaps for Black Undergraduate Students," *College Student Affairs Journal* 40, no. 2 (2022): 100–114. Estela Mara Bensimon and Yolanda Watson Spiva argue for using the term "institutional performance gap" in "The End of 'Equity Gaps' in Higher Education," Diverse: Issues in Higher Ed, August 24, 2022, https://www.diverseeducation.com/opinion/article/15295980/the-end-of-equity-gaps-in-higher-education

9. Artze-Vega et al., *Norton Guide*, xvii.

10. Jade McKay and Marcia Devlin, "'Low Income Doesn't Mean Stupid and Destined for Failure': Challenging the Deficit Discourse around Students from Low SES Backgrounds in Higher Education," *International Journal of Inclusive Education* 20, no. 4 (2016): 347–63, https://doi.org/10.1080/13603116.2015.1079273.

11. Elise Gahan, Sara Farooqui, and Cindy W. Leung, "'You Feel Out of Place': A PhotoVoice Study of the Impact of Food Insecurity on College Students," *Health Equity* 6, no. 1 (2022): 595–602; Mary E. Haskett et al., "The Role of University Students' Wellness in Links Between Homelessness, Food Insecurity, and Academic Success," *Journal of Social Distress and Homelessness* 30, no. 1 (2021): 59–65, https://doi.org/10.1080/10530789.2020.1733815; Richard Rickelle at al., "A Comparison of Experiences with Factors Related to Food Insecurity between College Students Who are Food Secure and Food Insecure: A Qualitative Study," *Journal of the Academy of Nutrition and Dietetics* (2022): https://doi.org/10.1016/j.jand.2022.08.001/.

12. Karen Weese, "When a Sudden, Small Expense Threatens an Entire College Career," *Washington Post,* January 30, 2022, https://www.washingtonpost.com/education/2022/01/30/college-poverty-expense-cost-dropout/

13. Emma Fernandez, "Colleges and Universities are Experiencing their Own Affordable Housing Crisis," Housing Matters, July 27, 2022, https://housingmatters.urban.org/articles/colleges-and-universities-are-experiencing-their-own-affordable-housing-crisis.

14. For citations about the impact of the COVID-19 pandemic on students economic, housing, and food security, visit https://jessamynneuhaus.com.

15. "The Very Wide Gap in College Graduation Rates," *Journal of Blacks in Higher Education*, November 7, 2022, https://www.jbhe.com/2022/11/the-very-wide-racial-gap-in-college-graduation-rates/.

16. Kristen A. Renn, "Low-Income, First-Generation College Students," Footnotes: The Magazine of the American Sociological Association 50, no. 2 (2023), https://www.asanet.org/footnotes-article/low-income-first-generation-college-students. For citations about the impact of the pandemic on first-generation students, visit https://jessamynneuhaus.com.

17. "Visualizing Health Equity: One Size Does Not Fit All Infographic," June 30, 2017, Robert Wood Johnson Foundation, https://www.rwjf.org/en/insights/our-research/infographics/visualizing-health-equity.html.

18. Hogan and Sathy, Inclusive Teaching, 4–5. See also Michel Estefan, Jesse Cordes Selbin, and Sarah Macdonald, "From Inclusive to Equitable Pedagogy: How to Design Course Assignments and Learning Activities that Address Structural Inequalities," Teaching Sociology 51, no. 3 (2023), https://doi.org/10.1177/0092055X231174515.

19. Irenee Beattie and Megan Thiele Strong, "Connecting in Class? College Class Size and Inequality in Academic Social Capital," Journal of Higher Education 87, no. 3 (2016): 332–62.

20. For citations on student biases about faculty, visit https://jessamyn neuhaus.com.

21. Beverly Irby et al., eds., Women of Color in STEM: Navigating the Double Bind in Higher Education (Information Age Publishing, 2021); Allison Mattheis et al., "'Maybe This Is Not the Place for Me': Gender Harassment and Discrimination in the Geosciences," PloS One 17, no. 5 (2022), https://doi.org/10.1371/journal.pone.0268562; Krista Lynn Minnotte and Daphene Pedersen, "Sexual Harassment, Sexual Harassment Climate, and the Well-Being of STEM Faculty Members," Innovative Higher Education 48 (2023): 601–18, https://doi.org/10.1007/s10755-023-09645-w; and Jamin Speer, "Bye by Ms. American Sci: Women and the Leaky STEM Pipeline," Economics of Education Review 93 (April 2023), https://doi.org/10.1016/j.econedurev.2023.102371.

22. Gabriella Gutiérrez y Muhs, ed., Presumed Incompetent: The Intersections of Race and Class for Women in Academia (University of Colorado Press, 2012).

23. For a detailed bibliography about teaching inequities, visit https://pictureaprofessor.com.

24. Stephanie Fryberg, "Constructing Junior Faculty of Color as Strugglers: The Implications for Tenure and Promotion," in The Future of Diversity: Academic Leaders Reflect on American Higher Education, ed. Daniel Little and Satya P. Mohanty (Palgrave Macmillan, 2021); Stephanie Lechuga-Peña, "Navigating Pre-Tenure and COVID-19: A Testimonio of a BIPOC Junior Faculty Mother," Affilia 37, no. 1 (2022): 13–19, https://doi.org/10.1177/08861099921104843; Gudrun Nyunt et al., "Tenure Undone: Faculty Experiences of Organizational Justice When Tenure Seems or Becomes Unattainable," Equity and Excellence in Education (2022), https://doi.org/10.1080/10665684.2021.2010013; Grace Park, "My Tenure Denial," in Yolanda Flores Niemann, Gabriella Gutiérrez y Muhs,

and Carmen G. González, eds., *Presumed Incompetent II: Race, Class, Power and Resistance of Women in Academia* (University of Colorado Press, 2020), 280–89; Patricia Perez, *The Tenure-Track Process for Chicana and Latina Faculty: Experiences of Resisting and Persisting in the Academy* (Rutledge, 2019); and Rachel Tudor, "Unconquered and Unconquerable: A Chickasaw Woman's Quest for Tenure," in Niemann, Gutiérrez y Muhs, and González, *Presumed Incompetent II*, 341–50.

25. Chavella Pittman, "Achieving Racial Equity in Tenure and Promotion," American Association of University Professors, Winter 2023, https://www.aaup.org/article/achieving-racial-equity-promotion-and-tenure.

26. TaLisa Carter and Miltonette Craig, "It Could Be Us: Black Faculty as 'Threats' on the Path to Tenure," *Race and Justice* 12, no. 3 (2022): 569, https://doi.org/10.1177/21533687221087366.

27. For citations on microaggressions, visit https://jessamynneuhaus.com.

28. Mart Elliot and Sarah J. Blithe, "Gender Inequality, Stress Exposure, and Well-Being among Academic Faculty," *International Journal of Higher Education* 10, no. 2 (2021): 240–52; Nicholas Hartlep and Daisy Ball, eds., *Racial Battle Fatigue in Faculty: Perspectives and Lessons from Higher Education* (Routledge, 2019); Evangela Q. Oates, "They Took My Hair—Racial Battle Fatigue in Academe: Accounts from the Plantation," in Teresa Y. Neely and Margie Montañez, *Dismantling Constructs of Whiteness in Higher Education* (Routledge, 2023); Melissa A. Martinez et al., "Sacrificing Body and Mind: Pretenure Women Faculty of Color, Their Health, and Well-Being," *Journal of Diversity in Higher Education* (2023), https://doi.org/10.1037/dhe0000462; Kerrie G. Wilkins-Yel, "'I Can't Push off My Own Mental Health': Chilly STEM Climates, Mental Health, and STEM Persistence Among Black, Latina, and White Graduate Women," *Sex Roles* 86, no. 3–4 (2022): 208–36, https://doi.org/10.1007/s11199-021-01262-1; and Ruth Enid Zambrana et al., "Workplace Stress and Discrimination Effects on the Physical and Depressive Symptoms of Underrepresented Minority Faculty," *Stress and Health* 37, no. 1 (2021): 175–85, https://doi.org/10.1002/smi.2983.

29. Vera Dolan, "'. . . But if You Tell Anyone, I'll Deny We Ever met': The Experiences of Academics with Invisible Disabilities in the Neoliberal University," *International Journal of Qualitative Studies in Education* 36, no. 4 (2023): 689–706, https://doi.org/10.1080/09518398.2021.1885075; Chang-kyu Kwon, "Resistance from the Margin: An Autoethnographic Account of Academic Ableism," *Human Resource Development Quarterly* 35, no. 1 (March 2024): 89–107, https://doi.org/10.1002/hrdq.21498; Sally Lindsay and Kristina Fuentes, "It Is Time to Address Ableism in Academia: A Systemic Review of Experiences and Impact of Ableism among Faculty and Staff," *Disabilities* 2, no. 2 (2022): 178–203, https://doi.org/10.3390/disabilities2020014; Cameron McKenzie and Maryam Khan, "The University and Social Work under Neoliberalism: Where's the Inclusion for Disabled Faculty?," *Social Inclusion* 11, no. 2 (2023): 136–46; Damian Mellifont,

"Ableist Ivory Towers: A Narrative Review Informing about the Lived Experiences of Neurodivergent Staff in Contemporary Higher Education," *Disability & Society* 38, no. 5 (2023): 865–86, https://doi.org/10.1080/09687599.2021.1965547; and Theodoto W. Ressa, "Disability, Race, and Immigration Intersectionality: Disempowering the Disabled through Institutionalized Ableism in American Higher Education," *Educational Forum* 87, no. 1 (2023): 17–32, https://doi.org/10.1080/00131725.2022.2065711.

30. Emily Kibler and Caroline J. Ketcham, "Ableism in Academia: Let's Talk about Desks," Elon University, Center for Engaged Learning, November 9, 2021, https://www.centerforengagedlearning.org/ableism-in-academia-lets-talk-about-desks/.

31. Bradley Irish, "How to Make Room for Neurodivergent Professors," *Chronicle of Higher Education*, March 2, 2023: https://www.chronicle.com/article/how-to-make-room-for-neurodivergent-professors.

32. Ai Binh T. Ho et al., "Cripping Neutrality: Student Resistance, Pedagogical Audiences, and Teachers' Accommodations," *Pedagogy: Critical Approaches to Teaching Literature, Language, Culture, and Composition* 20, no. 1 (2020): 127–39; Sheri Wells-Jensen, Emily K. Michael, and Mona Minkara, "How Blind Professors Win the First Day: Setting Ourselves Up for Success," in *Picture a Professor: Interrupting Biases about Faculty and Increasing Student Learning*, ed. Jessamyn Neuhaus (West Virginia University Press, 2022), 33–50.

33. For citations on gender stereotypes and faculty, visit https://jessamyn neuhaus.com.

34. Muninder K. Ahluwalia et al., "Mitigating the 'Powder Keg': The Experiences of Faculty of Color Teaching Multicultural Competence," *Teaching of Psychology* 46, no. 3 (2019): 187–96, https://doi.org/10.1177/0098628319848864; Celeste Atkin, "Teaching Up: Faculty of Color Teaching about Privilege," in *Gender, Race, and Class in the Lives of Today's Teachers: Educators at Intersections*, ed. Lata Murti and Glenda M. Flores (Springer, 2021); Guy A. Boysen, "Student Evaluations of Teaching: Can Teaching Social Justice Negatively Affect One's Career?," in *Navigating Difficult Moments in Teaching Diversity and Social Justice*, ed. Mary Kite, Kim Case, and Wendy Williams (American Psychological Association, 2021); Ginger Ko, "The Case for Humanities Training: A Woman of Color Teaching Social Justice in a Predominantly White Institution," *Theory in Action* 8, no. 4 (October 2015): 55–65, https://doi.org/10.3798/tia.1937-0237.15023; and Ryan Miller, Cathy Howell, and Laura Struve, "'Constantly, Excessively, and All the Time': The Emotional Labor of Teaching Diversity Courses," *International Journal of Teaching and Learning in Higher Education* 31, no. 3 (2019): 491–502.

35. As quoted in Glenn Colby, "Data Snapshot: Tenure and Contingency in U.S. Higher Education," AAUP, Spring 2023, https://www.aaup.org/article/data-snapshot-tenure-and-contingency-us-higher-education.

36. Thanks to Lillian Nave and Travis Thurston for introducing me to the acronym "VITAL."

37. For citations on contingent employment inequities, visit https://jess amynneuhaus.com.

38. Eric Fure-Slocum and Claire Goldsten, eds., *Contingent Faculty and the Remaking of Higher Education: A Labor History* (University of Illinois Press, 2024); Brenda J. Kirby and Clifford B. Donn, "A Comparative Analysis of Adjunct Faculty Collective Bargaining Agreements," *Journal of Higher Education Theory and Practice* 20, no. 3 (2020): 72–81, https://doi.org/10.33423 /jhetp.v20i3.2973; Gary Rhoades, "Taking College Teachers' Working Conditions Seriously: Adjunct Faculty and Negotiating a Labor-Based Conception of Quality," *Journal of Higher Education* 91, no. 3 (2021): 327–52, https://doi.org /10.1080/00221546.2019.1664196; Christian A. I. Schlaerth, "Adjuncts Unite! The Struggle to Unionize, Administrative Response, and Building a Bigger Movement," *Labor Studies Journal* 47, no. 1 (2022): 5–27, https://doi.org/10.1177 /0160449X211028660.

39. Albertus Barnes and Elisa Fredericks, "A Diamond in the Rough: Adjunct Faculty Opportunities and Challenges in Higher Learning Institutions," *Journal of Higher Education Theory and Practice* 21, no. 7 (2021): 83–102, https:// doi.org/10.33423/jhetp.v21i7.4489; Samantha Estrada Aguilera and Erica Martinez, "Average or Outlier? Introductory Statistics Adjunct Instructors' Beliefs, Practices, and Experience," *Qualitative Report* 28, no. 6 (2023): 1769–86; Liza Ann Bolitzer, "'A Two-Way Street': Adjunct Faculty's Learning from and with Students about Subject Matter," *College Teaching* 70, no. 1 (2022): 82–97, https://doi.org/10.1080/87567555.2021.1901067; and Kelly Chen, Zeynep Hansen, and Scott Lowe, "Why Do We Inflate Grades? The Effect of Adjunct Faculty Employment on Instructor Grading Standards," *Journal of Human Resources* 56, no. 3 (2021): 878–921, https://doi.org/10.3368/jhr.56.3.0518-9493R2. On support for VITAL pedagogical learning and development, see Kim Buch, Heather McCullough, and Jessica Kapota, "Virtual Faculty Learning Communities: An Innovative Approach to Supporting Adjunct Faculty," *Journal of Faculty Development* 37, no. 1 (2023): 15–23; Roy Fuller, and Marie Kendall Brown, eds., *Adjunct Faculty Voices: Cultivating Professional Development and Community at the Front Lines of Higher Education* (Routledge, 2017); Caroline Gelman, Jill Gandel, and Margaret Bausman, "A Multi-Faceted, Adjunct-Centered Initiative to Support Part-Time Faculty," *Journal of Teaching in Social Work* 42, no. 1 (2022): 82–99, https://doi.org/10.1080/08841233.2021.2013000; and Hellen Machelle Skinner, Brooke McAtee, and Rachel Huston, "Finding Innovative Strategies to Enhance Adjunct Faculty Support and Retention," *Journal of Nursing Education* (2023): 1–4, https://doi.org/10.3928/01484834-20230315-02.

40. Lauren Barbeau and Claudia Cornejo Happel, *Critical Teaching Behaviors: Defining, Documenting, and Discussing Good Teaching* (Stylus, 2023), 97–107; David Gooblar, *The Missing Course: Everything They Never Taught You about College Teaching* (Harvard University Press, 2019), 206–19; Alenius Saroyan et al., "Assumptions Underlying Workshop Activities," in *Rethinking Teaching in Higher*

Education: From a Course Design Workshop to a Faculty Development Framework, ed. Alenius Saroyan and Cheryl Amundsen (Stylus, 2004), 25–26.

41. Cynthia J. Finelli et al., "Reducing Student Resistance to Active Learning: Strategies for Instructors," *Journal of College Science Teaching* 47, no. 5 (2018): 80–91, https://doi.org/10.2505/4/jcst18_047_05_80; Cosette Lemelin et al., "Mitigating Student Resistance to Active Learning by Constructing Resilient Classroom," *Bioscene: Journal of College Biology Teaching* 47, no. 2 (December 2021): 3–9; Madison Andrews et al., "Explanation and Facilitation Strategies Reduce Student Resistance to Active Learning," *College Teaching* 70, no. 4 (2022): 530–40, https://doi.org/10.1080/87567555.2021.1987183; Harriet Schwartz, *Connected Teaching: Relationship, Power, and Mattering in Higher Education* (Stylus, 2019), 79–82; and Melody Pugh, "Just to Get the Grade: Learning Ecologies and Invisible Student Resistance," *Pedagogy: Critical Approaches to Teaching Literature, Language, Culture, and Composition* 20, no. 1 (2020): 59–71.

42. For citations and a detailed discussion about SET, see Jessamyn Neuhaus, "Figuring Out Student Feedback on Teaching: Strategies for Reducing Potential Personal and Professional Harm to Faculty," Picture a Professor, January 2023, https://pictureaprofessor.com.

43. Megan Weir, "Hitting Un-Mute: Let's Talk about the Impact of Abusive Teaching Evaluations," International Society of Critical Health Psychology, November 2, 2021, https://ischp.net/2018/11/01/hitting-un-mute-lets-talk-about-the-impact-of-abusive-teaching-evaluations.

44. Artze-Vega et al., *Norton Guide* 177; Tamara Glenz, "The Importance of Learning Students' Names," *Journal on Best Teaching Practices* 1, no. 1 (April 2014): 21–22; Rita Kohli and Daniel G. Solórzano, "Teachers, Please Learn Our Names! Racial Microagressions [*sic*] and the K–12 Classroom," *Race Ethnicity and Education* 15, no. 4 (2012): 441–62, https://doi.org/10.1080/13613324.2012.674026; Yvette Denise Murdoch, Lim Hyejung, and Alin Kang, "Learning Students' Given Names Benefits EMI Classes," *English in Education* 52, no. 3 (2018): 225–47, https://doi.org/10.1080/04250494.2018.1509673; Molly Townes O'Brien, Tania Leiman, and James Duffy, "The Power of Naming: The Multifaceted Value of Learning Students' Names," *QUT Law Review* 14, no. 1 (2014): 114–28, https://doi.org/10.5204/qutlr.v14i1.544; and Keisha Payne et al., "Names: A New Dimension of Transformation," *Race, Ethnicity and Education* 21, no. 4 (2018): 564–71, https://doi.org/10.1080/13613324.2016.1248832.

45. Addy et al., *What Inclusive Instructors Do*, 75–76; Hogan and Sathy, *Inclusive Teaching*, 95–96; LaSonya L. Moore et al., "The Power of a Name: Nontraditional Names, Teacher Efficacy, and Expected Learning Outcomes," *Journal of English Learner Education* 1, no. 11 (2020): 83–103.

46. Jessamyn Neuhaus, "Embodied Identity, Empowering Pedagogy, and Transformative Learning," in Neuhaus, *Picture a Professor*, 2.

47. Shanique Brown and Jennifer Gómez, "What BIPOC Professors Need from Students," Inside Higher Ed, March 3, 2022, https://www.insidehighered

.com/advice/2022/03/04/advice-how-grad-students-and-others-should-interact
-bipoc-women-professors-opinion; Cathy N. Davidson and Christina Katopodis, *The New College Classroom* (Harvard University Press, 2022), 41–44; and Ty-Ron Douglas and Sydney Freeman, "Why Do I Have to Call You Doctor?," Diverse: Issues in Higher Education, August 25, 2020, https://www.diverseeducation .com/opinion/article/15107622/why-do-i-have-to-call-you-doctor; Carrie J. Preston, "Do You Make Them Call You 'Professor?,'" *Chronicle of Higher Education*, November 2, 2016, https://www.chronicle.com/article/do-you-make-them-call -you-professor.

48. "Deadnaming: How Using the Wrong Name Can Affect Mental Health," PsychCentral, November 16, 2021, https://psychcentral.com/health /deadnaming.

49. Erin M. Adams, "Transforming Higher Education for the Betterment of Trans* Students," *Vermont Connection* 44, no. 1 (2023), https://scholarworks .uvm.edu/tvc/vol44/iss1/14/; Tamar Austin and Jay L. Austin, "Trans*script," in *Transnarratives: Scholarly and Creative Work on the Trans Experience*, ed. Kristi Carter and James Bruton (Women's Press, 2021), 91–103; Dot Brauer, "Complexities of Supporting Transgender Students' Use of Self-Identified First Names and Pronouns," *College and University* 92, no. 3 (2017): 2–13; Sofia Melendez and Archie Crowley, "Pronoun Practices in the Higher Education Classroom," *Journal of Language and Sexuality* 11, no. 2 (2022): 264–77, https://doi.org/10.1075 /jls.20022.cro; Alex Meyers, *Supporting Transgender Students* (University of New Orleans Press, 2021).

50. Z Nicolazzo, "The Spectre of the Tranny: Pedagogical (Im)possibilities," *Pedagogy, Culture, and Society* 29, no. 5 (2021): 811–24, https://doi.org/10 .1080/14681366.2021.1912163; Julia Sinclair-Palm and Kit Chokly, "'It's a Giant Faux Paus': Exploring Young Trans People's Beliefs about Deadnaming and the Term Deadname," *Journal of LGBT Youth* 20, no. 2 (2023): 370–89, https:// doi.org/10.1080/19361653.2022.2076182; Stephen Turton, "Deadnaming as Disformative Utterance," *Gender and Language* 15, no. 1 (2021), https://doi.org /10.1558/genl.18816; and Stanley R. Vance Jr., "The Importance of Getting the Name Right for Transgender and Other Gender Expansive Youth," *Journal of Adolescent Health* 63, no. 4 (2018): 379–80, https://doi.org/10.1016/j.jadohealth .2018.07.022.

Chapter 2

1. Jessica Bursztynsky, "UI Professor Leaves after Email Scandal Refusing to Accommodate Student," *Daily Illini*, September 12, 2017: https://dailyillini .com/news-stories/campus-life/2017/09/12/ui-professor-leaves-refusing -accommodate-student/; Daily Princetonian Editorial Board, "The N Word Is Not Your Educational Tool," *Daily Princetonian*, November 20, 2022, https:// www.dailyprincetonian.com/article/2022/11/princeton-professor-editorial-n

-word-scanlan; Brad Evans, "SUNY Plattsburgh Students Protest Racist Photo Posted on Social Media," NBC5, February 16, 2018, https://www.mynbc5.com /article/suny-plattsburgh-students-protest-racist-photo-posted-on-social-media /18210002#; Brandon Griggs, "A Black Yale Graduate Student Took a Nap in Her Dorm's Common Room. So a White Student Called Police," CNN, May 12, 2018, https://www.cnn.com/2018/05/09/us/yale-student-napping-black-trnd /index.html; Brianna Hatch, "A Professor Alleged Racial Profiling by a Campus Police Officer. Then Things Escalated," *Chronicle of Higher Education*, August 6, 2022, https://www.chronicle.com/article/a-professor-alleged-racial -profiling-by-a-campus-police-officer-then-things-escalated; Scott Jaschik, "The Admissions Tour That Went Horribly Wrong," Inside Higher Ed, May 6, 2018, https://www.insidehighered.com/admissions/article/2018/05/07/colorado -state-investigates-why-native-american-students-admissions; and Kelly Meyerhofer, "UW-Madison Student Apologizes for Racist Social Media Video, Calling Comments 'Completely Inexcusable,'" *Milwaukee Journal Sentinel*, June 8, 2023, https://www.jsonline.com/story/news/education/2023/06/06/university-of -wisconsin-student-audrey-godlewski-apologizes-for-racist-comments-in-social -media-vide/70291633007/.

2. Brendan T. Johns and Melody Dye, "Gender Bias at Scale: Evidence from the Usage of Personal Names," *Behavior Research Methods* 51 (2019): 1601–18; Rosine Mpozenzi, "Ever Been Mistaken for the Other Black Student in Your Class by a White Professor?," *CogBlog—A Cognitive Psychology Blog*, Colby College, May 16, 2022, https://web.colby.edu/cogblog/2022/05/16/ever-been -mistaken-for-the-other-black-student-in-your-class-by-a-white-professor/.

3. Derald Wing Sue et al., "Racial Microaggressions in Everyday Life: Implications for Clinical Practice," *American Psychologist* 62, no. 4 (2007): 271–86, https://doi.org/10.1037/0003-066X.62.4.271.

4. For citations on microaggressions, visit https://jessamynneuhaus.com.

5. Chavella T. Pittman and Niya Boyd, "Addressing Destructive Behaviour in the Classroom: Interview with Chavella T. Pittman," OneHE, n.d., https:// onehe.org/resources/addressing-destructive-behaviour-in-the-classroom -interview-with-chavella-pittman/.

6. Kelly A. Hogan and Viji Sathy, *Inclusive Teaching: Strategies for Promoting Equity in the College Classroom* (West Virginia University Press, 2022), 150.

7. Hogan and Sathy, *Inclusive Teaching*, 150.

8. Loretta J. Ross, "Speaking Up without Tearing Down," Southern Poverty Law Center, *Learning for Justice Magazine* 61, Spring 2019, https://www .learningforjustice.org/magazine/spring-2019/speaking-up-without-tearing -down.

9. Chavella Pittman, "10 in the Moment Responses for Addressing Micro and Macroaggressions in the Classroom," Scholarly Teacher, May 17, 2023, https://www.scholarlyteacher.com/post/10-in-the-moment-responses-for -addressing-micro-and-macroaggressions-in-the-classroom.

10. I should note that apologies can't be faked; they need to be rooted in some genuine regret. See Daniël Cuypers et al., eds., *Public Apology Between Ritual and Regret: Symbolic Excuses on False Pretenses or True Reconciliation out of Sincere Regret?* (Rodopi, 2013); Shike Li et al., "When Apologizing Hurts: Felt Transgression and Restoration Efforts," *Journal of Organizational Behavior* 44, no. 1 (2023): 42–63, https://doi.org/10.1002/job.2672.

11. Tai Saint-Louis, "Doing Too Much: Fired White Professor Wrote 9-Page Apology for Confusing 2 Black Students," *Black Enterprise*, December 12, 2021, https://www.blackenterprise.com/doing-too-much-fired-white-professor-wrote-9-page-apology-for-confusing-2-black-students/.

12. Oluremi Bolanle, "Workplace Conflict and Willingness to Cooperate: The Importance of Apology and Forgiveness," *International Journal of Conflict Management* 27, no. 2 (2016): 172–98, https://doi.org/10.1108/IJCMA-12-2014-0092; Guglielmo Faldetta, "Forgiving the Unforgivable: The Possibility of the 'Unconditional' Forgiveness in the Workplace," *Journal of Business Ethics* 180 (2022): 91–103, https://doi.org/10.1007/s10551-021-04885-2; Harriet Lerner, "The Power of Apologizing: What It Takes to Be Really Sorry," *Psychotherapy Networker*, March/April 2018, https://www.psychotherapynetworker.org/article/power-apologizing/?srsltid=AfmBOool4M8jn3hF33LcH4zdXlFl3hmiCChdKqx2vXXwsWBtAUKYc5aE; James Slack, "A Workplace Etiquette of Apology," Sage Publications, Business Cases, January 9, 2024, https://doi.org/10.4135/9781071926949.

Chapter 3

1. Shaylene E. Nancekivell et al., "A Slippery Myth: How Learning Style Beliefs Shape Reasoning about Multimodal Instruction and Related Scientific Evidence," *Cognitive Science* 45, no. 10 (October 2021): e13047, https://doi.org/10.1111/cogs.13047; Kris Vasquez, "Learning Styles as Self-Fulfilling Prophecy," in *Getting Culture: Incorporating Diversity across the Curriculum*, ed. Regan A. R. Guring and Loreto R. Prieto (Routledge, 2009, 2023); and Todd Zakrajsek, *The New Science of Learning: How to Learn in Harmony with Your Brain Third Edition* (Stylus, 2022), 169–171.

2. Thomas J. Tobin and Kirsten T. Behling, *Reach Everyone, Teach Everyone: Universal Design for Learning in Higher Education* (West Virginia University Press, 2018), 21.

3. Tobin and Behling, *Reach Everyone*, 25–6.

4. Tobin and Behling, *Reach Everyone*, 25. On multiple modes of instruction, see Kelly A. Hogan and Viji Sathy, *Inclusive Teaching: Strategies for Promoting Equity in the College Classroom* (West Virginia University Press, 2022), 117–18.

5. CAST, "The UDL Guidelines," https://udlguidelines.cast.org/.

6. As quoted in Cathy N. Davidson and Christina Katopodis, *The New College Classroom* (Harvard University Press, 2022), 51.

7. Tobin and Behling, *Reach Everyone*, 134.

8. Anwar Alsalamah, "Using Captioning Services with Deaf and Hard of Hearing Students in Higher Education: A Systematic Review," *American Annals of the Deaf* 165, no. 1 (Spring 2020): 114–27; Morton Ann Gernsbacher, "Video Captions Benefit Everyone," *Policy Insights from the Behavioral and Brain Sciences* 2, no. 1 (October 2015): 195–202, https://doi.org/10.1177/2372732215602130; N. Sooryah and K. R. Soundarya, "Live Captioning for Live Lectures—An Initiative to Enhance Language Acquisition in Second Language Learners, through Mobile Learning," *Webology* 17, no. 2 (2020): 238–43, https://doi.org/10.14704/WEB/V17I2/WEB17027.

9. Jeffrey W. Alstete, John P. Meyer, and Nicholas J. Beutell, "Enriching Management Learning with Differentiated Instruction," *International Journal of Educational Management* 35, no. 3 (2021): 640–54; Angela Danley and Carla Williams, "Choice in Learning: Differentiating Instruction in the College Classroom," *InSight: A Journal of Scholarly Teaching* 15 (2020): 83–104; Wendy McCarty et al., "Renewing Teaching Practices: Differentiated Instruction in the College Classroom," *Journal of Curriculum, Teaching, Learning and Leadership in Education* 1, no. 1 (2016): article 5; and Windi D. Turner, Oscar J. Solis, and Doris H. Kincade, "Differentiating Instruction for Large Classes in Higher Education," *International Journal of Teaching and Learning in Higher Education* 29, no. 3 (2017): 490–500.

10. For citations on diversifying the curriculum, visit https://jessamyn neuhaus.com.

11. Carlos Enrique George Reyes et al., "Post-Pandemic Study Habits in University Students," Institute for the Future of Education, June 14, 2022, https://observatory.tec.mx/edu-bits-2/post-pandemic-study-habits-in-university -students/.

12. Susan Boyle, Karen L. Rizzo, and Jonte C. Taylor, "Reducing Language Barriers in Science for Students with Special Educational Needs," *Asia-Pacific Science Education* 6, no. 2 (2021): 364–87, https://doi.org/10.1163/23641177 -BJA10006; Jennifer D. Green and Beth Dillard, "Scaffolding the Scaffold: Creating Graphic Organizers to Support Your Students' Learning," *Transformative Dialogues: Teaching and Learning Journal* 14, no. 2 (September 2021), https:// journals.psu.edu/td/article/view/1495; S. Jay Kuder, Amy Accardo, and John Woodruff, *College Success for Students on the Autism Spectrum: A Neurodiversity Perspective* (Taylor and Francis, 2023); and Xue Wang et al., "Benefits of Interactive Graphic Organizers in Online Learning: Evidence for Generative Learning Theory," *Journal of Educational Psychology* 113, no. 5 (2021): 1024–37, https://doi .org/10.1037/edu0000606.

13. Hogan and Sathy, *Inclusive Teaching*, 27–48.

14. Hogan and Sathy, *Inclusive Teaching*, 21.

15. Michelle D. Miller, *A Teacher's Guide to Learning Student Names: Why You Should, Why It's Hard, How You Can* (University of Oklahoma Press, 2024).

16. Katelyn M. Cooper et al., "What's in a Name? The Importance of Students Perceiving That an Instructor Knows Their Names in a High-Enrollment Biology Classroom," *CBE—Life Sciences Education* 16, no. 1 (2017), https://doi.org/10.1187/cbe.16-08-0265. See also Hogan and Sathy, *Inclusive Teaching*, 147.

17. Sandra L. Faulkner et al., "'Treat Me Like a Person, Rather Than Another Number': University Student Perceptions of Inclusive Classroom Practices," *Communication Education* 70, no. 1 (2021): 92–111, https://doi.org/10.1080/03634523.2020.1812680.

18. Sheri Wells-Jensen, Emily K. Michael, and Mona Minkara, "How Blind Professors Win the First Day: Setting Ourselves Up for Success," in *Picture a Professor: Interrupting Biases about Faculty and Increasing Student Learning*, ed. Jessamyn Neuhaus (West Virginia University Press, 2022), 42–43.

19. Isis Artze-Vega et al., *The Norton Guide to Equity-Minded Teaching* (W. W. Norton, 2023), 129–30; Kelly E. Theisen, "Commonalities and Research: A One-Two Punch to Combat STEM Fears and Biases on the First Day of Class," in Neuhaus, *Picture a Professor*, 68–80; and Reba Wissner, "Where's the Professor? First-Day Active Learning for Navigating Students' Perceptions of Young Professors," in Neuhaus, *Picture a Professor*, 81–97.

20. Fen Kennedy, "Collaborative Rubric Creation as a Queer, Transgender Professor's Tactic for Building Trust in the Classroom," in Neuhaus, *Picture a Professor*, 118–32; and Erik Simmons, "Black Man in a Strange Land: Using Principles of Psychology and Behavior Science to Thrive in the Classroom," in Neuhaus, *Picture a Professor*, 167–82.

21. Sandy Sufian, "The Prejudicial Logic of Productivity," Inside Higher Ed, April 11, 2023, https://www.insidehighered.com/opinion/views/2023/04/11/prejudicial-logic-productivity.

22. Rebecca Pope-Ruark, *Unraveling Faculty Burnout: Pathways to Reckoning and Renewal* (Johns Hopkins University Press, 2022). See also Sheila A. Boamah et al., "Striking a Balance between Work and Play: The Effects of Work-Life Interference and Burnout on Faculty Turnover Intentions and Career Satisfaction," *International Journal of Environmental Research and Public Health* 19, no. 2 (2022): 809, https://doi.org/10.3390/ijerph19020809; Asia Eaton and Leah R. Warner, "Social Justice Burnout: Engaging in Self-Care While Doing Diversity Work," in *Navigating Difficult Moments in Teaching Diversity and Social Justice*, ed. Mary E. Kite, Kim Case, and Wendy Williams (American Psychological Association, 2021): 31–43; and Yin Xu and Yike Wang, "Job Stress and University Faculty Members' Life Satisfaction: The Mediating Role of Emotional Burnout," *Frontiers in Psychology* 14 (2023), https://doi.org/10.3389/fpsyg.2023.1111434.

23. Samantha Primiano, Ananya Krishnan, and Thurka Sangaramoorthy, "Plagues, Pathogens, and Pedagogical Decolonization: Reflecting on the Design of a Decolonized Pandemic Syllabus," *Teaching & Learning Anthropology Journal* 3, no. 2 (2020), https://doi.org/10.5070/T33249635; and Sulafa Zidani, "Whose

Pedagogy Is It Anyway? Decolonizing the Syllabus through a Critical Embrace of Difference," *Media, Culture & Society* 43, no. 5 (2021): 970–78, https://doi.org/10.1177/0163443720980922.

24. This section is based on my open-access chapter in *Picture a Professor* titled "Figuring Out Student Feedback on Teaching: Strategies for Reducing Potential Personal and Professional Harm to Faculty." Available for download on https://pictureaprofessor.com.

25. Lauren Barbeau and Claudia Cornejo Happel, *Critical Teaching Behaviors: Defining, Documenting, and Discussing Good Teaching* (Stylus, 2023).

26. Barbeau and Happel, *Critical Teaching Behaviors*, 128–40; Karron G. Lewis, "Using Midsemester Student Feedback and Responding to It," *New Directions in Teaching & Learning* 87 (Autumn 2002): 33–44, https://doi.org/10.1002/tl.26; and Rebecca L. Taylor et al., "Seven Principles for Good Practice in Midterm Student Feedback," *International Journal for Academic Development* 25, no. 4 (2020): 350–62, https://doi.org/10.1080/1360144x.2020.1762086.

27. Caitlin M. Cunningham and Theresa L. White, "What Are They Trying to Tell Me? Large-Scale Viability of the *Start, Stop, Continue* Teaching Evaluation Method," *Innovations in Education and Teaching International* 59, no. 1 (2022): 60–69, https://doi.org/10.1080/14703297.2020.1810099; and Alice E. Hoon et al., "Use of the 'Stop, Start, Continue' Method Is Associated with the Production of Constructive Qualitative Feedback by Students in Higher Education," *Assessment & Evaluation in Higher Education* 40, no. 5 (2014): 755–67, https://doi.org/10.1080/02602938.2014.956282.

28. Gilberto Sarfati, "We Can Work It Out: Faculty Interpretation of Student Evaluations of Teaching," *Journal of Further and Higher Education* 46, no. 5 (2022): 708–20, https://doi.org/10.1080/0309877X.2021.2002282; and Courtney Vengrin, "Engaging the Fear: How to Utilize Student Evaluations, Accept Feedback, and Further Teaching Practice," in *Teaching in the University: Learning from Graduate Students and Early Career Faculty*, ed. Donna Westfall-Rudd, Courtney Vengrin, and Jeremy Elliott-Engel (Virginia Tech University, 2022).

29. Barbeau and Happel, *Critical Teaching Behaviors*, 128.

30. Dan Li and Steve Benton, "Creating Fair Student Evaluations of Teaching," *Anthology*, March 26, 2020, https://www.anthology.com/blog/creating-fair-student-evaluations-of-teaching.

Chapter 4

1. Betsy Barre, "The Workload Dilemma," Wake Forest University Center for the Advancement of Teaching, January 22, 2021, https://cat.wfu.edu/2021/01/the-workload-dilemma/; Peter Felten, "From Pandemic to Endemic Pedagogy: Being CLEAR in Our Teaching," *New Directions for Teaching and Learning* 2022, no. 169 (Spring 2022): 39–46, https://doi.org/10.1002/tl.20481; and Benjamin Motz et al., "A Pandemic of Busywork: Increased Online Coursework Following

the Transition to Remote Instruction Is Associated with Reduced Academic Achievement," *Online Learning* 25, no. 1 (2021): 70–85, https://doi.org/10.24059 /olj.v25i1.2475.

2. Paul Hanstedt, *Creating Wicked Students: Designing Courses for a Complex World* (Stylus, 2018), 12; and Christine Harrington and 50 College Students, *Keeping Us Engaged: Student Perspectives (and Research-Based Strategies) on What Works and Why* (Stylus, 2021), 86.

3. Jan L. Plass, Roxana Moreno, and Roland Brünken, eds., *Cognitive Load Theory* (Cambridge University Press, 2010), https://doi.org/10.1017 /CBO9780511844744; Tracy A. H. Taylor et al., "Teaching in Uncertain Times: Expanding the Scope of Extraneous Cognitive Load in the Cognitive Load Theory," *Frontiers in Psychology* 13 (2022). https://doi.org/10.3389/fpsyg.2022 .665835; and Susanne Vogel et al., "Stress Affects the Neural Ensemble for Integrating New Information and Prior Knowledge," *Neuroimage* 173 (June 2018): 176–87, https://doi.org/10.1016/j.neuroimage.2018.02.038.

4. This isn't the same problem as aligning specific assignments to course learning goals but lack of such alignment would increase the odds of students perceiving an assignment as busywork. See Lauren Barbeau and Claudia Cornejo Happel, *Critical Teaching Behaviors: Defining, Documenting, and Discussing Good Teaching* (Stylus, 2023), 13–14; and Aeron Haynie and Stephanie Spong, *Teaching Matters: A Guide for Graduate Students* (West Virginia University Press, 2022), 35–37.

5. Meghan Brink, "Public Opinion on Value of Higher Ed Remains Mixed," Inside Higher Ed, July 11, 2022, https://www.insidehighered.com/news /2022/07/12/most-americans-skeptical-value-college-degree; Aurore J. Kamssu and R. Barbara Kouam, "The Effects of the COVID-19 Pandemic on University Student Enrollment Decisions and Higher Education Resource Allocation," *Journal of Higher Education Theory and Practice* 21, no. 12 (2021): 143–53, https:// doi.org/10.33423/jhetp.v21i12.4707; and Rick Seltzer, "Why Aren't People Going to College?," Higher Ed Dive, September 28, 2022, https://www.highereddive .com/news/why-arent-people-going-to-college/632915/.

6. Miranda P. Dotson et al., "'Emotional Distancing': Change and Strain in U.S. Young Adult College Students' Relationships during COVID-19," *Emerging Adulthood* 10, no. 2 (2022): 546–57, https://doi.org/10.1177/21676968211065531; and Kristen Lewis, "Understanding Youth Disconnection in the Age of Coronavirus," in *Community Quality-of-life Indicators: Best Cases IX*, ed. Frank Ridzi, Chantal Stevens, and Lyle Wray (Springer International Publishing, 2022): 105–23, https://doi.org/10.1007/978-3-031-06940-6_7.

7. James M. Lang, *Small Teaching: Everyday Lessons from the Science of Learning* Second Edition (Jossey-Bass, 2021), 159.

8. Erin M. Bentrim and Gavin W. Henning, eds., *The Impact of a Sense of Belonging in College: Implications for Student Persistence, Retention, and Success* (Stylus, 2022); and Peter Felten and Leo M. Lambert, *Relationship-Rich*

Education: How Human Connections Drive Success in College (Johns Hopkins University Press, 2020). "Sense of belonging" can be defined as "the feeling of acceptance and support that comes with knowing that one is part of a group. In an academic setting, it refers to a student's feeling of acceptance, inclusion, support, and respect in a learning environment." Isis Artze-Vega et al., *The Norton Guide to Equity-Minded Teaching* (W. W. Norton, 2023), 33.

9. For citations on diverse and intersecting contributing factors to students' sense of belonging, visit https://jessamynneuhaus.com.

10. "Our sense of truth and how the world works is formed socially, not individually." Sarah Rose Cavanagh, *Hivemind: The New Science of Tribalism in Our Divided World* (Grand Central Publishing, 2019), 27.

11. Cathy N. Davidson and Christina Katopodis, *The New College Classroom* (Harvard University Press, 2022), 12–16; Joshua R. Eyler, *How Humans Learn: The Science and Stories behind Effective College Teaching* (West Virginia University Press, 2018), 164–67; Anastassis Kozanitis and Lucian Nenciovici, "Effect of Active Learning versus Traditional Lecturing on the Learning Achievement of College Students in Humanities and Social Sciences: A Meta-Analysis," *Higher Education* 86, no. 4 (2022): 1–18, https://doi.org/10.1007/s10734-022-00977-8; Katie A. L. McCallister, *Beyond the Lecture: Interacting with Students and Shaping the Classroom Dynamic* (Rowman & Littlefield, 2021); Larry D. Spence, *Maybe Teaching Is a Bad Idea: Why Faculty Should Focus on Learning* (Stylus, 2022), 39–45; and Henk G. Schmidt et al., "On the Use and Misuse of Lectures in Higher Education," *Health Professions Education* 1, no. 1 (2015): 12–18, https://doi.org/10.1016/j.hpe.2015.11.010.

12. For citations on interactive lectures, visit https://jessamynneuhaus.com.

13. As discussed in Kevin M. Gannon, *Radical Hope: A Teaching Manifesto* (West Virginia University Press, 2020), 23.

14. Frank Heppner, *Teaching the Large College Class: A Guidebook for Instructors with Multitudes* (Jossey-Bass, 2007), 92.

15. Amy E. Covill, "College Students' Perceptions of the Traditional Lecture Method," *College Student Journal* 45, no. 1 (2011): 92–101; and Louis Deslauriers et al., "Measuring Actual Learning versus Feeling of Learning in Response to Being Actively Engaged in the Classroom," *Proceedings of the National Academy of Sciences* 116, no. 39 (2019): 19251–257, https://doi.org/10.1073/pnas.1821936116. A 2022 study found that student comfort with the standard lecture format may enable them to build some supportive networks with the students in class, even if they're not actually *learning* as much as content as they could be. Colin Loughlin and Åsa Lindberg-Sand, "The Use of Lectures: Effective Pedagogy or Seeds Scattered on the Wind?," *Higher Education* 85, no. 2 (2023): 283–99, https://doi.org/10.1007/s10734-022-00833-9. Recent research suggests a careful combination of traditional lecture and in-class activity effectively facilitates learning. Jennifer Calabrese, "A Pilot Study to Compare Lecture and Active Learning," *Journal of*

Occupational Therapy Education 7, no. 2 (2023): https://doi.org/10.26681/jote .2023.070208; and Corbin M. Campbell, *Great College Teaching: Where It Happens and How to Foster It Everywhere* (Harvard University Press, 2023), 24–27.

16. Felten and Lambert, *Relationship-Rich Education*, 30.

17. Danielle Bissonette and Dawn M. Szymanski, "Minority Stress and LGBQ College Students' Depression: Roles of Peer Group and Involvement," *Psychology of Sexual Orientation and Gender Diversity* 6, no. 3 (2019): 308–17, https://doi.org/10.1037/sgd0000332; Derrick R. Brooms and Arthur R. Davis, "Staying Focused on the Goal: Peer Bonding and Faculty Mentors Supporting Black Males' Persistence in College," *Journal of Black Studies* 48, no. 3 (April 2017): 305–26, https://doi.org/10.1177/0021934717692520; Elizabeth M. Lee and Jacob Harris, "Counterspaces, Counterstructures: Low-Income, First-Generation, and Working-Class Students' Peer Support at Selective Colleges," *Sociological Forum* 35, no. 4 (December 2020): 1135–56, https://doi.org/10.1111 /socf.12641; and Garth Stahl et al., "'I Tell My Brothers That It Can Be Done': Indigenous Males Navigating Elite Australian Higher Education," *Research in Post-compulsory Education* 28, no. 3 (2023): 418–38, https://doi.org/10.1080 /13596748.2023.2221118.

18. Henriikka Juntunen et al., "Feeling Exhausted and Isolated? The Connections between University Students' Remote Teaching and Learning Experiences, Motivation, and Psychological Well-Being during the COVID-19 Pandemic," *Educational Psychology* 42, no. 10 (2022): 1241–62, https://doi.org /10.1080/01443410.2022.2135686; and Mahyudin Ritonga et al., "Online Learning during the Covid-19 Pandemic Period: Studies on the Social Presence and Affective and Cognitive Engagement of Students," *Pegem Journal of Education and Instruction* 12, no. 1 (2022): 207–12, https://doi.org/10.47750/pegegog.12.01.21.

19. Michelle Pacansky-Brock, Michael Smedshammer, and Kim Vincent-Layton, "Humanizing Online Teaching to Equitize Higher Education," *Current Issues in Education* 21, no. 2 (2020), http://dx.doi.org/10.13140/RG.2.2.33218 .94402.

20. Flower Darby with James M. Lang, *Small Teaching Online: Applying Learning Science in Online Classes* (Jossey-Bass, 2019), 76, 81. Darby uses the online Community of Inquiry (CoI) model, which includes three interdependent elements of connection: social presence, cognitive presence, and teaching presence. Darby, *Small Teaching Online*, 79.

21. Kevin Kelly and Todd Zakrajsek, *Advancing Online Teaching: Creating Equity-Based Digital Learning Environments* (Stylus, 2021), 15. See also Emmy Vrieling-Teunter et al., "Facilitating Peer Interaction Regulation in Online Settings: The Role of Social Presence, Social Space and Sociability," *Frontiers in Psychology* 13 (April 2022), https://doi.org/10.3389/fpsyg.2022.793798.

22. Beth McMurtrie, "A 'Stunning' Level of Disconnection: Professor are Reporting Record Numbers of Students Checked Out, Stressed Out, and

Unsure of Their Future," *Chronicle of Higher Education*, April 5, 2022, https://www.chronicle.com/article/a-stunning-level-of-student-disconnection.

23. For citations on loneliness, visit https://jessamynneuhaus.com.

24. Robert Eaton, Steven V. Hunsaker, and Bonnie Moon, *Improving Learning and Mental Health in the College Classroom* (West Virginia University Press, 2023), 5–12.

25. Sarah Rose Cavanagh, *Mind over Monsters: Supporting Youth Mental Health with Compassionate Challenge* (Beacon Press, 2023), 22.

26. Cavanagh, *Mind over Monsters*, 24, 27, 37, 54.

27. Bradley E. Cox et al., "Pedagogical Signals of Faculty Approachability: Factors Shaping Faculty-Student Interaction Outside the Classroom," *Research in Higher Education* 51, no. 8 (December 2010): 767–88, https://doi.org/10.1007/s11162-010-9178-z; Fizza Sabir, Robert Matthews, and Poulomee Datta, "Are Teachers Approachable or Unapproachable: Insights from Undergraduate University Students," *Curriculum and Teaching* 36, no. 2 (December 2021): 41–58, https://doi.org/10.7459/ct/36.2.04; Gerda Hagenauer, Franziska Muehlbacher, and Mishela Ivanova, "'It's Where Learning and Teaching Begins—Is This Relationship'—Insights on the Teacher-Student Relationship at University from the Teachers' Perspective," *Higher Education* 85, no. 4 (2023): 819–35, https://doi.org/10.1007/s10734-022-00867-z; and Zach Taylor et al., "Finding Affinity between Faculty Members and College Students: Which Salient Identities Do Faculty Members Disclose?," *Journal of Faculty Development* 36, no. 1 (January 2022): 23–32. See also "The Faculty Approachability Project," https://www.facultyapproachabilityproject.com/.

28. Artze-Vega et al., *Norton Guide*, 19; and Beth McMurtrie, "Repairing Gen Ed: Colleges Struggle to Help Students Answer the Question, 'Why Am I Taking This Class?,'" *Chronicle of Higher Education* 69, no. 19 (May 26, 2023): https://www.chronicle.com/article/repairing-gen-ed.

29. This is an example of what higher education scholar Amy Johnson asked participants to describe as a "bad educational experience" in her workshop "Creating Fearless Classrooms: Designing Spaces Where Students Can Embrace Risk," at the August 9, 2023, Conference on High Impact Instructional Practices conferences at East Tennessee State University. In a large room packed with college faculty, every person could instantly recall a significantly negative experience we had in school and, moreover, for most of us, a teacher or professor played a prominent role in that negative experience.

30. Rebecca Pope-Ruark, *Unraveling Faculty Burnout: Pathways to Reckoning and Renewal* (Johns Hopkins University Press, 2022), 38–39.

31. Pope-Ruark, *Unraveling Faculty Burnout*, 8, 135–59.

32. "Polysynchronous" refers to facilitating multiple forms of interaction (student to content, student to student, student to instructor) in multiple modalities. I believe it to be a more accurate term than "HyFlex."

33. Courtney Adams Wooten and Megan A. Condis, "Collegiality as a Dirty Word? Implementing Collegiality Statements in Institutions of Higher Education," *Academic Labor: Research and Artistry* 2, article 3 (2018), https://digitalcommons.humboldt.edu/alra/vol2/iss1/3/; and Bharat Mehra, Laurie Bonnici, and Steven L. MacCall, "Collegiality as a Weapon to Maintain Status Quo in a White-privileged and Entrenched LIS Academy," in *Antiracist Library and Information Science: Racial Justice and Community* 52, ed. Kimberly Black and Bharat Mehra (Emerald, 2023):123–138.

34. Pope-Ruark, Unraveling Faculty *Burnout*, 92–96.

Chapter 5

1. For citations on stereotype threat, visit https://jessamynneuhaus.com.

2. Amber R. Dickinson and Ursula W. Kreitmair, "The Importance of Feeling Cared For: Does a Student's Perception of How Much a Professor Cares about Student Success Relate to Class Performance?," *Journal of Political Science Education* 17, no. 3 (2021): 356–70, https://doi.org/10.1080/15512169.2019.1659803.

3. Jessamyn Neuhaus, *Geeky Pedagogy: A Guide for Intellectuals, Introverts, and Nerds Who Want to Be Effective Teachers* (West Virginia University Press, 2019), 53–54.

4. Student Experience Project, "Your Syllabus as a Tool to Promote Student Equity, Belonging, and Growth," https://library.studentexperienceproject.org/courses/syllabus.

5. Millie Cordaro, "Pouring from an Empty Cup: The Case for Compassion Fatigue in Higher Education, *Building Healthy Academic Communities Journal* 4, no. 2 (November 2020): 17–28, https://doi.org/10.18061/bhac.v4i2.7618; and Xiajun Yu et al., "The Cost of Caring: Compassion Fatigue Is a Special Form of Teacher Burnout," *Sustainability* 14, no. 10 (2022): 6071, https://doi.org/10.3390/su14106071.

6. Kelly A. Hogan and Viji Sathy, *Inclusive Teaching: Strategies for Promoting Equity in the College Classroom* (West Virginia University Press, 2022), 159–63; and Kimberly Sarmiento, *199 Mistakes New College Instructors Make and How to Prevent Them: Insider Secrets to Avoid Classroom Blunders* (Atlantic Publishing Group, 2016), 95.

7. Sara Rose Cavanagh, *The Spark of Learning: Energizing the College Classroom with the Science of Emotion* (West Virginia University Press, 2016), 65.

8. Catherine J. Denial, *A Pedagogy of Kindness* (University of Oklahoma Press, 2024).

9. The transparency in learning and teaching (TILT) framework can be especially useful for making these types of revisions. Mary-Ann Winkelmes, Allison Boye, and Suzanne Tapp, eds., *Transparent Design in Higher Education Teaching and Leadership: A Guide to Implementing the Transparency Framework Institution-Wide to Improve Learning and Retention* (Stylus, 2019).

Chapter 6

1. Triada Konstantina Papapanou et al., "Strong Correlations Between Social Appearance Anxiety, Use of Social Media, and Feelings of Loneliness in Adolescents and Young Adults," *International Journal of Environmental Research and Public Health* 20, no. 5 (2023): 4296, https://doi.org/10.3390/ijerph20054296; and Jonathan Haidt, *The Anxious Generation: How the Great Rewiring of Childhood Is Causing an Epidemic of Mental Illness* (Penguin Press, 2024).

2. Sarah Rose Cavanagh, *Mind over Monsters: Supporting Youth Mental Health with Compassionate Challenge* (Beacon Press, 2023), 229; Aleena Chia, Ana Jorge, and Tero Karppi, eds., Reckoning with Social Media: Disconnection in the Age of the Techlash (Rowman & Littlefield, 2021); Sarah M. Coyne et al., "Does Time Spent Using Social Media Impact Mental Health?: An Eight Year Longitudinal Study," *Computers in Human Behavior* 104 (2020): article 106160, https://doi.org/10.1016/j.chb.2019.106160; Michela Drusian, Paolo Magaudda, and Cosimo Marco Scarcelli, eds., *Young People and the Smartphone: Everyday Life on the Small Screen* (Palgrave Macmillan, 2022); and Samuel Hardman Taylor, Pengfei Zhao, and Natalya N. Bazarova, "Social Media and Close Relationships: A Puzzle of Connection and Disconnection," *Current Opinion in Psychology* 45 (2022): article 101292, https://doi.org/10.1016/j.copsyc.2021.12.004.

3. James M. Lang, *Small Teaching: Everyday Lessons from the Science of Learning*, second edition (Jossey-Bass, 2021), 198, 205.

4. David Gooblar, *The Missing Course: Everything They Never Taught You about College Teaching* (Harvard University Press, 2019), 63–64.

5. On using unessays in history classes, see *Teaching History: A Journal of Methods* 47, no. 1 (Fall 2022), https://doi.org/10.33043/TH.47.1. See also Bryan A. Banks, "The Unessay: A Creative and Audience-Focused Assignment," *Perspectives on History* 61, no. 6 (September 20, 2023), https://www.historians .org/research-and-publications/perspectives-on-history/september-2023/the -unessay-a-creative-and-audience-focused-assignment; and Kevin M. Gannon, *Radical Hope: A Teaching Manifesto* (West Virginia University Press, 2020), 92–94.

6. Isis Artze-Vega et al., *The Norton Guide to Equity-Minded Teaching* (W. W. Norton, 2023), 42–43; Jennifer R. Bechkoff, "Gamification Using a Choose-Your-Own-Adventure Type Platform to Augment Learning and Facilitate Student Engagement in Marketing Education," *Journal for Advancement of Marketing Education* 27, no. 1 (2019): 13–19; Jonathan Ross Gilbert and Mario Gonzalez-Fuentes, "Choose-Your-Own-Adventure in Marketing Education: Empowering Students to Increase Engagement and Rigor through Mass Customization," *Marketing Education Review* 33, no. 2 (2023): 163–69, https:// doi.org/10.1080/10528008.2022.2159440; Christine Harrington and 50 College Students, *Keeping Us Engaged: Student Perspectives (and Research-Based Strategies) on What Works and Why* (Stylus, 2021), 30–33; and Andrew P. Mills,

"Letting Students Choose: Investigating the Menu Approach to Graded Work," *American Association of Philosophy Teachers Studies in Pedagogy* 5 (2019): 68–88, https://doi.org/10.5840/aaptstudies2019121043.

7. Paul Hanstedt, *Creating Wicked Students: Designing Courses for a Complex World* (Stylus, 2018), 11–39.

8. Artze-Vega et al., *Norton Guide*, 21–36. See also Richard M. Felder and Rebecca Brent, "Random Thoughts: The 10 Worst Teaching Mistakes I.—Mistakes 5–10," *Chemical Engineering Education* 42, no. 4 (Fall 2008): 201–2; and Margaret Vaughn, "What Is Student Agency and Why Is It Needed Now More Than Ever?," *Theory into Practice* 59, no. 2 (2020): 114, https://doi.org/10.1080/00405841.2019.1702393.

9. "I find it strange that teachers and institutions would predetermine outcomes before students even arrive on the scene. I argue, instead, for *emergent outcomes*, ones that are cocreated by teachers and students and revised on the fly [original emphasis]." Jesse Stommel, "How to Ungrade," in *Ungrading: Why Rating Students Undermines Learning (and What to Do Instead)*, ed. Susan D. Blum (West Virginia University Press, 2020), 30.

10. Peter C. Brown, Henry L. Roediger III, and Mark A. McDaniel, *Make It Stick: The Science of Successful Learning* (Harvard University Press, 2014), 102; and Terry Doyle and Todd Zakrajsek, *The New Science of Learning: How to Learn in Harmony with Your Brain*, third edition (Stylus, 2022), 95–99.

11. James M. Lang, "Why Students Hate Group Projects (and How to Change That)," *Chronicle of Higher Education*, June 17, 2022; https://www.chronicle.com/article/why-students-hate-group-projects-and-how-to-change-that; and Nadia Tamez-Robledo and Jeffery R. Young, "Group Project Horror Stories—and How to Avoid Them," *Edsurge*, podcast, August 29, 2023, https://www.edsurge.com/news/2023-08-29-group-project-horror-stories-and-how-to-avoid-them.

12. Cathy N. Davidson and Christina Katopodis, *The New College Classroom* (Harvard University Press, 2022), 142–67; and Robert John Robertson and Shannon Riggs, "Collaborative Assignments and Projects," in *High-Impact Practices in Online Education*, ed. Kathryn E. Linder and Chrysanthemum Mattison Hayes (Stylus, 2018), 71–84.

13. Corbin M. Campbell, *Great College Teaching: Where It Happens and How to Foster It Everywhere* (Harvard University Press, 2023), 24–28.

14. Kelly A. Hogan and Viji Sathy, *Inclusive Teaching: Strategies for Promoting Equity in the College Classroom* (West Virginia University Press, 2022), 38.

15. Stephen D. Brookfield and Stephen Preskill, *Discussion as a Way of Teaching: Tools and Techniques for Democratic Classrooms*, second edition (Jossey-Bass, 2005), 42

16. Jay R. Howard, *Discussion in the College Classroom: Getting Your Students Engaged and Participating in Person and Online* (Jossey-Bass, 2015), 134–35; Cass M. Johnson, "Rethinking Online Discourse: Improving Learning through Discussions in the Online Classroom," *Education and Information Technologies*

21, no. 6 (2016): 1483–1507, https://doi.org/10.1007/s10639-015-9395-3; Saba Fatma, "Strategies to Improve Classroom Discussions," *International Journal of Advance Research, Ideas and Innovations In Technology* 7, no. 2 (2021): 715–20; and Jennifer H. Herman and Linda B. Nilson, *Creating Engaging Discussions: Strategies for "Avoiding Crickets" in Any Size Classroom and Online* (Stylus, 2018).

17. Hogan and Sathy, *Inclusive Teaching*, 117.

18. Flower Darby with James M. Lang, *Small Teaching Online: Applying Learning Science in Online Classes* (Jossey-Bass, 2019), 81–84.

19. Darby, *Small Teaching Online*, 193; and Cathy L. Green, "Personal Learning Networks: Defining and Building a PLN," in *Learning in the Digital Age*, ed. Tutaleni I. Asino (Oklahoma State University, 2020), https://open.library .okstate.edu/learninginthedigitalage/chapter/personal-learning-networks _defining-and-building-a-pln/.

20. Robert Drago and Michelle Setnikar, "Where to Start? Asset-Based Approaches for Practitioners in Higher Education," *Vermont Connection* 44, no. 1 (April 2023): article 20, https://scholarworks.uvm.edu/tvc/vol44/iss1/20.

21. Melissa Eblen-Zayas, interview with John Kane and Rebecca Mushtare, "Reflect to Deflect," *Tea for Teaching*, podcast and transcript, November 16, 2022, https://teaforteaching.com/263-reflect-to-deflect/.

22. Lang, *Small Teaching*, 109.

23. Bradley J. Irish, "How to Make Room for Neurodivergent Professors," *Chronicle of Higher Education*, March 2, 2023, https://www.chronicle.com/article /how-to-make-room-for-neurodivergent-professors.

24. Rebekkah McLellan, "Stop Telling Us 'You Hide It So Well," Inside Higher Ed, June 16, 2022, https://www.insidehighered.com/views/2022/06/17 /how-disabled-and-neurodivergent-faculty-live-opinion.

25. Hogan and Sathy, *Inclusive Teaching*, 214–15; Howard, *Discussion in the College Classroom*, 34; Kimberly Sarmiento, *199 Mistakes New College Instructors Make and How to Prevent Them: Insider Secrets to Avoid Classroom Blunders* (Atlantic Publishing Group, 2016). 183.

26. Cavanagh, *Mind over Monsters*, 100.

27. Nicholas D. Hartlep and Daisy Ball, eds., *Racial Battle Fatigue in Faculty: Perspectives and Lessons from Higher Education* (Routledge, 2019).

28. Lang, *Small Teaching*, 210–11.

29. Davidson and Katopodis, *New College Classroom*, 47–48.

30. M. Barton Laws et al., "Factors Associated with Patient Recall of Key Information in Ambulatory Specialty Care Visits: Results of an Innovative Methodology," *PLoS One* 13, no. 2 (2018), https://doi.org/10.1371/journal.pone .0191940.

31. For example, advice about office hours often presumes that you have an on-campus office—a luxury that VITAL faculty and faculty teaching exclusively online may not enjoy.

32. Hogan and Sathy, *Inclusive Teaching*, 171.

33. Peter Felten and Leo M. Lambert, *Relationship-Rich Education: How Human Connections Drive Success in College* (Johns Hopkins University Press, 2020), 4.

34. Janelle T. Billingsley and Noelle M. Hurd, "Discrimination, Mental Health and Academic Performance among Underrepresented College Students: The Role of Extracurricular Activities at Predominantly White Institutions," *Social Psychology of Education* 22 (2019): 421–46, https://doi.org/10.1007/s11218-019-09484-8; and Maude Guilmette et al. "Past and Present Participation in Extracurricular Activities Is Associated with Adaptive Self-Regulation of Goals, Academic Success, and Emotional Wellbeing among University Students," *Learning and Individual Differences* 73, no. 3 (2019): 8–15, https://doi.org/10.1016/j.lindif.2019.04.006.

35. Christopher V.H.-H. Chen et al., "Caring for Our Communities of Practice in Educational Development," *To Improve the Academy: A Journal of Educational Development* 41, no. 1 (2022): https://doi.org/10.3998/tia.460; Linda C. Hodges and Patrice McDermott, "Building Community: From Faculty Development to Pedagogical Innovation and Beyond," in *The Palgrave Handbook of Academic Professional Development Centers*, ed. Otherine Johnson Neisler (Springer International Publishing, 2022): 393–403; Tracy Smith and Melba Spooner, "Constellations of Support: A Community Development Model," *To Improve the Academy* 40, no. 2 (Winter 2021), https://doi.org/10.3998/tia.505; and Audrey J. Tocco et al., "Learning Communities Promote Pedagogical Metacognition in Higher Education Faculty," in *To Improve the Academy* 42, no. 1 (Spring 2023), https://doi.org/10.3998/tia.2044.

36. Klara Bolander Laksov and Cormac McGrath, "Failure as a Catalyst for Learning: Towards Deliberate Reflection in Academic Development Work," *International Journal for Academic Development* 25, no. 1 (2020): 1–4, https://doi.org/10.1080/1360144X.2020.1717783.

37. Harriet L. Schwartz, *Connected Teaching: Relationship, Power, and Mattering in Higher Education* (Stylus, 2019), 130.

38. Celeste Atkins, "Teaching Up: Bringing My Blackness into the Classroom," in *Picture a Professor: Interrupting Biases about Faculty and Increasing Student Learning*, ed. Jessamyn Neuhaus (West Virginia University Press, 2022), 279.

39. Candace N. Hall, "Centering Joy and Community for the Wellbeing of Black Faculty," *Journal of Faculty Development* 37, no. 1 (2023): 76.

40. Niya Bond, "The Future of Faculty Development Is Feminist," Inside Higher Ed, April 14, 2022, https://www.insidehighered.com/advice/2022/04/15/providing-holistic-professional-development-faculty-members-need-opinion.

41. Marcia Chatelain, "Is Twitter Any Place for a [Black Academic] Lady?," in *Bodies of Information: Intersectional Feminism and the Digital Humanities*, ed. Elizabeth Losh and Jacqueline Wernimont (University of Minnesota Press, 2019): 172–84; Mandy Johnson et al., "Twitter: A Tool for Communities of Practice,"

Southeastern Regional Association of Teacher Educators Journal 28, no. 1 (2019): 61–75; and Lua Tian, Candice Freeman, and Jill Stefaniak, "'Like, Comment, and Share'—Professional Development through Social Media in Higher Education: A Systematic Review," *Educational Technology Research and Development* 68 (2020): 1659–83, https://doi.org/10.1007/s11423-020-09790-5.

42. Linda C. Hodges et al., "Supporting Academic Continuity by Building Community: The Work of a Faculty Development Center during COVID-19," *Journal on Centers for Teaching and Learning* 12 (2020): 26–45, https://openjournal .lib.miamioh.edu/index.php/jctl/article/view/208; and Mays Imad, "Transcending Adversity: Trauma-Informed Educational Development," *To Improve the Academy* 39, no. 3 (Spring 2021), https://doi.org/10.3998/tia.17063888.0039.301.

43. As quoted in Darby, *Small Teaching Online,* 89.

44. Student comments by Morgan Gerscheidle, Liam Sample, and Peter Basile. Used by permission.

Chapter 7

1. https://twitter.com/Jessifer/status/726424167420145664?ref=jesse -stommel, April 30, 2016. By the way, my #4WordPedagogy was "Nerd out about teaching."

2. Or, more accurately, my andragogical practices, because college educators teach adults, not children. However, in both K–12 as well as higher education, "pedagogy" is the word most people use. There are compelling reasons why some scholars of college teaching and learning insist on using "andragogy," but until that term is better recognized and understood, I believe that it's more likely to promote academic gatekeeping than to improve teaching and learning.

3. Karen Hao, "A U.S. Government Study Confirms Most Facial Recognition Systems Are Racist," MIT Technology Review, December 20, 2019, https://www.technologyreview.com/2019/12/20/79/ai-face-recognition-racist-us -government-nist-study/; Lindsay McKenzie, "Time to Rethink AI Proctoring?," Inside Higher Ed, May 27, 2021, https://www.insidehighered.com/news/2021 /05/28/are-colleges-checking-ais-work-remote-exam-proctoring; and Katherine Mangan, "The Surveilled Student: New Ways of Monitoring Health and Academic Performance Won't Just Disappear When the Pandemic Subsides," *Chronicle of Higher Education,* February 15, 2021, https://www.chronicle.com/article/the -surveilled-student.

4. John Locke and Jessamyn Neuhaus, interview with John Kane and Rebecca Mushtare, "Remote Proctoring," *Tea for Teaching,* podcast and transcript, September 30, 2020, https://teaforteaching.com/155-remote-proctoring/; Charles Logan, "Refusal, Partnership, and Countering Educational Technology's Harms," Hybrid Pedagogy, October 21, 2020, https://hybridpedagogy.org /refusal-partnership-countering-harms/; and Sarah Silverman et al., "What Happens When You Close the Door on Remote Proctoring? Moving toward

Authentic Assessments with a People-Centered Approach," *To Improve the Academy* 39, no. 3 (Spring 2021), https://doi.org/10.3998/tia.17063888.0039.308.

5. Aaron Ansuini et al., "Rethinking What It Means to Return to Normal," *Art Education* 75, no. 2 (2022): 46–48, https://doi.org/10.1080/00043125.2021.2020036; Lee Skallerup Bessette, "'There's No Normal to Get Back To': The State of Higher Education," Public Books, March 16, 2023, https://www.publicbooks.org/state-of-higher-ed-after-covid/; and Dawn Hodges, "Higher Education Cannot Return to Normal," *Dean & Provost* 23, no. 7 (March 2022): 3–7, https://doi.org/10.1002/dap.31003.

6. Committee on Developments in the Science of Learning, *How People Learn: Brain, Mind, Experience, and School* (National Academies Press, 2000), 57–58.

7. Susan D. Blum, "Just One Change (Just Kidding): Ungrading and Its Necessary Accompaniments," in *Ungrading: Why Rating Students Undermines Learning (and What to Do Instead)*, ed. Susan D. Blum (West Virginia University Press, 2020), 57.

8. Tor Grenness, "'If You Don't Cheat, You Lose': An Explorative Study of Business Students' Perceptions of Cheating Behavior," *Scandinavian Journal of Educational Research* 67, no. 3 (2023): 1122–36, https://doi.org/10.1080/00313831.2022.2116479; and James M. Lang, *Cheating Lessons: Learning from Academic Dishonesty* (Harvard University Press, 2013).

9. Mary Ellen Fromuth et al., "Academic Entitlement: Its Relationship with Academic Behaviors and Attitudes," *Social Psychology of Education* 22, no. 2 (November 2019): 1153–67, https://doi.org/10.1007/s11218-019-09517-2.

10. When students use the phrase "We had to teach ourselves," it may mean (a) the professor utilized student-centered self-directed pedagogical techniques that made passivity impossible, or (b) the professor left students to flounder and fail without giving scaffolds, supports, and opportunities to practice. The pandemic exacerbated this contradictory use of the phrase. See, for example, Marissa Jacobs, "Students Are Not Paying to Teach Themselves," The Shield, March 17, 2020, https://usishield.com/33011/opinion/students-are-not-paying-to-teach-themselves/.

11. Margaret Finders and Joaquin Muñoz, "Cameras On: Surveillance in the Time of COVID-19," Inside Higher Ed, March 2, 2021, https://www.insidehighered.com/advice/2021/03/03/why-its-wrong-require-students-keep-their-cameras-online-classes-opinion; S. L. Nelson and Annette Vee, "The View from 'Zoom University': Surveillance and Control in Higher Ed's Pandemic Pedagogy Pivot," Enculturation: A Journal of Rhetoric, Writing, and Culture, February 20, 2022, https://enculturation.net/zoom_university; and Matt Reed, "Should Showing Faces Be Mandatory?," *Confessions of a Community College Dean*, blog, Inside Higher Ed, May 12, 2020, https://www.insidehighered.com/blogs/confessions-community-college-dean/should-showing-faces-be-mandatory.

12. Maha Bali, "Students Talk to Me About Webcams," *Reflecting Aloud*, blog, March 25, 2021, https://blog.mahabali.me/educational-technology-2/students -talk-to-me-about-webcams/; Rebecca Barrett-Fox, "A Reminder of Who Is Hurt by Insisting that Students Share Images of Personal Lives," *Rebecca Barrett-Fox*, blog, April 6, 2020: https://anygoodthing.com/2020/04/06/a-reminder-of-who -is-hurt-by-insisting-that-students-share-images-of-their-personal-lives/; Denise Chapman and Guido O. Andrade de Melo, "Zooming While Black: Creating a Black Aesthetic and Counter Hegemonic Discourse in a Digital Age," in *The Routledge Handbook of Media Education Futures Post-Pandemic*, ed. Yonty Friesem et al. (Routledge, 2023); 37–45; Taharee Jackson, "COVID-19 and Videoclassism: Implicit Bias, Videojudgment, and Why I'm Terrified to Have You Look over My Shoulder," LinkedIn, May 27, 2020, https://www.linkedin.com/pulse/covid -19-videoclassism-implicit-bias-videojudgment-why-jackson/; and Ripudaman Singh Minhas, "The Elephant in the Zoom: Recognizing and Reconciling My Internalized Racism," *CMAJ* 192, no. 40 (2020): E1169–70, https://doi.org/10 .1503/cmaj.201737.

13. Samuel Amponsah et al., "Academic Experiences of 'Zoom-Fatigue' as a Virtual Streaming Phenomenon during the COVID-19 Pandemic," *International Journal of Web-Based Learning and Teaching Technologies* 17, no. 6 (January 2022): 1–17, https://doi.org/10.4018/IJWLTT.287555; Mehmet Engin Deniz et al., "Zoom Fatigue, Psychological Distress, Life Satisfaction, and Academic Well-Being," *Cyberpsychology, Behavior, and Social Networking* 25, no. 5 (May 2022): 270–77, https://doi.org/10.1089/cyber.2021.0249; and Chandra K. Massner, "Who's Zooming Who: A Case Study of Videoconferencing's Effects on Faculty and Students," *International Journal of Technology in Education and Science* 6, no. 4 (2022): 602–19, https://doi.org/10.46328/ijtes.412.

14. Especially for many neurodivergent students or students from a culture where direct eye contact is not necessarily a sign of respect.

15. Michel Foucault, *Discipline and Punish: The Birth of the Prison*, trans. Alan Sheridan (Vintage Books, 1979), 201. See also Danielle L. Couch, Priscilla Robinson, and Paul A. Komesaroff, "COVID-19—Extending Surveillance and the Panopticon," *Journal of Bioethical Inquiry* 17, no. 4 (2020): 809–14, https:// doi.org/10.1007/s11673-020-10036-5.

16. Beth McMurtrie, "Students Crossing Boundaries: Rudeness, Disruptions, Unrealistic Demands. Where to Draw the Line?," *Chronicle of Higher Education*, November 14, 2023, https://www.chronicle.com/article/students -crossing-boundaries.

17. Kalley Huang, "Alarmed by A.I. Chatbots, Universities Are Changing How They Teach," *New York Times*, January 16, 2023, https://www.nytimes.com /2023/01/16/technology/chatgpt-artificial-intelligence-universities.html; and John Warner, "Freaking Out about ChatGPT—Part 1," *Just Visiting*, blog, Inside Higher Ed, December 5, 2022, https://www.insidehighered.com/blogs/just -visiting/freaking-out-about-chatgpt%E2%80%94part-i.

18. Joseph M. Keegin, "ChatGPT Is a Plagiarism Machine," *Chronicle of Higher Education*, May 23, 2023, https://www.chronicle.com/article/chatgpt-is-a-plagiarism-machine; and Jeffrey R. Young, "ChatGPT Has Colleges in Emergency Mode to Shield Academic Integrity," EdSurge, January 24, 2023, https://www.edsurge.com/news/2023-01-24-chatgpt-has-colleges-in-emergency-mode-to-shield-academic-integrity.

19. Flower Darby, "Teaching and the Academy: The Road Forward after Three Years of Disruption," Conference on Instruction & Technology, SUNY Oswego, May 24, 2023.

Chapter 8

1. If you're thinking that the student should have told me about their medical device, think again. It's illegal for instructors to require students disclose any medical or health-related information for any reason; it's a violation of trust and of the law.

2. Yassenia Manzo, "In Lak'ech: The Interconnectedness between Faculty and Students of Color," in *Presumed Incompetent II: Race, Class, Power, and Resistance of Women in Academia*, ed. Yolanda Flores Niemann, Gabriella Gutiérrez y Muhs, and Carmen G. González (Utah State University Press, 2020), 297; Sherri Wells-Jensen, Emily K. Michael, and Mona Minkara, "How Blind Professors Win the First Day: Setting Ourselves Up for Success," in *Picture a Professor: Interrupting Biases about Faculty and Increasing Student Learning*, ed. Jessamyn Neuhaus (West Virginia University Press, 2022), 37; Sarah Rose Cavanagh, *The Spark of Learning: Energizing The College Classroom with the Science of Emotion* (West Virginia University Press, 2016), 194; Sarah Mayes-Tang, "Sharing Our Stories to Build Community, Highlight Bias, and Address Challenges to Authority," in *Picture a Professor*, 262; Chavella Pittman, "Addressing Incivility in the Classroom: Effective Strategies for Faculty at the Margins," in *Difficult Subjects: Insights and Strategies for Teaching about Race, Sexuality, and Gender*, ed. Badia Ahad-Legardy and OiYan A. Poon (Stylus, 2018): 58, 63; and Christine Stanley, "Coloring the Academic Landscape: Faculty of Color Breaking the Silence in Predominantly White Colleges and Universities," *American Educational Research Journal* 43, no. 4 (2006): 706, https://doi.org/10.3102/00028312043004701.

3. Some of the behaviors that aren't "disruptions" but rather threats requiring us to immediately end the class and call campus security include: when a student "violates your personal space," "seems irrational," "implies or makes a direct threat to harm themselves or others," "displays a firearm," or "physically confronts or attacks another student." Aeron Haynie and Stephanie Spong, *Teaching Matters: A Guide for Graduate Students* (West Virginia University Press, 2022), 103.

4. Cavanagh, *Spark of Learning*, 195.

5. Haynie and Spong, *Teaching Matters*, 100.

Chapter 9

1. Peter Felten, Rachel M. Forsyth, and Kathryn A, Sutherland, "Building Trust in the Classroom: A Conceptual Model for Teachers, Scholars, and Academic Developers in Higher Education," *Teaching and Learning Inquiry* 11 (2023): 6, https://doi.org/10.20343/teachlearninqu.11.20.

2. Dennis E. Clayson, "Initial Impressions and the Student Evaluation of Teaching," *Journal of Education for Business* 88, no. 1 (2013): 26–35, https://doi.org/10.1080/08832323.2011.633580; and Kelly A. Hogan and Viji Sathy, *Inclusive Teaching: Strategies for Promoting Equity in the College Classroom* (West Virginia University Press, 2022), 84–85.

3. For citations on first day activities, visit https://jessamynneuhaus.com.

4. Karen Costa, 99 *Tips for Creating Simple and Sustainable Educational Videos: A Guide for Online Teachers and Flipped Classes* (Stylus, 2020), 40; Hogan and Sathy, *Inclusive Teaching*, 87.

5. Tracie Marcella Addy et al., *What Inclusive Instructors Do: Principles and Practices for Excellence in College Teaching* (Stylus, 2021), 47–50; Cynthia Briggs, Rebecca Boyle, and Alejandra Chavez Stuart, "Creating Inclusive Syllabi: Recommendations from the Field," *Journal of Educational Research & Practice* 12, no. 0 (2023): 94–102, https://doi.org/10.5590/JERAP.2022.12.0.06; and Kimberly LaPiene, Terry Pettijohn II, and Linda Palm, "An Investigation of Professor and Course First Impressions as a Function of a Syllabus Welcome Statement in College Students," *College Student Journal* 56, no. 3 (September 2022): 281–87.

6. For citations on syllabus design, visit https://jessamynneuhaus.com.

7. Isis Artze-Vega et al., *The Norton Guide to Equity-Minded Teaching* (W. W. Norton, 2023), 129.

8. Peter Felten and Leo M. Lambert, *Relationship-Rich Education: How Human Connections Drive Success in College* (Johns Hopkins University Press, 2020), 20.

9. Cathy Davidson and Christina Katopodis, *The New College Classroom* (Harvard University Press, 2022), 223.

10. On TILT in Higher Ed, see https://tilthighered.com. For a critique of "transparency," see Margaret Bearman and Rola Ajjawi, "From 'Seeing through' to 'Seeing With': Assessment Criteria and the Myths of Transparency," *Frontiers in Education* 3, no. 96 (2018): https://doi.org/10.3389/feduc.2018.00096.

11. For citations on rubrics, visit https://jessamynneuhaus.com.

12. Gary Chu, "The Point-less Classroom: A Math Teacher's Ironic Choice in Not Calculating Grades," in Susan Blum, ed., *Ungrading: Why Rating Students Undermines Learning (and What to Do Instead)* (West Virginia University Press, 2020), 167; and Bill Latham, "Teachable Moments: The Grading Conference," Teaching Professor, October 17, 2022: https://www.teachingprofessor.com/topics/from-the-archive/teachable-moments-the-grading-conference/.

13. Flower Darby with James M. Lang, *Small Teaching Online: Applying Learning Science in Online Classes* (Jossey-Bass, 2019), 98–99.

14. Kathy Glyshaw, "The Clock Strikes at Midnight: An Argument Against the 'Pumpkin Rule,'" Faculty Focus, February 2, 2022, https://www.facultyfocus.com/articles/effective-classroom-management/the-clock-strikes-at-midnight-an-argument-against-the-pumpkin-rule/.

15. Beckie Supiano, "The Attendance Conundrum: Students Find Policies Inconsistent and Confusing. They Have a Point," *Chronicle of Higher Education* 68, no. 13 (2022), https://www.chronicle.com/article/the-attendance-conundrum. See also Sofoklis Goulas, Silvia Griselda, and Rigissa Megalokonomou, "Compulsory Class Attendance versus Autonomy," *Journal of Economic Behavior & Organization* 212 (August 2023): 935–81, https://doi.org/10.1016/j.jebo.2023.06.018; Andrea Lofgren, "College Students and Class Attendance: How Poverty and Illbeing Affect Student Success through Punitive Attendance Policies," *College Teaching* (September 2023): 1–9, https://doi.org/10.1080/87567555.2023.2255714; and Laura E. McClelland and Kimberly F. Case, "Is Class Worth Their Time? College Student Perspectives on Class Structure and Attendance," *Studies in Educational Evaluation* 78 (September 2023), https://doi.org/10.1016/j.stueduc.2023.101281.

16. Anita Acai, Lucy Mercer-Mapstone, and Rachel Guitman, "Mind the (Gender) Gap: Engaging Students as Partners to Promote Gender Equity in Higher Education," *Teaching in Higher Education* 27, no. 1 (February 2022): 18–38, https://doi.org/10.1080/13562517.2019.1696296; Alison Cook-Sather and Sophia Abbot, "Translating Partnerships: How Faculty-Student Collaboration in Explorations of Teaching and Learning Can Transform Perceptions, Terms, and Selves," *Teaching & Learning Inquiry* 4, no. 2 (September 2016): 36–49, https://doi.org/10.20343/teachlearninqu.4.2.5; and Alison Cook-Sather, Catherine Bovill, and Peter Felten, *Engaging Students as Partners in Learning and Teaching: A Guide for Faculty* (Jossey-Bass, 2014); and Natasha A. Jankowski et al., eds. *Student-Focused Learning and Assessment: Involving Students in the Learning Process in Higher Education* (Peter Lang, 2020).

17. Alison Cook-Sather et al., "How Can Students-as-Partners Work Inform Assessment?," *International Journal for Students as Partners* 7, no. 1 (2023): 218–34, https://doi.org/10.15173/ijsap.v7i1.5453; and Alison Cook-Sather and Peter Felten, "Where Student Engagement Meets Faculty Development: How Student-Faculty Pedagogical Partnership Fosters a Sense of Belonging," *Student Engagement in Higher Education* 1, no. 2 (2017), https://sehej.raise-network.com/raise/article/view/cook.

18. Robert Talbert, "Promoting Student Growth with Engagement Credit," *Grading for Growth*, blog, May 20, 2024: https://gradingforgrowth.com/p/promoting-student-growth-with-engagement.

19. Lorrie Comeford, "Attendance Matters! Supporting First Year Students' Success with a Structured Attendance Policy," *Student Success* 14, no. 1 (2023): 71–75, https://doi.org/10.5204/ssj.2420.

20. Eva Blondeel, Patricia Everaert, and Evelien Opdecam, " A Little Push in the Back: Nudging Students to Improve Procrastination, Class Attendance and Preparation," *Studies in Higher Education* (November 2023): 1–20, https://doi.org/10.1080/03075079.2023.2288170; Mandar Chandrachood, "Revitalizing Classroom Attendance: Reviving Interest in Medical Education by Tackling Challenges and Embracing Solutions," *GAIMS Journal of Medical Sciences* 4, no. 1 (January–June 2024): 1–2; Mickaël Antoine Joseph et al., "Using Digital Badges to Enhance Nursing Students' Attendance and Motivation," *Nurse Education in Practice* 52 (March 2021): 103033, https://doi.org/10.1016/j.nepr.2021.103033; Robert Pinter et al., "Enhancing Higher Education Student Class Attendance through Gamification," *Acta Polytechnica Hungarica* 17, no. 2 (January 2020): 13–33, https://doi.org/10.12700/APH.17.2.2020.2.2; Bipul Kumar Sarker, "Enhanced Student Class Attendance by Using Concept of Flipped Classroom Approach," *Journal of Social, Humanity, and Education* 3, no. 2 (February 2023): 105–17, https://doi.org/10.35912/jshe.v3i2.1240; and Robert J. Weijers et al., "'I'll Be There': Improving Online Class Attendance with a Commitment Nudge During COVID-19," *Basic and Applied Social Psychology* 44, no. 1 (2022): 12–24, https://doi.org/10.1080/01973533.2021.2023534.

21. To view a sample attendance contract visit https://jessamynneuhaus.com.

22. Michelle D. Miller, *Remembering and Forgetting in the Age of Technology: Teaching, Learning, and the Science of Memory in a Wired World* (West Virginia University Press, 2022), 189–98.

23. Kevin M. Gannon, *Radical Hope: A Teaching Manifesto* (West Virginia University Press, 2020), 85.

24. Gannon, *Radical Hope*, 88.

25. Jeannie D. DiClementi and Mitchell M. Handelsman, "Empowering Students: Class-Generated Course Rules," *Teaching of Psychology* 32, no. 1 (2005): 18–21, https://doi.org/10.1207/s15328023top3201_4; Jesica Siham Fernández, "Creating Classroom Community Agreements," Inside Higher Ed, June 14, 2023, https://www.insidehighered.com/opinion/career-advice/teaching/2023/06/14/benefits-creating-community-classroom-agreements-opinion; Hogan and Sathy, *Inclusive Teaching*, 113–14; Cara E. Jones, "Transforming Classroom Norms as Social Change: Pairing Embodied Exercises with Collaborative Participation in the WGS Classroom (with Syllabus)," *Radical Teacher* 107 (2017): 14–31, https://doi.org/10.5195/rt.2017.322; and Kenya Z. Mejia et al., "Insights into Power Relations from the Co-designing of Classroom Norms between Students and Faculty," *2021 IEEE Frontiers in Education Conference* (2021): 1–5, https://doi.org/10.1109/FIE49875.2021.9637134.

26. Boston University's Faculty of Computing & Data Sciences policy "Using Generative AI in Coursework" is an example of a policy that strikes a good balance between these extremes: https://www.bu.edu/cds-faculty/culture-community/gaia-policy/.

27. Susan D'Agostino, "Turnitin's AI Detector: Higher-Than-Expected False Positives," Inside Higher Ed, June 1, 2023, https://www.insidehighered

.com/news/quick-takes/2023/06/01/turnitins-ai-detector-higher-expected-false
-positives; and William Walters, "The Effectiveness of Software Designed to
Detect AI-Generated Writing: A Comparison of 16 AI Text Detectors," *Open
Information Science* (October 2023), https://doi.org/10.1515/opis-2022-0158.

28. Weixin Liang et al., "GPT Detectors Are Biased against Non-Native
English Writers," *Patterns* 4, no. 7 (2023): 100779, https://doi.org/10.1016/j
.patter.2023.100779.

29. Alise de Bie, "Respectfully Distrusting 'Students as Partners' Practice
in Higher Education Applying a Mad Politics of Partnership," *Teaching in Higher
Education* 27, no. 6 (2022): 717–37, https://doi.org/10.1080/13562517.2020
.1736023; Jenny Marie and Stuart Sims, "Control, Freedom and Structure in
Student-Staff Partnerships," in *Advancing Student Engagement in Higher Education: Reflection, Critique and Challenge,* ed. Tom Lowe (Routledge, 2023): 123–34;
and Kelly E. Matthews, "Rethinking the Problem of Faculty Resistance to Engaging with Students and Partners in Learning and Teaching in Higher Education,"
International Journal for the Scholarship of Teaching & Learning 13, no. 2 (2019):
https://doi.org/10.20429/ijsotl.2019.130202.

30. Chanelle Wilson and Alison Cook-Sather, "Rippling the Patterns of
Power: Enacting Anti-Racist Pedagogy with Students as Co-teachers," in *Picture
a Professor: Interrupting Biases about Faculty and Increasing Student Learning,*
ed. Jessamyn Neuhaus (West Virginia University Press, 2022), 201–18. See
also Mick Healey and Ruth L. Healey, "'It Depends': Exploring the Context-
Dependent Nature of Students as Partners Practices and Policies," *International
Journal for Students as Partners* 2, no. 1 (2018): 1–10, https://doi.org/10.15173
/ijsap.v2i1.3472; Ruth Healey and Derek France, "'Every Partnership [. . . is] an
Emotional Experience': Towards a Model of Partnership Support for Addressing the Emotional Challenges of Student-Staff Partnerships," *Teaching in Higher
Education* 29, no. 8 (January 2022): 1–19, https://doi.org/10.1080/13562517
.2021.2021391; and Lucy Mercer-Mapstone, Maisha Islam, and Tamara Reid,
"Are We Just Engaging 'The Usual Suspects'? Challenges in and Practical Strategies for Supporting Equity and Diversity in Student-Staff Partnership Initia-
tives," *Teaching in Higher Education* 26, no. 2 (2021): 227–45, https://doi.org/10
.1080/13562517.2019.1655396.

31. Erik Simmons, "Black Man in a Strange Land: Using Principles of Psychology and Behavior Science to Thrive in the Classroom," in Neuhaus, *Picture
a Professor,* 173.

32. Elizabeth A. Norell, *The Present Professor: Authenticity and Transformation Teaching* (University of Oklahoma Press, 2024).

33. Jessamyn Neuhaus, *Geeky Pedagogy: A Guide for Intellectuals, Introverts,
and Nerds Who Want to Be Effective Teachers* (West Virginia University Press,
2019), 113–23. My understanding of gratitude practices has been most influenced by Kerri Howells, *Gratitude in Education: A Radical View* (Sense Publishers, 2012).

34. Ideally, this kind of evidence of our teaching efficacy will be used during formal reviews as well. See Lauren Barbeau and Claudia Cornejo Happel, *Critical Teaching Behaviors: Defining, Documenting, and Discussing Good Teaching* (Routledge, 2023).

Chapter 10

1. Jessamyn Neuhaus, *Manly Meals and Mom's Home Cooking: Cookbooks and Gender in Modern America* (John Hopkins University Press, 2003); and Jessamyn Neuhaus, *Housework and Housewives in American Advertising: Married to the Mop* (Palgrave Macmillan, 2011).

2. Joshua R. Eyler, *How Humans Learn: The Science and Stories behind Effective College Teaching* (West Virginia University Press, 2018), 171–217.

3. Peter C. Brown, Henry L. Roediger III, and Mark A. McDaniel, *Make It Stick: The Science of Successful Learning* (Harvard University Press, 2014), 7, 92.

4. Orit Alfi, Avi Assor, and Idit Katz, "Learning to Allow Temporary Failure: Potential Benefits, Supportive Practices and Teacher Concerns," *Journal of Education for Teaching* 30, no. 1 (2004): 27–41, https://doi.org/10.1080/0260747032000162299; Eyler, *How Humans Learn*, 173; Kevin Gannon, *Radical Hope: A Teaching Manifesto* (West Virginia University Press, 2020), 137–38; Naomi Steenhof, Nicole N. Woods, and Maria Mylopoulos, "Exploring Why We Learn from Productive Failure: Insights from the Cognitive and Learning Sciences," *Advances in Health Sciences Education* 25, no. 5 (2020): 1099, https://doi.org/10.1007/s10459-020-10013-y; and Krystal Nunes et al., "Science Students' Perspectives on How to Decrease the Stigma of Failure," *FEBS Open Bio* 12, no. 1 (January 2022): 34, https://doi.org/10.1002/2211-5463.13345.

5. Eyler, *How Humans Learn*, 172–73.

6. Anne Lamott, *Bird by Bird: Some Instructions on Writing and Life* (Anchor Books, 1994), 21–22.

7. S. Lee and D. Shapiro, "Completing College: National and State Report with Longitudinal Data Dashboard on Six- and Eight-Year Completion Rates," Signature Report 22 (National Student Clearinghouse Research Center, 2023), 2–3.

8. Brian N. Weidner and Ellen Skolar, "Teaching for a FAIL (First Attempt in Learning) in the Ensemble Classroom," *Music Educators Journal* 108, no. 2 (2021): 25, https://doi.org/10.1177/00274321211060332.

9. David Cannon, "Learning to Fail, Failing to Recover," in *Failing Students in Higher Education*, ed. Moira Peelo and Terry Wareham (Society for Research into Higher Education and Open University Press, 2002), 79–80; and Jennifer L. Woodrum and Jeffrey H. Khan, "Perfectionist Concerns and Psychological Distress: The Role of Spontaneous Emotion Regulation during College Students' Experiences with Failure," *Journal of Counseling Psychology* 69, no. 2 (2022): 246–56, https://doi.org/10.1037/cou0000580.

10. For citations on how students' individual traits affect their experiences of failure, visit https://jessamynneuhaus.com.

11. Beomkyu Choi, "I'm Afraid of Not Succeeding in Learning: Introducing an Instrument to Measure Higher Education Students' Fear of Failure in Learning," *Studies in Higher Education* 46, no. 11 (2021): 2107–21, https://doi .org/10.1080/03075079.2020.1712691; Krista De Castella, Don Byrne, and Martin Covington, "Unmotivated or Motivated to Fail? A Cross-Cultural Study of Achievement Motivation, Fear of Failure, and Student Disengagement," *Journal of Educational Psychology* 105, no. 3 (2013): 861, https://doi.org/10.1037 /a0032464; Meredith A. Henry et al., "Quantifying Fear of Failure in STEM: Modifying and Evaluating the Performance Failure Appraisal Inventory (PFAI) for Use with STEM Undergraduates," *International Journal of STEM Education* 8, article 43 (2021): 1–28, https://doi.org/10.1186/s40594-021-00300-4; Meredith A. Henry et al., "*FAIL* Is Not a Four-Letter Word: A Theoretical Framework for Exploring Undergraduate Students' Approaches to Academic Challenge and Responses to Failure in STEM Learning Environments," *CBE—Life Sciences Education* 18, no. 1 (2019): 1–17, https://doi.org/10.1187/cbe.18-06-0108; Kalif E. Vaughn, Neha Srivatsa, and Allyson S. Graf, "Effort Praise Improves Resilience for College Students with High Fear of Failure," *Journal of College Student Retention: Research, Theory & Practice* 25, no. 2 (2023): 378–97, https://doi.org/10 .1177/1521025120986517; Laura Harrison, *Teaching Struggling Students: Lessons Learned from Both Sides of the Classroom* (Palgrave Macmillan, 2019), 37–39; and Dietrich Wagner and Taiga Brahm, "Fear of Academic Failure as a Self-Fulfilling Prophecy," *Higher Education Transitions* (May 2017): 13–30.

12. Mohsen Haghbin, Adam McCaffrey, and Timothy A. Pychyl, "The Complexity of the Relations between Fear of Failure and Procrastination," *Journal of Rational-Emotive & Cognitive-Behavior Therapy* 30 (2012): 249–63, https://doi .org/10.1007/s10942-012-0153-9; Jose Parlade and Cebrail Karayigit, "Examining Procrastination and Fear of Failure among College Students," *Cognition, Brain, Behavior* 26, no. 4 (2022): 199–213, https://doi.org/10.24193/cbb.2022 .26.11; and Subhan Ajrin Sudirman et al., "Putting Off until Tomorrow: Academic Procrastination, Perfectionism, and Fear of Failure," *International Journal of Islamic Educational Psychology* 4, no. 1 (2023): 136–53.

13. Rebecca D. Cox, "'It Was Just That I Was Afraid': Promoting Success by Addressing Students' Fear of Failure," *Community College Review* 37, no. 1 (2009): 77, https://doi.org/10.1177/0091552109338390. Cox's research showed that "students' strategies for balancing their hopes and fears had greater influence on their approaches to college course work than did their cognitive-academic preparation" (54). See also Rebecca D. Cox, *The College Fear Factor: How Students and Professors Misunderstand Each Other* (Harvard University Press, 2009).

14. Sarah Rose Cavanagh, *Mind over Monsters: Supporting Youth Mental Health with Compassionate Challenge* (Beacon Press, 2023), 45.

15. For citations on productive struggle, visit https://jessamynneuhaus.com.

16. Brown, Roediger, and McDaniel, *Make It Stick*, 94.

17. Kayla Benson, Alvin Nicholas, and Kanako Taku, "Complex Outcomes of Failure: How Loss of Success Yields Wisdom alongside Depression," *Journal of Loss and Trauma* 27, no. 8 (2022): 693, https://doi.org/10.1080/15325024 .2022.2037896.

18. Rebecca Whittle et al., "The 'Present-Tense' Experience of Failure in the University: Reflections from an Action Research Project," *Emotion, Space and Society* 37 (2020), https://doi.org/10.1016/j.emospa.2020.100719.

19. Jennifer A. Mangels et al., "Emotion Blocks the Path to Learning under Stereotype Threat," *Social Cognitive and Affective Neuroscience* 7, no. 2 (2012): 230–41, https://doi.org/10.1093/scan/nsq100; Eyler, *How Humans Learn*, 200–201; Ebony McGee, "'Black Genius, Asian Fail': The Detriment of Stereotype Lift and Stereotype Threat in High-Achieving Asian and Black STEM Students," *AERA Open* 4, no. 4 (2018): https://doi.org/10.1177/2332858418816658; Kevin L. Nadal et al., "The Legacies of Systemic and Internalized Oppression: Experiences of Microaggressions, Imposter Phenomenon, and Stereotype Threat on Historically Marginalized Groups," *New Ideas in Psychology* 63, no. 1 (December 2021): 100895, https://doi.org/10.1016/j.newideapsych.2021.100895; and Robert J. Rydell et al., "The Effect of Negative Performance Stereotypes on Learning," *Journal of Personality and Social Psychology* 99, no. 6 (October 2010): 883, https://doi.org/10.1037/a0021139. One 2022 study did *not* find a link between stereotype threat and decreased learning: Sabrina König et al., "Stereotype Threat in Learning Situations? An Investigation among Language Minority Students," *European Journal of Psychology of Education* 38, no. 2 (2023): 841–64, https://doi.org/10.1007/s10212-022-00618-9.

20. Rola Ajjawi et al., "Persisting Students' Explanations of and Emotional Responses to Academic Failure," *Higher Education Research & Development* 39, no. 2 (2020): 196, https://doi.org/10.1080/07294360.2019.1664999.

21. Ajjawi et al., "Persisting Students' Explanations," 190–91.

22. Kelly A. Hogan and Viji Sathy, *Inclusive Teaching: Strategies for Promoting Equity in the College Classroom* (West Virginia University Press, 2022), 30–33.

23. Jessamyn Neuhaus, *Geeky Pedagogy: A Guide to Intellectuals, Introverts, and Nerds Who Want to Be Effective Teachers* (University of West Virginia Press, 2019), 69–70.

24. Joshua Eyler, *Failing Our Future: How Grades Harm Students and What We Can Do about It* (Johns Hopkins University Press, 2024).

25. Susan D. Blum, "Why Ungrade? Why Grade?," in *Ungrading: Why Rating Students Undermines Learning (and What to Do Instead)*, ed. Susan D. Blum (West Virginia University Press, 2020), 2; and David Clark and Robert Talbert, *Grading for Growth: A Guide to Alternative Grading Practices That Promote Authentic Learning and Student Engagement in Higher Education* (Routledge, 2023), 13–16.

26. Aaron Blackwelder, "What Going Gradeless Taught Me about Doing the 'Actual Work,'" in Blum, *Ungrading*; and Arthur Chiaravalli, "Grades Stifle

Student Learning. Can We Learn to Teach Without Grades?," in Blum, *Ungrading*. See also Jesse Stommel, *Undoing the Grade: Why We Grade and How to Stop* (Hybrid Pedagogy, 2023).

27. Horace T. Crogman et al., "Ungrading: The Case for Abandoning Institutionalized Assessment Protocols and Improving Pedagogical Strategies," *Education Sciences* 13, no. 11 (2023): 1091, https://doi.org/10.3390/educsci13111091; Erin M. Eggleston and Shelby Kimmel, "Ungrading: Reflections through a Feminist Pedagogical Lens," *Feminist Pedagogy* 4, no. 2, article 7 (2023), https://digitalcommons.calpoly.edu/feministpedagogy/vol4/iss2/7; Tim Gorichanaz, "'It Made Me Feel Like It Was Okay to Be Wrong': Student Experiences with Ungrading," *Active Learning in Higher Education* 25, no. 1 (2022): 67–80, https://doi.org/10.1177/14697874221093640; Jenny Inker et al., "Pushing Back against AI: Using Ungrading to Promote Critical Thinking and Intrinsic Motivation," *Innovation in Aging* 7, supplement 1 (2023): 324–25, https://doi.org/10.1093/geroni/igad104.1082; Lindsay C. Masland, "Ungrading: The Joys of Doing Everything Wrong," *Zeal: A Journal for the Liberal Arts* 1, no. 2 (2023): 88–93; and Marcia Rapchak, Africa S. Hands, and Merinda Kaye Hensley, "Moving toward Equity: Experiences with Ungrading," *Journal of Education for Library and Information Science* 64, no. 1 (January 2023): 89–98, https://doi.org/10.3138/jelis-2021-0062.

28. Gannon, *Radical Hope*, 138.

29. "In the rush of daily activity at my university, I still struggle professionally to 'see' my students clearly and to accept them as being fully human, unique individuals whose lives include many more important aspects for their consideration than anything in my curriculum." Mark W. F. Condon, "Practicing What I Preach," in *Oops: What We Learn When Our Teaching Fails*, ed. Brenda Miller Power and Ruth Shagoury Hubbard (Stenhouse, 1996), 172.

30. Clark and Talbert, *Grading for Growth*, 19; Jesse Stommel, "How to Ungrade," in Blum, *Ungrading*, 28.

31. He left a complete paper on my door months after the class was over. Taking the coward's way out, I never contacted him about it.

32. Stephen Brookfield, *The Skillful Teacher: On Technique, Trust, and Responsiveness in the Classroom*, second edition (Jossey-Bass, 2006), 213–14.

33. Brookfield, *The Skillful Teacher*, 214.

34. Margaret Jaworski, "The Negativity Bias: Why the Bad Stuff Sticks," HealthCentral, updated February 19, 2020, https://www.healthcentral.com/mental-health/negativity-bias?legacy=psycom.

35. Harriet Schwartz, *Connected Teaching: Relationship, Power, and Mattering in Higher Education* (Stylus Publications, 2019), 116, 117.

36. Brookfield, *The Skillful Teacher*, 262.

37. Shawn R. Simonson, Brittnee Earl, and Megan Frary, "Establishing a Framework for Assessing Teaching Effectiveness," *College Teaching* 70, no. 2 (2022): 164, https://doi.org/10.1080/87567555.2021.1909528.

38. John Horton, "Failure Failure Failure Failure Failure Failure: Six Types of Failure within the Neoliberal Academy," *Emotion, Space and Society* 35 (May 2020): 100672, https://doi.org/10.1016/j.emospa.2020.100672.

Chapter 11

1. Rola Ajjawi et al., "Persisting Students' Explanations of and Emotional Responses to Academic Failure," *Higher Education Research & Development* 39, no. 2 (2020): 191–92, https://doi.org/10.1080/07294360.2019.1664999.

2. Moira Peelo, "Setting the Scene," in *Failing Students in Higher Education*, ed. Moira Peelo and Terry Wareham (Society for Research into Higher Education and Open University Press, 2002), 3.

3. Karen Hinett, "Failing to Assess or Assessing Failure," in *Failing Students in Higher Education*, ed. Peelo and Wareham, 178.

4. Joshua R. Eyler, *How Humans Learn: The Science and Stories behind Effective College Teaching* (West Virginia University Press, 2018), 174.

5. Corbin M. Campbell, ed., *Reframing Rigor: New Understandings for Equity and Student Success* (Jossey-Bass, 2018); K. C. Culver, John M. Braxton, and Ernest T. Pascarella, "What We Talk about When We Talk about Rigor: Examining Conceptions of Academic Rigor," *Journal of Higher Education* 92, no. 7 (2021): 1140–63; and Kevin Gannon, "Why Calls for a 'Return to Rigor' Are Wrong," *Chronicle of Higher Education*, May 22, 2023: https://www.chronicle.com/article/why-calls-for-a-return-to-rigor-are-wrong.

6. Nancy J. Frank, "Dealing with the Aftermath of Student Failure: Strategies for Nurse Educators," *Journal of Professional Nursing* 36, no. 6 (November–December 2020): 515, https://doi.org/10.1016/j.profnurs.2020.04.009. I agree with Frank that ideally "students should learn of their failure in person rather than seeing the failing grade on the learning management system or academic transcript" (515).

7. Frank, "Dealing with the Aftermath," 516.

8. Frank, "Dealing with the Aftermath," 515.

9. Harriet L. Schwartz, *Connected Teaching: Relationship, Power, and Mattering in Higher Education* (Stylus, 2019), 124–25.

10. Schwartz, *Connected Teaching*, 125.

11. John Horton, "Failure Failure Failure Failure Failure Failure: Six Types of Failure within the Neoliberal Academy," *Emotion, Space and Society* 35 (May 2020): https://doi.org/10.1016/j.emospa.2020.100672.

12. Schwartz, *Connected Teaching*, 127–28.

13. Shirley Brown, "Student Counselling and Students' Failures," in *Failing Students in Higher Education*, ed. Peelo and Wareham, 148–49; and Klara Bolander Laksov and Cormac McGrath, "Failure as a Catalyst for Learning: Towards Deliberate Reflection in Academic Development Work," *International*

Journal for Academic Development 25, no. 1 (2020): 1, https://doi.org/10.1080 /1360144X.2020.1717783.

14. Sheryl Sandberg, *Lean in: Women, Work, and the Will to Lead* (Alfred A. Knopf, 2013).

15. Ashley Hartman Annis, "Which Way Is Feminism Leaning? A Critique of Sandberg's 'Feminist Manifesto,'" *Feminist Collections* 37, no. 1–2 (2016): 1–5; and Pamela Eddy and Kelly Ward, "Problematizing Gender in Higher Education: Why Leaning In Isn't Enough," in *Critical Approaches to Women and Gender in Higher Education*, ed. Pamela L. Eddy, Kelly Ward, and Tehmina Khwaja (Palgrave Macmillan, 2017), 13–39.

Chapter 12

1. Donna Mejia, "The Superpowers of Visual Ambiguity: Transfiguring My Experience of Colorism and Multiheritage Identity for Educational Good," in *Picture a Professor: Interrupting Biases about Faculty and Increasing Student Learning*, ed. Jessamyn Neuhaus (West Virginia University Press, 2022), 248–49.

2. Kelly A. Hogan and Viji Sathy, *Inclusive Teaching: Strategies for Promoting Equity in the College Classroom* (West Virginia University Press, 2022), 33–35.

3. For citations on scaffolding, visit https://jessamynneuhaus.com.

4. Sara Rose Cavanagh, "Honeybees, Social Neuroscience, and Team Dynamics: Lessons for Building Community," Anchor Session, POD Network Annual Conference, Pittsburgh, PA, November 17, 2019.

5. For citations on effective feedback, visit my website, https://jessamyn neuhaus.com.

6. Shana K. Carpenter, Steven C. Pan, and Andrew C. Butler, "The Science of Effective Learning with a Focus on Spacing and Retrieval Practice," *Nature Reviews Psychology* 1, no. 9 (2022): 496–511, https://doi.org/10.1038/s44159-022 -00089-1; Gregory M. Donoghue and John A. C. Hattie, "A Meta-Analysis of Ten Learning Techniques," *Frontiers in Education* 6 (2021), https://doi.org/10.3389 /feduc.2021.581216; Alyson Froehlich and Elizabeth Bond Rogers, "Four Keys to Unlocking Equitable Learning: Retrieval, Spacing, Interleaving, and Elaborative Encoding," in *Teaching and Learning for Social Justice and Equity in Higher Education: Virtual Settings*, ed. Laura Parson and C. Casey Ozaki (Springer International, 2022): 249–75, https://doi.org/10.1007/978-3-030-88608-0_10; Kathleen P. McDermott, "Practicing Retrieval Facilitates Learning," *Annual Review of Psychology* 72 (2021): 609–33, https://doi.org/10.1146/annurev-psych-010419 -051019; and Michelle D, Miller, *Remembering and Forgetting in the Age of Technology: Teaching, Learning, and the Science of Memory in a Wired World* (West Virginia University Press, 2022), 107–14.

7. Hogan and Sathy, *Inclusive Teaching*, 27–29; Marsha C. Lovett et al., *How Learning Works: Eight Research-Based Principles for Smart Teaching*, second

edition (Wiley, 2023), 130–61; and Larry D. Spence, *Maybe Teaching Is a Bad Idea: Why Faculty Should Focus on Learning* (Stylus, 2022), 139–44.

8. James M. Lang, *Small Teaching: Everyday Lessons from the Science of Learning*, second edition (Jossey-Bass, 2021), 117.

9. For citations on flipping the classroom, active learning, and interleaving, visit https://jessamynneuhaus.com.

10. He later married one of his students, so, yeah, the guy had issues.

11. Susan D. Blum, *"I Love Learning; I Hate School": An Anthropology of College* (Cornell University Press, 2016), 10.

12. Laila I. McCloud, "Keeping Receipts: Thoughts on Ungrading from a Black Woman Professor," *Zeal: A Journal for the Liberal Arts* 1, no. 2 (2023): 101.

13. Hogan and Sathy, *Inclusive Teaching*, 29–30; Jayme Dyer, "Ungrading Has an Equity-Related Achilles Heel," Grading for Growth, January 8, 2024, https://gradingforgrowth.com/p/ungrading-has-an-equity-related-achilles; Juuso Nieminen, "Ungrading = Inclusive Assessment?," Grow Beyond Grades, n.d., https://www.teachersgoinggradeless.com/blog/ungrading-inclusive-assessment; and Beckie Supiano, "The Unintended Consequences of 'Ungrading': Does Getting Rid of Grades Make Things Worse for Disadvantaged Students?," *Chronicle of Higher Education* 68, no. 18 (2022), https://www.chronicle.com/article/the-unintended-consequences-of-ungrading.

14. Robert Talbert, "Grading for Growth: Toward More Humane, Authentic, and Trustworthy Ways to Evaluate Student Work," Zoom presentation, January 10, 2024.

15. David Clark and Robert Talbert, *Grading for Growth: A Guide to Alternative Grading Practices That Promote Authentic Learning and Student Engagement in Higher Education* (Routledge, 2023), 28–29.

16. Cathrine Becker, "Discrimination in the Classroom: Calls for Detracking and Anonymous Grading," *Sociological Imagination* 8, no. 1 (2023): 1–7; Clark and Talbert, *Grading for Growth*, 20–23; David Contreras, "Gender Differences in Grading: Teacher Bias or Student Behaviour?," *Education Economics* (September 2023): 1–24, https://doi.org/10.1080/09645292.2023.2252620; Lewis Doyle, Matthew J. Easterbrook, and Peter R. Harris, "Roles of Socioeconomic Status, Ethnicity and Teacher Beliefs in Academic Grading," *British Journal of Educational Psychology* 93, no. 1 (2023): 91–112, https://doi.org/10.1111/bjep.12541; Bruno Ferman and Luiz Felipe Fontes, "Assessing Knowledge or Classroom Behavior? Evidence of Teachers' Grading Bias," *Journal of Public Economics* 216, no. 1 (December 2022): 104773, https://doi.org/10.1016/j.jpubeco.2022.104773; Luke Green, "[GPA] in, [GPA] Out: Uncovering Inequity and Flaws in Grading Policies," *AASA Journal of Scholarship and Practice* 18, no. 4 (Winter 2022): 40–50; Kim Gower, "Let Them Eat Cake: Why the Inherent Bias in Professor Grading Should Change to Individual Performance Assessments," *Journal of Organizational Psychology* 27, no. 5 (2021): 149–54, https://doi.org/10.33423/jop

.v21i5.4724; and Laura J. Link and Thomas R. Guskey, "How Traditional Grading Contributes to Student Inequities and How to Fix It," *Educational, School, and Counseling Psychology Faculty Publications* 53 (Fall 2019), https://uknowledge.uky .edu/edp_facpub/53/. See also Joe Feldman, *Grading for Equity: What It Is, Why It Matters, and How It Can Transform Schools and Classrooms*, second edition (Corwin, 2023),

17. Colin Rogers, "Developing a Positive Approach to Failure," in *Failing Students in Higher Education*, ed. Moira Peelo and Terry Wareham (Society for Research into Higher Education and Open University Press, 2002), 123. See also Alexandra Mihai, "Space to Fail. And Learn," *The Educationalist*, blog, March 11, 2024, https://educationalist.substack.com/p/space-to-fail-and-learn.

18. Hogan and Sathy, *Inclusive Teaching*,79, 78-79.

19. Kevin M. Gannon, *Radical Hope: A Teaching Manifesto* (West Virginia University Press, 2020), 138, 137, 147.

20. Spence, *Maybe Teaching Is a Bad Idea*, 130.

21. Spence, *Maybe Teaching Is a Bad Idea*, 124, 132.

22. Robert Grassinger et al., "Smart Is Who Makes Lots of Errors? The Relevance of Adaptive Reactions to Errors and a Positive Error Climate for Academic Achievement," *High Ability Studies* 29, no. 1 (April 2018): 37–49, https:// doi.org/10.1080/13598139.2018.1459294; Yunteng He, "Constructive Error Climate: A Classroom Assessment Technique in Science Classes," *Journal of College Science Teaching* 49, no. 4 (2020): 37–40, https://doi.org/10.1080/0047231x .2020.12315638; Patricia Köpfer, "Teachers' Perspectives on Dealing with Students' Errors," *Frontiers in Education* 7 (2022), https://doi.org/10.3389/feduc .2022.868729; James McMillan and Stephanie Moore, "Better Being Wrong (Sometimes): Classroom Assessment That Enhances Student Learning and Motivation," *Clearing House: A Journal of Educational Strategies, Issues and Ideas* 93, no. 2 (2020): 85–92, https://doi.org/10.1080/00098655.2020.1721414; and Qian Zhao et al., "The Effects of Teachers' Error Orientations on Students' Mathematics Learning: The Role of Teacher Emotions," *Sustainability* 14, no. 10 (May 2022): 6311, https://doi.org/10.3390/su14106311.

23. Joshua R, Eyler, *How Humans Learn: The Science and Stories behind Effective College Teaching* (West Virginia University Press, 2018), 208–9.

24. Mejia, "Superpowers of Visual Ambiguity," 248–49. For citations on productive failure in STEM, visit https://jessamynneuhaus.com.

25. Mejia, "Superpowers of Visual Ambiguity," 248.

26. Tracie Marcella Addy et al., *What Inclusive Instructors Do: Principles and Practices for Excellence in College Teaching* (Stylus, 2021), 107; Brandi Bohney et al., "Fail Forward! Perspectives on Failure in the Writing Classroom," *Journal of Teaching Writing* 33, no. 2 (2018), 73–78, https://journals.indianapolis.iu .edu/index.php/teachingwriting/article/view/23308; and Nekesha B. Williams, "Failing Forward: Helping Undergraduate Researchers in Geosciences Cultivate Strong Science Identities and Growth Mindsets," in *Confronting Failure:*

Approaches to Building Confidence and Resilience in Undergraduate Researchers, ed. Lisa A. Corwin and Louise K. Harrodian with Jennifer M. Heemstra (Council on Undergraduate Research, 2022), 10–23.

27. Donna Mejia, interview with John Kane and Rebecca Mush tare, "Fumble Forward," *Tea for Teaching*, podcast and transcript, December 14, 2022, https://teaforteaching.com/267-fumble-forward/.

28. Erik Simmons, "Black Man in a Strange Land: Using Principles of Psychology and Behavior Science to Thrive in the Classroom," in Neuhaus, *Picture a Professor*, 172. See also Liz Norell, "Reflection, Curiosity and Psychological Safety with Liz Norell," interview with Lillian Nave, *Think UDL*, podcast, March 1, 2024, https://thinkudl.podbean.com/e/reflection-curiosity-and-psychological-safety-with-liz-norell/.

29. Jennie Weiner et al., "Keep Safe, Keep Learning: Principals' Role in Creating Psychological Safety and Organizational Learning during the COVID-19 Pandemic," *Frontiers in Education* 5 (2021), 3, https://doi.org/10.3389/feduc.2020.618483.

30. Weiner et al., "Keep Safe, Keep Learning," 4.

31. Ruoying Xie et al., "Under Psychological Safety Climate: The Beneficial Effects of Teacher-Student Conflict," *International Journal of Environmental Research and Public Health* 19, no. 15 (2022): 9300, https://doi.org/10.3390/ijerph19159300.

32. Sara Abercrombie, Kira J. Carbonneau, and Carolyn J. Hushman, "(Re)Examining Academic Risk Taking: Conceptual Structure, Antecedents, and Relationship to Productive Failure," *Contemporary Educational Psychology* 68 (January 2022): 102029, https://doi.org/10.1016/j.cedpsych.2021.102029.

33. Abraham Carmeli and Jody Hoffer Gittell, "High-Quality Relationships, Psychological Safety, and Learning from Failures in Work Organizations," *Journal of Organizational Behavior* 30, no. 6 (August 2009): 712, https://doi.org/10.1002/job.565.

34. Adelaide H. McClintock, Sara Kim, and Esther K. Chung, "Bridging the Gap Between Educator and Learner: The Role of Psychological Safety in Medical Education," *Pediatrics* 149, no. 1 (January 2022): e20211055028, https://doi.org/10.1542/peds.2021-055028.

35. Shenghao Han, Dewen Liu, and Yilian Lv, "The Influence of Psychological Safety on Students' Creativity in Project-Based Learning: The Mediating Role of Psychological Empowerment," *Frontiers in Psychology* 13 (April 2022): 2; Sarah Rose Cavanagh, *Mind over Monsters: Supporting Youth Mental Health with Compassionate Challenge* (Beacon Press, 2023), 22; and Ji Eun Park and Jung-Hee Kim, "Nursing Students' Experiences of Psychological Safety in Simulation Education: A Qualitative Study," *Nurse Education in Practice* 55 (August 2021): 103163, https://doi.org/10.1016/j.nepr.2021.103163.

36. "I never thought of it that way before" may not work in some teaching contexts and for some instructors but this is teaching gold for me. It models

discussion-based learning, and it empowers students as full participants building knowledge in class.

37. Gannon, *Radical Hope*, 146.

38. Krystal Nunes et al., "Science Students' Perspectives on How to Decrease the Stigma of Failure," *FEBS Open Bio* 12, no. 1 (January 2022): 24, https://doi.org/10.1002/2211-5463.13345.

39. Rebecca Whittle et al., "The 'Present-Tense' Experience of Failure in the University: Reflections from an Action Research Project," *Emotion, Space and Society* 37, no. 8 (November 2020): 9, https://doi.org/10.1016/j.emospa.2020.100719. See also Heather Haeger and Natasha Oehlman, "'You're Invited to the Rejection Party' and Other Strategies for Normalizing Rejection and Failure as Part of the Research Process," in Corwin and Charkoudian, *Confronting Failure*, 148–60.

40. Veselin Jungic et al., "Experiencing Failure in the Classroom and across the University," *International Journal for Academic Development* 25, no. 1 (2020): 40–41, https://doi.org/10.1080/1360144X.2020.1712209. See also Deanna L. Fassett and John T. Warren, "'You Get Pushed Back': The Strategic Rhetoric of Educational Success and Failure in Higher Education," *Communication Education* 53, no. 1 (2004): 21–39, https://doi.org/10.1080/0363452032000135751.

41. T. H. White, *The Once and Future King* (Putnam, 1958), 183.

Chapter 13

1. Sarah Rose Cavanagh, *Mind over Monsters: Supporting Youth Mental Health with Compassionate Challenge* (Beacon Press, 2023), 183–86.

2. Parker Palmer, *The Courage to Teach: Exploring the Inner Landscape of a Teacher's Life*, tenth anniversary edition (John Wiley and Sons, 2007), 39–40.

3. T. Scott Bledsoe and Janice J. Baskin, "Recognizing Student Fear: The Elephant in the Classroom," *College Teaching* 62, no. 1 (2014): 33, https://doi.org/10.1080/87567555.2013.831022.

4. Cavanagh, *Mind over Monsters*, 91–92.

5. Bruce D. Perry, "Fear and Learning: Trauma-Related Factors in the Adult Education Process," *New Directions for Adult & Continuing Education* 2006, no. 110 (Summer 2006): 26, https://doi.org/10.1002/ace.215. See also Joshua R. Eyler, *How Humans Learn: The Science and Stories behind Effective Teaching* (West Virginia University Press, 2018), 182.

6. For citations on trauma-informed pedagogy, visit https://jessamyn neuhaus.com.

7. Jennifer V. Pemberton and Ellen K. Edeburn, "Becoming a Trauma-Informed Educational Community with Underserved Students of Color: What Educators Need to Know," *Curriculum and Teaching Dialogue* 23, no. 1–2 (2021): 181–96; Jill M. Wood, "Teaching Students at the Margins: A Feminist

Trauma-Informed Care Pedagogy," in *Lessons from the Pandemic: Trauma-Informed Approaches to College, Crisis, Change*, ed. Janice Carello and Phyllis Thompson (Palgrave Macmillan, 2021): 23–37; Megan Paceley et al., "Trauma-Informed Approaches to Teaching Students with Marginalized Identities during Times of Crisis," in *Trauma-Informed Pedagogies: A Guide for Responding to Crisis and Inequality in Higher Education*, ed. Phyllis Thompson and Janice Carello (Palgrave Macmillan, 2022): 93–104; Alex Shervin Venet, *Equity-Centered Trauma-Informed Education* (W. W. Norton, 2021); and Tiffany R. Williams, Tenesha L. Walker, and Whitney N. Wyatt, "Conceptualizing Racism through a Systemic Trauma Lens: Impacts on Black College Students," *Journal of Psychotherapy Integration* 32, no. 1 (*March 2022*): 49–63. For a critique of discourse about trauma-informed teaching and racial identity, see Simona Goldin, Addison Duane, and Debi Khasnabis, "Interrupting the Weaponization of Trauma-Informed Practice: '. . . Who Were You Really Doing the 'Saving' For?,'" *Educational Forum* 86, no. 1 (2022): 5–25, https://doi.org/10.1080/00131725.2022.1997308.

8. For citations on pandemic era trauma-informed teaching, visit https://jessamynneuhaus.com/.

9. Peter Felten and Leo M. Lambert, *Relationship-Rich Education: How Human Connections Drive Success in College* (Johns Hopkins University Press, 2020), 42; Virginia R. Downing et al., "Fear of Negative Evaluation and Student Anxiety in Community College Active-Learning Science Courses," *CBE—Life Sciences Education* 19, no. 2 (June 2020), https://doi.org/10.1187/cbe.19-09-0186; Karen Kangas Dwyer and Marlina M. Davidson, "Take a Public Speaking Course and Conquer the Fear," *Journal of Education and Educational Development* 8, no. 2 (2021): 255–69, https://doi.org/10.22555/joeed.v8i2.456; Jose Parlade and Cebrail Karayigit, "Examining Procrastination and Fear of Failure among College Students," *Cognition, Brain, Behavior* 26, no. 4 (2022): 199–213, https://doi.org/10.24193/cbb.2022.26.11; Nicole E. Rader, Sarah A. Rogers, and Jeralynn S. Cossman, "Physical Health, Mental Health, and Fear of Crime among College Students: A Consideration of Sex Differences," *Violence against Women* 26, no. 1 (2020): 3–23, https://doi.org/10.1177/1077801219826749; and Jo Lauren Weaver and Jacqueline M. Swank, "An Examination of College Students' Social Media Use, Fear of Missing Out, and Mindful Attention," *Journal of College Counseling* 24, no. 2 (July 2021): 132–45, https://doi.org/10.1002/jocc.12181.

10. Bledsoe and Baskin, "Recognizing Student Fear," 34.

11. Bledsoe and Baskin, "Recognizing Student Fear," 34.

12. Sarah Rose Cavanagh, *The Spark of Learning: Energizing the College Classroom with the Science of Emotion* (West Virginia University Press, 2016), 182–91; John Jerrim, "Test Anxiety: Is It Associated with Performance in High-Stakes Examinations?," *Oxford Review of Education* 49, no. 3 (2023): 321–41, https://doi.org/10.1080/03054985.2022.2079616; and David Putwain and Wendy Symes,

"The Four Ws of Test Anxiety: What Is It, Why Is It Important, Where Does It Come From, and What Can Be Done about It?," *Psychologica* 63, no. 2 (December 2020): 31–52, https://doi.org/10.14195/1647-8606_63-2_2.

13. Laura G. Burgess et al., "The Influence of Social Contagion within Education: A Motivational Perspective," *Mind, Brain, and Education* 12, no. 4 (2018): 164–74, https://doi.org/10.1111/mbe.12178; Brandi N. Frisby, "The Influence of Emotional Contagion on Student Perceptions of Instructor Rapport, Emotional Support, Emotion Work, Valence, and Cognitive Learning," *Communication Studies* 70, no. 4 (2019): 492–506, https://doi.org/10.1080/10510974.2019.1622584; and Qiyong Zhang and Jiamei Lu, "What Is Emotional Contagion? The Concept and Mechanism of Emotional Contagion," *Advances in Psychological Science* 21, no. 9 (2013): 1596, https://doi.org/10.3724/SP.J.1042.2013.01596.

14. Palmer, *Courage to Teach*, 37.

15. Palmer, *Courage to Teach*, 35–38

16. Sara E. Brownell and Kimberly D. Tanner, "Barriers to Faculty Pedagogical Change: Lack of Training, Time, Incentives, and . . . Tensions with Professional Identity?," *CBE—Life Sciences Education* 11, no. 4 (Winter 2012): 339–46, https://doi.org/10.1187/cbe.12-09-0163; Linda C. Hodges, "Preparing Faculty for Pedagogical Change: Helping Faculty Deal with Fear," *To Improve the Academy* 24, no. 1 (2006): 121–34, https://doi.org/10.1002/j.2334-4822.2006.tb00454.x; Jennifer McCrickerd, "Understanding and Reducing Faculty Reluctance to Improve Teaching," *College Teaching* 60, no. 2 (April–June 2012): 56–64, https://doi.org/10.1080/87567555.2011.633287; Harriet L. Schwartz, *Connected Teaching: Relationship, Power, and Mattering in Higher Education* (Stylus, 2019), 121; Mary L. Sinclair and Sarah R. Faltin Osborn, "Faculty Perceptions to Imposed Pedagogical Change: A Case Study," *Nebraska Educator* 1 (2014): 78–100; and Anne M. Walder, "Obstacles to Innovation: The Fear of Jeopardising a Professorial Career," *British Journal of Education* 3, no. 6 (June 2015): 1–16.

17. Mark Capofari et al., "Course Design Unbundled: A Trauma-Informed Modality of Faculty Development," *Journal of Faculty Development* 37, no. 3 (2023): 72–75; Kelly M. Elkins et al., "Unlocking Barriers to Learning: Trauma-Informed Faculty Professional Development," *Journal of Faculty Development* 37, no. 2 (2023): 13–17; Elisabeth Counselman-Carpenter et al., "Trauma-Informed Macro Strategies to Support Faculty Resiliency," *Journal of Faculty Development* 37, no. 2 (May 2023): 12–14; and Mays Imad, "Transcending Adversity: Trauma-Informed Educational Development," *To Improve the Academy* 39, no. 3 (Spring 2021): https://doi.org/10.3998/tia.17063888.0039.301.

18. Perry, "Fear and Learning," 24.

19. Perry, "Fear and Learning," 25.

20. Palmer, *Courage to Teach*, 40.

21. Palmer, *Courage to Teach*, 40, 41, 45, 46.

22. Perry, "Fear and Learning," 24.

23. Bledsoe and Baskin, "Recognizing Student Fear," 36.

Chapter 14

1. Gloria M. Rodriguez, "Power and Agency in Education: Exploring the Pedagogical Dimensions of Funds of Knowledge," *Review of Research in Education* 37 (2013): 102. See also Eugene Matusov, Katherine von Duyke, and Shakhnoza Kayumova, "Mapping Concepts of Agency in Educational Contexts," *Integrated Psychological & Behavior Science* 50, no. 3 (September 2016): 420–46, https://doi.org/10.1007/s12124-015-9336-0.

2. Rola Ajjawi et al., "'Attending Lectures in Your Pyjamas': Student Agency in Constrained Circumstances," *Higher Education* 86 (2023): 1365, https://doi.org/10.1007/s10734-022-00976-9.

3. Anna Drake et al., "Invisible Labor, Visible Change: Non-Tenure-Track Faculty Agency in a Research University," *Review of Higher Education* 42, no. 4 (Summer 2019): 1635–64, https://doi.org/10.1353/rhe.2019.0078; Leslie D. Gonzales, "Faculty Agency in Striving University Contexts: Mundane yet Powerful Acts of Agency," *British Educational Research Journal* 41, no. 2 (April 2015): 303–23, https://doi.org/10.1002/berj.3140; Elizabeth Niehaus and KerryAnn O'Meara, "Invisible but Essential: The Role of Professional Networks in Promoting Faculty Agency in Career Advancement," *Innovative Higher Education* 40 (2015): 159–71, https://doi.org/10.1007/s10755-014-9302-7; Anne Pathiranage and Thashmee Karunaratne, "Teachers' Agency in Technology for Education in Pre- and Post-COVID-19 Periods: A Systemic Literature Review," *Education Sciences* 13, no. 9 (2023): 917, https://doi.org/10.3390/educsci13090917; Rosemary J. Perez, et al., "Graduate Students' Agency and Resistance after Oppressive Experiences," *Studies in Graduate and Postdoctoral Education* 11, no. 1 (2020): 57–71, https://doi.org/10.1108/SGPE-06-2019-0057; Anita Samuel, "Zones of Agency: Understanding Online Faculty Experiences of Presence," *International Review of Research in Open and Distributed Learning* 21, no. 4 (2020): 79–95, https://doi.org/10.19173/irrodl.v21i4.4905; and Stephen Secules et al., "Supporting the Narrative Agency of a Marginalized Engineering Student," *Journal of Engineering Education* 107, no. 2 (April 2018): 186–218, https://doi.org/10.1002/jee.20201.

4. KerryAnn O'Meara and Corbin M. Campbell, "Faculty Sense of Agency in Decisions about Work and Family," *Review of Higher Education* 34, no. 3 (Spring 2011): 448, https://doi.org/10.1353/rhe.2011.0000; and Dawn Culpepper et al., "Who Gets to Have a Life? Agency in Work-Life Balance for Single Faculty," *Equity & Excellence in Education* 53, no. 4 (2020): 535, https://doi.org/10.1080/10665684.2020.1791280; and Drake et al., "Invisible Labor," 636.

5. Päivi Kristiina Hökkä, Katja Vähäsantanen, and Salme Mahlakaarto, "Teacher Educators' Collective Professional Agency and Identity—Transforming Marginality to Strength," *Teaching and Teacher Education* 63 (2017): 37, https://doi.org/10.1016/j.tate.2016.12.001.

6. Hökkä, Vähäsantanen, and Mahlakaarto, "Teacher Educators' Collective Professional Agency," 37. See also Guopeng Fu and Anthony Clarke,

"Connected by Emotion: Teacher Agency in an Online Science Education Class during COVID-19," *Journal of Research on Science Teaching* (2023): 17, https://doi .org/10.1002/tea.21886; and Chris Winberg, "'Extreme Teaching': Exercising Agency in Difficult Contexts," in *Theorising Learning to Teach in Higher Education*, ed. Brenda Leibowitz, Vivienne Bozalek, and Peter Kahn (Routledge, 2017), 174.

7. Heng Luo et al., "Impact of Student Agency on Learning Performance and Learning Experience in a Flipped Classroom," *British Journal of Educational Technology* 50, no. 2 (March 2019): 819–34, https://doi.org/10.1111/bjet.12604; Nita Mennega and Martina Jordaan, "Developing Personal Agency: Students' Reactions to Changes to a Community Service–Learning Module during COVID-19 Lockdown," *International Journal of Learning in Higher Education* 30, no. 2 (2023): 171–93, https://doi.org/10.18848/2327-7955/CGP/v30i02/171-193; and Maria Hvid Stenalt and Berit Lassesen, "Does Student Agency Benefit Student Learning? A Systemic Review of Higher Education Research," *Assessment & Evaluation in Higher Education* 47, no. 5 (2022): 653–69, https://doi.org/10.1080/02602938 .2021.1967874.

8. Juuso Henrik Nieminen et al., "Student Agency in Feedback: Beyond the Individual," *Assessment & Evaluation in Higher Education* 47, no. 1 (2022): 99, https://doi.org/10.1080/02602938.2021.1887080; and Juuso Henrik Nieminen and Laura Tuohilampi, "'Finally Studying for Myself'—Examining Student Agency in Summative and Formative Self-Assessment Models," *Assessment & Evaluation in Higher Education* 45, no. 7 (2020): 1034, 1033, https://doi.org/10 .1080/02602938.2020.1720595.

9. Kevin M. Gannon, *Radical Hope: A Teaching Manifesto* (West Virginia University Press, 2020), 24.

10. Margaret Vaughn, "What Is Student Agency and Why Is It Needed Now More Than Ever?," *Theory into Practice* 59, no. 2 (2020): 110, https://doi.org /10.1080/00405841.2019.1702393.

11. Margaret Vaughn, *Student Agency in the Classroom: Honoring Student Voice in the Curriculum* (Teachers College Press, 2021), 61–62.

12. Secules et al., "Supporting the Narrative Agency," 187.

13. Vaughn, "What Is Student Agency," 112. See also Sarah Rose Cavanagh, *Mind over Monsters: Supporting Youth Mental Health with Compassionate Challenge* (Beacon Press, 2023), 145.

14. Andy Cavagnetto, Brian Hand, and Joshua Premo, "Supporting Student Agency in Science," *Theory into Practice* 59, no. 2 (December 2019): 128, 129, https://doi.org/10.1080/00405841.2019.1702392.

15. Cavagnetto, Hand, and Premo, "Supporting Student Agency," 130, 131.

16. Dana Robertson et al., "Cultivating Student Agency through Teachers' Professional Learning," *Theory into Practice* 59, no. 2 (2020): 193, https://doi.org /10.1080/00405841.2019.1705090.

17. Lindsey Moses et al., "Educators' Perspectives on Supporting Student Agency," *Theory into Practice* 59, no. 2 (2020): 214, https://doi.org/10.1080/00405841.2019.1705106.

18. Fu and Clarke, "Connected by Emotion," 2.

19. Crina Damşa et al., "Teachers' Agency and Online Education in Times of Crisis," *Computers in Human Behavior* 121 (August 2021), https://doi.org/10.1016/j.chb.2021.106793.

20. Alcione Negrão Ostorga, *The Right to Teach: Creating Spaces for Teacher Agency* (Rowman & Littlefield, 2018), 29–30.

21. Robertson et. al., "Cultivating Student Agency," 194.

22. Niehaus and O'Meara, "Invisible but Essential," 160.

23. Damşa et al., "Teachers' Agency."

24. Tom Romano, "Fear, Incompetence, and Fraud," in Brenda Miller Power and Ruth Shagoury Hubbard, eds., *Oops: What We Learn When Our Teaching Fails* (Stenhouse, 1999), 30.

25. Parker J. Palmer, *The Courage to Teach: Exploring the Inner Landscape of a Teacher's Life,* tenth anniversary edition (John Wiley, 2007), 37.

26. Ostorga, *The Right to Teach,* xv; and Damşa et al., "Teachers' Agency," 1.

27. As quoted in KerryAnn O'Meara, "A Career with a View: Agentic Perspectives of Women Faculty," *Journal of Higher Education* 86, no. 3 (2015): 355, https://doi.org/10.1080/00221546.2015.11777367.

Conclusion

1. Jessamyn Neuhaus, *Geeky Pedagogy: A Guide for Intellectuals, Introverts, and Nerds Who Want to Be Effective Teachers* (West Virginia University Press, 2019), 144.

2. Travis N. Thurston, "Introduction," in *Resilient Pedagogy: Practical Teaching Strategies to Overcome Distance, Disruption, and Distraction,* ed. Travis Thurston, Kacy Lundstrom, and Christopher González (Utah State University, 2021), 2.

3. Thurston, "Introduction," *Resilient Pedagogy,* 4.

4. James M. Lang, *Distracted: Why Students Can't Focus and What You Can Do about It* (Basic Books, 2020), 243.

INDEX